Praise for
GREED IS GOOD

"I've never laughed so hard at something so serious as investing."
—Fred Berry, "Rerun" from TV's *What's Happenin'* and president,
Show Us The Money Management Inc.

"Hoenig is the voice of finance for Generation X."
—*Forbes*

*"Greed Is Good is great. In a most entertaining way, Jonathan Hoenig packs the book with
practical information and investing advice that is a joy to read."*
—Leo Melamed, Chairman Emeritus and Senior Policy Advisor, Chicago Mercantile Exchange

*"In his book Greed Is Good Jonathan Hoenig does a superb job defining investment basics:
what stocks, bonds and mutual funds are, and why any person would want to invest in any of
them. This book is an excellent read for the 20-something age group that understands the
importance of developing a successful investment program but doesn't know where to begin."*
—David P. Brady, CFA and Senior Portfolio Manager, Stein Roe Young Investor Fund

"Hoenig is a marvel."
—Jim Russell, general manager, PRI's *Marketplace*

*"Jonathan Hoenig deploys an engaging and entertaining style to convey substance of
uncommon sense. Who would have thought a cunning Gen-Xer would provide so much
insight and information not only to his cohorts, but even to those boomers willing to
listen and learn."*
—Michael Medved, film critic, radio host

" 'Capitalist Pig' is a show of a different stripe."
—*Wall Street Journal*

*"While he may claim to be no Jack Kerouac, Jonathan Hoenig takes a very beat approach
to the pan-investment landscape. If you've never read an investment guide before, read
this one. If you have, read it anyway—you'll find yourself looking at finance from a very
different, and illuminating, point of view."*
—Patrick H. Arbor, former chairman, Chicago Board of Trade

GREED IS Good

GREED IS

Good

The Capitalist Pig
Guide to Investing

Jonathan Hoenig

HarperBusiness
A Division of HarperCollinsPublishers

The following figures are used with permission: *Stocks, Bonds, Bills and Inflation*; *Large Company Stocks*; *Rates of Return by Decade*; *Risk Tolerance Spectrum*; *Diversified Portfolios in a Bear Market*; *Power of Compounding*; *World Stock Market Capitalization*. © 1998 Ibbotson Associates, Inc. All rights reserved. [Certain portions of this work were derived from copyrighted works of Roger G. Ibbotson and Rex Sinquefield.]

Unless otherwise indicated, all photos courtesy of Photofest.

HarperCollins books may be purchased for educational, business, or sales promotional use. For information please write: Special Markets Department, HarperCollins Publishers, Inc., 10 East 53rd Street, New York, NY 10022.

FIRST EDITION

Designed by Joel Avirom and Jason Snyder

Library of Congress Cataloging-in-Publication Data

Hoenig, Jonathan.
    Greed is good: the capitalist pig guide to investing/Jonathan Hoenig.
        p. cm.
    Includes index.
    ISBN 0-88730-984-4
    1. Investment—United States. 2. Stock exchanges—United States. I. Title.
HG4910.H585 1999
332.6—dc21   99-20597

99 00 01 02 03 ❖/RRD 10 9 8 7 6 5 4 3 2 1

My own power is as great as the power of money.

The properties of money are my own properties and faculties. What I am and can do is, therefore, not at all determined by my individuality. I am ugly, but I can buy the most beautiful woman for myself. Consequently, I am not ugly, for the effect of ugliness, its power to repel, is annulled by money. As an individual I am lame, but money provides me with twenty-four legs. Therefore, I am not lame. I am a detestable, dishonorable, unscrupulous and stupid man, but money is honored and so also is its possessor.

Money is the highest good, and so its possessor is good. Besides, money saves me the trouble of being dishonest; therefore, I am presumed honest. I am stupid, but since money is the real mind of all things, how should its possessor be stupid? Moreover, he can buy talented people for himself, and is not he who has power over the talented more talented then they? I who can have, through the power of money, everything for which the human heart longs, do I not possess all human abilities?

—*Karl Marx*

CONTENTS

ACKNOWLEDGMENTS

Many thanks: Alan Blum, Adrian Zackheim, Amy Lambo, Ben Emkin, Blum Family, Bonnie Bertram, Brian Musburger, CQG, Cathy Martin, Charlie D'Francesca, Clark Golembo, Craig Musburger, Dan Roth, Dan Weil, David Lauren, David Morton, Debbie Englander, Deborah Clark, Everybody I forgot, Everyone @ HarperBusiness, Frank Sennett, Fred Stuart, Gordon Rubinstein, Hal Lux, Henry Feldman, Jamie Ceaser, Inez Wilson, Jason Chaet, Jim Berger, Jim Harris, Jim Henderson, Jim Russell, John Callaway, John Cravens, Joie Chen, Jonay Wellner, Joseph Silich, Ken Kurson, Leo Melamed, Linda Ellerbee, Lisa Berkowitz, Lisa Hepner, Lisa Jackson, Lori Greenberg, Maudine Johnson, Michele Jacob, Mitch Rosen, Pamela Van Geensen, Patrick Arbor, Rheva Phillips, Rick Morris, Robert Feder, Susan Godfrey, Ted Cox, Tim Schellhardt.

My infinite appreciation to my agent Todd Musburger, and my editorial assistants: Leigh Ann Hirschman and Jodi Anderson.

As my editor, I discovered Laureen Rowland to be one of the most talented visionaries I've met. This entire project was spearheaded by her from the start. I am eternally grateful for her support, enthusiasm, and kindness.

*Written in honor of my mother, Ann Hoenig
and grandmother Esther Shlensky.*

*In memory of my father, David Hoenig
and brother, Stephen Hoenig.*

PREFACE: PREPARE FOR PIG

I had just made a vanilla latte, the warm foam peaking over the flimsy cardboard cup. Starbucks was packed with seemingly hundreds of baby boomers barking about their frou-frou drinks. "My frappuccino is *lacking*," one shrieked, and I checked my watch to see how long it had been since I had tasted fresh air or seen the sun.

Five-fifteen an hour doesn't exactly inspire dedication, and as an inquisitive high school student I was beginning to realize that working was a downright drag. Minutes melted into months as I spent hours contemplating just *why* I subjected myself to the crabby nature of corporate coffee.

I was working for the same reason we all work: *for the money*. **Starbucks** (merely the McDonald's of our day) was the low-paying service-sector job designed to keep me out of trouble for the summer and put a few bucks in my postpubescent pocket. Despite the rhetoric of imported coffee, high-priced tchotchkes, and upscale espresso machines, this was grunge work for grunge times. I was making money, but not much. A few hours after school each week didn't exactly qualify me for the American Express Gold Card. In hindsight, it never would have. Working a forty-hour week for five bucks an hour will gross you just north of $10,000 a year . . . before taxes. That's good money, *if you're fifteen, Amish, or inhabiting a corrugated cardboard box.*

Starbucks: The masses who line up for venti vanilla lattes at $3.50 a pop might have bought a few shares of the company itself. Shares in Starbucks have rocketed 780 percent since 1992.

Admittedly, my paychecks were slowly adding up. That can happen . . . when you're (yikes) living at home. Now, I wasn't particularly focused on saving money—I continued to buy all the normal *accoutrements de adolescence*: compact discs, movie tickets, Gap garb, and the like. But I did make it a habit to deposit my paltry paycheck directly into my bank account, rather than cashing it and jaunting off on a Tori Spelling–style shopping spree of adolescent excess. Although I had not been actively saving for much of anything, I couldn't help but notice that as the weeks went by, the money started to pile up.

MONEY ON THE MIND

I had always been interested in money. Though no one in my family was a stockbroker or anything like that, growing up in the "go-go" 1980s, I learned that cash was key. From an early age I saw how money allows you to work the system. It acts as a catalyst for change. In short, it gets you what you want.

As a young boy, I was fascinated by the stock listings. I didn't really understand how the whole deal worked, but the notion of being able to make money without actually doing much of anything jazzed me no end. Besides, the 1980s were in full swing: Donald Trump, J. R. Ewing, and **Henry Kravis** were the media demigods of the day. Caving in to my relentless inquiries, my father bought me a few shares of stock of my very own. Not much money, mind you—a couple hundred dollars of a well-known aerospace company: Boeing. I didn't have much stock, but what I had was all mine. When other kids were following the World Series, I followed that stock. I followed it for years.

So with my Starbucks savings starting to soar, I realized that for the first time I could afford to buy stock *with my own money*. With some caffeinated cash in the bank and some parental cosignage in effect, I opened a tiny account at a local discount brokerage.

Henry Kravis is one of the most legendary and successful financiers in history. During the 1980s, he pioneered the LBO, or leveraged buyout, a technique he used in 1988 when he staged the then-record $24.8 billion acquisition of RJR Nabisco. This story was later dramatized in the excellent bestseller *Barbarians at the Gate.*

CHOICES, CHOICES . . .

But what to buy? I pondered that point for a few weeks, as I clocked in and **kvetched** at work. A particularly soapy-eyed regular in whom I had confided my investment fantasies suggested

kvetch (kə-vech): Yiddish word meaning "to complain habitually."

Starbucks, and not for refreshment. A few hundred dollars later, I invested my meager stash in shares of Starbucks stock. My check was sent to a local brokerage firm and I quickly became **part owner**, sharing in the potential rewards and, to some extent, risk in the burgeoning coffee kingdom. On break (15 minutes), I check the paper. My tiny stake in the equity market (12 shares of Starbucks stock) is on the rise. Shit, I'm making money! *Serious money.* More in one day than I had in a whole week of mopping floors, scooping up coffee grounds, and listening to people whine about the temperature of their grande mochas.

> When you own stock, you become **part owner** in a particular company.

Cleaning the coffee grinds from under my fingernails, my shirt soaked with sweat, I knew I was in the wrong business. While I was making mochas, money—real money—was being made on Wall Street. I had to get in. The first precept of capitalism was already clear: It's always better to own than be owned. And once you've experienced that feeling, there's no going back. Spreading the word to my friends became my mission. With a newfound passion (and growing portfolio) I decided to preach the gospel of greed. This was the birth of "Capitalist Pig."

ON THE AIR

Jonathan at the mike

I started "Capitalist Pig" the radio program while still a junior at Northwestern University, in 1996. It began on WNUR-FM, Northwestern's not-for-profit, volunteer-run radio station. The impetus to invent a more entertaining (and educational) look at the markets was born out of the same frustration I had experienced ten years prior: I was still obsessed with markets and money, a topic none of my friends seemed to know anything about.

My show was originally sandwiched in between the Haitian music show and the contemporary classical music show. It was pretty obvious nobody knew where to put a serious but entertaining look at the stock market. I wasn't surprised. Business broadcasting had long been the domain of the boorish and boring. There had never been a frank, honest, and, yes, entertaining look at the markets, especially one that specifically addressed the financial needs and concerns of young people.

From the beginning "Capitalist Pig" was different. It focused not on the bullshit minutiae that nobody understands (or even cares about) but on the more important long-term factors of business and finance, topics of interest and relevance to younger investors. So I didn't spend the first 15 minutes yapping about fiscal policy or monetary indicators; I went straight to the practical financial advice that matters. It had always frustrated me as an ardent listener of business broadcasting that the hosts (and guests) seemed to be talking to someone else, someone older, richer. Someone with far less hair than I. As the markets continued to climb higher and higher, I as a young person felt we were being left behind. I created "Capitalist Pig," kind of a "morning zoo" program about money, to fill that niche.

Talking about the **Nikkei's** performance while rocking to "Turning Japanese" seemed downright bizarre next to *Moneyline*, *Wall Street Week*, and everything that had come before. Even the station managers, students themselves, were skeptical about putting a finance show on a station more known for Morphine than money.

The show is interesting and informative, just like any other program. But unlike most others, "Capitalist Pig" is always aiming to entertain. From the start, guests have been topnotch, from *über*-entrepreneur Michael Bloomberg to the legendary (and quite raucous) **Rukeyser**. Even Howard Schultz (CEO, Starbucks Coffee) managed to make a telephonic appearance. Sound bites from *Wall Street*, *Trading Places*, and most of Michael J. Fox's films from the eighties also play a big role, as does a nice dollop of hard-core Toto. The show's soundtrack is, to use a familiar refrain, *totally eighties.*

The response was huge. Calls from all over Chicagoland came in each Saturday, and WNUR was flooded with news crews from CNN, MTV, and Fox News Channel. Support flowed from everywhere—even **Congress**. Looking to capitalize (but of course!) I shopped the show around to a few local media outlets, after which it was promptly picked up by a large commercial Chicago radio station, WMVP. My audience went from a few hundred to several hundred thousand in a matter of months, now

The **Nikkei 225** is the most recognized and popular index of Japanese stocks.

Lou Dobbs hosts *Moneyline* on CNNfn, CNN's 24-hour business news channel.

For over 25 years, **Louis Rukeyser** *has hosted* Wall Street Week *on PBS stations nationwide.*

GREED IS GOOD

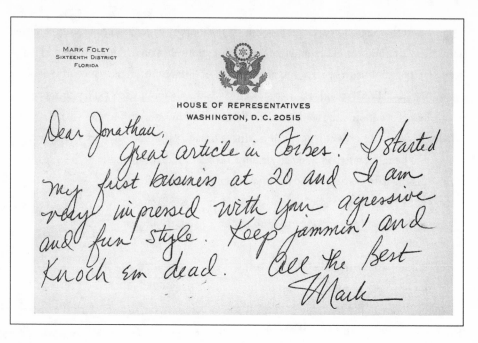

MARK FOLEY
SIXTEENTH DISTRICT
FLORIDA

HOUSE OF REPRESENTATIVES
WASHINGTON, D. C. 20515

Dear Jonathan,
Great article in Forbes! I started my first business at 20 and I am very impressed with your agressive and fun style. Keep jammin' and knock em dead.
All the Best
Mark

broadcasting to over 18 states. Additionally, I began working as a commentator for Public Radio International's *Marketplace* and writing an investment column for *POV* magazine, in addition to publishing my own 'zine, *Capitalist Pig Report*.

While at the helm of the investment banking firm Drexel Lambert's junk bond department, **Michael Milken** almost single-handedly helped finance the "merger mania" of the 1980s. In 1988, he was charged with securities fraud; in 1990, he was sentenced to 10 years in prison, ordered to pay $600 million in fines, and permanently barred from engaging in the securities business.

LEARNING TO LOVE (AND LOATHE) MONEY

"Capitalism" . . . such an ugly word! Connotes the images of a greedy **Michael Milken** firing hundreds of factory workers, or a pompous Donald Trump erecting another ostentatious phallic skyscraper into the sky. Capitalism always seems to get a bad rap, even by those who have benefited the most from its unmistakable reach. While I was still attending classes at Northwestern University, I was also struck with how taboo it was to talk about being interested in money, especially among my circle of liberal, moderately affluent kids from the suburbs. I had female friends who would disclose erotic lesbian fantasies before they'd admit to wanting a big house in the suburbs. Having an interest in, learning about, or (God forbid) having more money was like admitting to a felony. And as I spoke of mutual funds between bong hits, my friends looked at me with a mixture of scorn and disbelief. It was almost as if they were saying, *"How could you?"*

That feeling changed, of course, when graduation came. Once Mommy and/or Daddy severed the umbilical cord of cash, most of us begin to understand the contextual importance of money. For many of us, it's during this time that we being the process of reforming our previous misconceptions about the power of money.

LIVING IN THE EIGHTIES

Estimated price: $105 at Cheap Jack's Vintage Clothing, New York, New York

It was during those formative years in the 1980s that many of our feelings towards money, material wealth, and consumption were formed. Even if you resisted the urge to buy a Michael Jackson **zipper jacket**, anyone who grew up during the 1980s couldn't help but be influenced by the imagery of the era. For those of us who grew up on a steady diet of **Square Pegs** and Rick Springfield, the eighties were a petrie dish of misguided thought. And I'm not talking about feathered hair, acid washed jeans, or Wham's "Wake Me Up Before You Go-Go." You see, if you have a misconception about money, chances are it was developed in the 1980s.

In 1984, **Newsweek** proclaimed the decade to be "The Year of the Yuppie." Seemingly the entire nation was focused on conspicuous consumption. Prime-time television was packed with images of wealth: *Dallas, Silver Spoons, Lifestyles of the Rich and Famous,* and *Fantasy Island*

Square Pegs, *an early eighties television show starring Sarah Jessica Parker, brought "Valley-speak" to the forefront of the American lexicon. The show was canceled after only one year.*

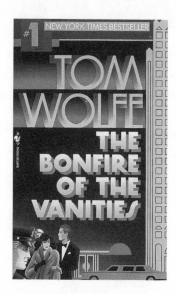

Tom Wolfe's Bonfire of the Vanities *is the quintessential 1980s novel and is required reading for capitalists of any age.*

tempted our young minds with the trappings of material success. The cultural obsession with wealth accompanied a meteoric rise in the stock market, and a particularly sick political brew known as Reaganomics put wealth on display.

Under the weight of Reaganomics and slowing economic growth the era came crashing down into a mess of styling mousse, Perrier, and John Hughes teen angst films. The poor made less and paid more in taxes, while the rich made more and paid less in taxes. Reagan's notions about "trickle-down economics"—that economic prosperity of the affluent would eventually trickle down to the less well off—bombed . . . big time. Reaganomics had prompted a massive redistribution of wealth: According to *The Complete Book of Greed*, "The richest 1 percent of Americans wound up with their income tax rates lowered by 25 percent. By the end of the decade, on average, they were paying $40,000 less in income taxes than at the beginning of the decade. However, the median American family was actually paying $400 more in taxes."

Which was it for your family? Did a parent get laid off from work in the midst of a corporate leveraged buyout? Or were Mom and Dad among the lucky ones who during the 1980s mined a mint of cash? No matter on what side of the coin your family landed, your parents' socioeconomic state inevitably influenced your feelings about wealth.

YUPPIE FALLOUT: MONEY AND HAPPINESS

It seems to be that the "Yuppie's Demise," if you will, was due not so much to the crash of 1987, nor even to the resulting recession of the early 1990s. It was due to yuppies' harboring the false impression that money meant happiness. We are well positioned to be more successful than our parents' generation, simply because we are well positioned to learn from their unfortunate mistakes. In short, we've learned a thing or two since Taco ruled rock radio.

Having money won't make you happy. It is a means to an end, not an end unto itself. When you have money, you can work . . . *or not.* You can eat at the restaurants you enjoy without looking at the prices, or travel the world in something besides the backseat of a road-trippin' station wagon. Money is simply the catalyst. *It makes things happen.*

We have been done a great disservice by the established ruling class—a misguided assemblage of baby boomers who have always equated money with success. It doesn't work. Success has to be measured by each of us individually, on our own well-considered terms, not by the material trinkets we can afford to amass. The tchotchkes of prosperity are ultimately more of a hindrance than a help. *Success is not about making purchases.* If anything, it's about knowing why most purchases don't need to be made. During the latter part of the 1980s, the accessory of choice for the upwardly mobile (or moronic?) was the Vietnamese pot-bellied pig. According to *Forbes,* "Fashionable pet-seekers plunked down as much as $15,000" to own one, making this these little porkers (no relation) the "must-have" pet for every yuppie worth his Perrier. Years later, the same pigs are fetching $10. Many of the well-heeled buyers got fed up with slopping the swine, leading "many expensive oinkers [to] wind up in the slaughterhouse."

Don't own a pig. *Be one.* This book will show you how.

THE CAPITALIST PIG CREDO

The Capitalist Pig philosophy is not simply about getting rich. More than anything, it's about the desire to establish lives in which *we* are in control of our future, monetarily, personally, and professionally. It's about planning. It's about thinking. It's about not having to worry or hope. In the pages that follow, you'll learn to make sensible choices and anticipate probable

The Sharper Image catalog (a classic 80s edition shown above) has long been the definitive source for yuppie crap you'll never use. Among the indispensably useless products from the holiday 1998 edition include a vibrating tongue cleaner for $30 and a Model T golf cart for a mere $15,000.

Recommended books on **taxes**
and general personal finance:
J. K. Lasser's *Your Income Tax 1999*
(Macmillan); *The Ernst and Young
Tax Savers Guide* (John Wiley);
*The Wall Street Journal Guide
to Understanding Personal
Finance* (Fireside).

outcomes, to invest with the knowledge that the choices you make are congruent with your life goals. In this sense, it's a guide to becoming more aware of your resources, more prudent in your investments, and more demanding of your returns.

So what should you expect over the pages to come? *If you have come looking for the comprehensive guide to personal finance, I would strongly advise you to move on.* You will find no analysis of **taxes**, insurance, or mortgages within these pages. For one thing, I find these topics relentlessly boring. Sure, this stuff is an integral part of your overall financial state of being, but it's frankly too important to cram into this book, where I've decided to focus on the concepts and practices of investing.

We'll cover the basics of savings accounts on up through stocks, mutual funds—even options and futures. It is my hope that you'll learn not only the nuts and bolts of the various financial instruments covered, but also the more general conceptions of how to visualize life's resources as precious investments. We'll talk at great length about some of the concepts of what "investment" really should be.

We're going to focus on goals. Your goals. Because ultimately, they are the only reason to give a crap about money in the first place. I'm going to show you how to use a variety of investment "products"—stuff like stocks, bonds, and mutual funds—to help you reach your goals. And not just goals 30 years into the future. If you want to backpack in Borneo in a matter of months, there are still some solid steps you take to make getting there that much easier. We're also going to talk about investing in yourself—about getting the most satisfaction out of the money you spend on your own well-being. I'm not going to give you right answers, because there are none. Hopefully, I'll provide you with the philosophy, attitude, and tools you need to find your own path. You'll make the decisions that bring you the most satisfaction from your money, and consequently, from your life.

This is a book about investments, not a guide to getting rich. I know no secrets or schemes for turning a poor pauper into a wealthy prince. Reading this book won't turn you into a Kennedy. Or a Rockefeller. Frankly, nothing will. Frustrating as it might seem, there will always be those with more money than you. But that doesn't prevent you from becoming more aware of your resources and doing some simple planning that will easily allow you to reach every one of your goals. "I just want to be rich" doesn't mean much. Money isn't the end, but simply the means to an end: our goals.

But follow along and you *will* have more money. In fact, you'll be a millionaire. **BFD**. A million bucks doesn't get you very far anymore. **Inflation** and 15 years of a sweet stock market have sent the numbers of Americans with that type of disposable cash soaring: By the end of 1998, there were 4 million millionaires living in America. You'll be a millionaire, all right. You'll need to be.

BEGIN THE BEGUINE

I'm a big believer in the never-ending possibility of *everything*. Even if the idea of getting your finances in order sounds totally preposterous, so decidedly out of character for you, the fact remains that no matter what your financial situation, the ability to change begins with you. Not to sound too Tony Robbins but if you keep doing what you've been doing you'll keep getting what you've been getting. How do you get there? Good techniques include prudence, education, and patience. For those who flip ahead to the "sexy stuff" on speculating in Chapter 9, I wish you luck. Without a proper foundation rooted in saving and investing, the markets will chew you up and spit you out.

My hope has been to create a investment book that is like no other. An investment book that doesn't insult you, but doesn't bore you either. Something that most of the establishment will probably hate because it doesn't look like anything they've ever seen. And while I would never assume to speak for any generation, let alone my own, let it be said that a dramatic shout is being heard in America these days. *It's the voice of new money.* It's young people who are determined to be themselves. It's a unique set of beliefs and aspirations for the future, different from those of any generation that has come before. It's a group of diverse individuals who aren't interested in living a label, but a life. Each in our own unique fashion. I hope you'll find this book to be unique as well. This is the voice of new money. There's a lot to be said. I invite you to come along and listen.

BFD: Big fucking deal

Inflation is a rise in the general level of prices, where the buying power of the dollar decreases. Inflation is generally thought to occur because of an increase in demand for goods without a corresponding increase in the supply of goods.

PART 1:
PREPPING

1 | *GREED IS GOOD*

The point, ladies and gentlemen, is that greed, for lack of a better word, is good. Greed is right. Greed works. Greed clarifies, cuts through and captures the essence of the evolutionary spirit.

—Michael Douglas as Gordon Gekko, *Wall Street*

In the few years since "Capitalist Pig" was born out of my cramped college dorm room, I've given numerous speeches, presentations, and programs to a variety of audiences. Besides the cookies and coffee (and speaker's fees), one of the aspects of public speaking I have most enjoyed is taking questions and chatting with audience members about my favorite subject: greed.

Greed has been much maligned in our culture; there has been a big-time bastardization of a perfectly normal noun. Mere utterance of the word, which I tend to use a lot, prompts a disgusted look from almost everyone. "It's not good to be greedy!" most people say. I disagree. Big time. Greed, as the Gordon Gekko character in the movie *Wall Street* points out, can be focused on any number of ideals. Greed for life, love, independence, money—*whatever*. Greediness is next to godliness, as far as passion goes. It's not just about the money.

In the game called life, the object is to make yourself happy. Greed is the mechanism to get what you want. Wanting money is wanting choices. Being greedy is simply wanting the opportunity to have as much autonomy, freedom, and independence as possible. The pen might be mightier than the sword, but the checkbook beats 'em all hands down. You want to travel? You want an education? You want opportunity? You want choice? You might have the kindest heart, be the greatest person, or have the best work ethic, but at the end of the day, money talks. With money in the bank . . . anything is possible.

So being a "capitalist pig" isn't about having a driveway full of Porsches and knuckles full o' rings. It's simply about *becoming aware of your resources and spending them in ways that bring you the most satisfaction*. It's about seeing everything we do as an investment, and making our own informed choices about which investments are the right ones for us to make.

Whether your money is going toward stocks, bonds, graduate school, or groceries, I want you to start thinking about all of your spending, no matter how small, as an investment. Every damn dime should give you the maximum return possible. The return might be financial, like investing $100 in a mutual fund to earn 11 percent per annum, or it might not—like spending $1,000 on a once-in-a-lifetime vacation you'll never forget. Every penny should be deliberately expended—and then enjoyed—to the fullest extent.

GETTING DOWN TO GOALS

The hardest part of investing wisely is not acquiring money, but knowing *why* you're acquiring it in the first place. In short, you need some goals. At least ballpark goals, that is.

So what are your goals? At some point, will you want to travel? Buy some land? Start your own company? Retire in the lap of luxury? Don't just think ten minutes into the future; think ten years. What do you want? Twenty years? Forty years? It sounds like a lifetime away . . . and it is.

Yes, your goals will change—*and that's okay!* After building latrines in Afghanistan for a few months, you might just decide *against* spending the rest of your life working in social service. Conversely, a few years in big business might prompt you to seek out a less chaotic pasture. Maybe you'll work at a Club Med. Maybe you'll become a nun or priest. *Whatever.*

Regardless of the long-term twists your life takes, you've got to start making some decisions. You've got to look even six months into the future and ask yourself: *What do I want to be doing 180 days from now? What do I need to do to get there?*

Our goals are what drive us to do the things we do. In economic terms, we are "rational agents," meaning that the choices we make should be sound and thoughtful

ones, all directed toward effectively reaching our goals. That is the theory. Here is the practice: How rational is it to pay 17 percent interest to a credit card company on things we can't afford in the first place? How rational is it to buy a risky mutual fund just because it's splashed on the cover of *Money Magazine*? How rational is it to dump 100K on a diploma we might never even need, just because everyone says so? How rational is it to make a sequel to *The Love Boat*?

I don't know you. I'm not going to try and be "down" with you. I'm certainly not going to pretend to know what you want out of life. So unlike every other investment-book author out there, I'm just not going to give you a step-by-step guide to everything. Your goals are your own. Nobody can tell you what to do. My hope is, however, to get you thinking about those goals in an action-oriented way and illuminate the tools and techniques about money that can make your goals a lot easier to achieve.

RETHINKING RESOURCES

Entrain this upon your brain: *We inhabit a world of scarce resources.* There's just so much of everything to go around. Time. Money. Molecules. Everything. We'd love a fountain of youth, and I'd kill for a fountain of money . . . but it just ain't gonna happen. We've got to make the best of what we have.

Why give a rat's ass about resources? It is your resources that allow you to reach your goals. Whether you want to start a business or a band, travel to Cuba or loaf on the couch, your resources will take you there. The ability to marshal your **resources** effectively, to use them in appropriate and productive ways that work *for you* is the whole enchilada. It's the only thing you really need to know to get basically anything you want out of life.

Resources are your means—whether financial (like your money), emotional (your time and sanity), or otherwise—that you can invest as you see fit.

"Resources." It's a term you might be used to hearing within the context of the environment. *Save the rainforest! We're destroying our natural resources!*

The rainforest is a limited resource, for obvious reasons: *When it's gone, it's gone.* Nothing will bring back the trees after we've chopped them to the forest floor. In this case, wasting resources is tantamount to wasting opportunity; once the animal and plant species are gone, so are the medical breakthroughs and the cleaner earth they currently provide. The ramifications of these environmental decisions, these choices, will be with us forever.

The **rainforest** is the Earth's resource. Money and time are yours. The point is that we're not simply going to waste our own resources like we've screwed up the earth's. We're going invest our resources into projects that will give us a return. It might be financial, like making a few hundred dollars in a mutual fund. It might also be emotional, like the satisfaction of donating some of your time to charity. For many people, that provides a solid return on their "investment" of time. Whatever the resource, the point is to be smart. Be greedy. And to make the most of what you have by investing it in prudent ways.

The Clock Conundrum: Time as a Resource

In those precious moments between our miraculous birth and unavoidable demise exists the only "pure" resource we have as humans, our time. According to the National Census Bureau, we are born with an average of 85.12 years, or about 30,000 days, to spend in this lifetime. "Spend" is an appropriate term. Though we are seldom conscious of the choices we make day in and day out, every day we decide what to *do* with our time. Nobody forces you to go to work. Nobody makes you get out of bed in the morning. Or makes you get into one at night, for that matter. Every day you spend approximately 1/30,000 of your life. I'm sure you know that your time is important. The question is: How are you spending it?

We **allocate** our resources in different ways, none better than the next. What constitutes a sound investment of your time is completely up to you. Want to hang out at the beach all day? Cool. Want to become an astronaut? Fine. It's your choice. Nobody else really gives a shit, except maybe your parents, and past a certain point it's really none of their business anyway. You can do whatever you want; just be prepared to deal with the consequences of your decisions. When it comes to your time and your life, nothing is inherently the "right"

Tired but true. The **rainforest** is a useful *and* limited resource. How useful? Hundreds of plant and animal species inhabit the rainforest. It's a veritable medicine chest of potential cures for serious disease. The rainforest is essential to maintaining the earth's ecosystem and ozone layer. Rent *Gorillas in the Mist* or *Medicine Man*. You'll know exactly what I'm talking about.

To allocate: To distribute your resources for a particular purpose or to a certain person, entity, or thing.

thing to do. College, marriage, suburbia . . . *whatever.* Don't let me (or parents, educators, or *Entertainment Weekly*) determine the course of your days.

Cash Crunch: Money as a Resource

Time is one resource. Money is another. Money is the topic nobody wants to talk about, be it because they've got too much or they haven't got enough. Much has been written about why **money** is so totally taboo as a topic of conversation.

You probably have some of your own ideas.

Money affords you the opportunities, the choices, the *freedom* to pursue your goals—to get what you want. In capitalist America and indeed all throughout the world, money is the tool that makes it happen. If you aspire to the material world, if Range Rovers, imported olive oils, and Pottery Barn make your nipples perky, well then have no fear: Money will surely get you there. In contemporary capitalism, there's not much that money can't buy. Even other **people.**

But for most of us, those particular goals aren't the ones we're *most* interested in. You can't put a price tag on happiness, fulfillment, or love. You can't order that stuff out of a catalog. *This is true.* But money does facilitate **mazel**.

It's hard to be happy. It's hard to have love in your life. But I have to imagine that it's

Mazel: Yiddish word meaning "luck."

even harder when you're eating out of a soup can. Life is full of stressors. Why should money be one of them? As Charlie Sheen's character puts it in *Wall Street*, "There's no nobility in poverty." He's right.

THE CAPITALIST CATALYST

Greed—the kind of greed I'm interested in—is never just about money. While some *twisted individuals* spend their whole lives accumulating money and wealth for no specific purpose, money functions only as the means to help you achieve your dreams. I'm not just talking about the traditional American Dream. Here, late in the twentieth century, that ideal has become something decidedly more exciting than buying a house in the suburbs and putting up a white picket fence. The **American Dream** is, in fact, *your* dream. Whatever it is.

That's why we invest—to fulfill our dreams. Hell, even if you're not sure yet what your dreams are, you want to invest now so you can afford them once you've figured it out. When you've got money, you've got choices. When you're broke, you've got *bubkus*.

Ah, to have money! Banks will stand in line to lend you dough for your new home or entrepreneurial start-up, though you won't need it. You find yourself in a bad job and discover it's much easier to give your boss the finger when you've got a few grand stashed somewhere for safekeeping. With money in the bank you can make those choices. You can take advantage of the unexpected opportunity, be it the concert ticket, warehouse sale, or two-for-one night at the local Toss and Sauce.

Between 1947–1951, William J. Levitt defined suburbia in Levittown, a development of 17,311 identical houses build in Hempstead, NY. The development came to so symbolize the **American Dream** *that when Soviet Premier Nikita Khrushchev visited American in 1959, President Eisenhower encouraged him to visit Levittown to see the American Dream incarnate. Khrushchev took a pass.*

We have goals. We have wants. It's the resources that get you there. Simply put, resources give us the freedom to get what we want.

FUTURE SHOCK

Take a look at your parents. I know, it's difficult, but do your best. While our lives will take a decidedly different tack from theirs, we most certainly will encounter a lot of the **michagais** they have been through. Some of us will have children. Some of us are going to get cancer. But all of us are going to grow older. Understanding some of the hardships and experiences of older generations isn't placating the past, it's simply doing field research for the future.

Michagais (me-shu-GAS): Yiddish word for "craziness, madness, or lunacy."

Was it not Mr. Peter Brady, a young'un himself, who so eloquently stated, "When it's time to change/You've got to rearrange/who you are and what you want to be!" Things do change. For me as a **bachelor**, my living expenses are few and far between. But I can imagine a time, distant as it may seem, when I might be weighed down with other expenses.

Home sweet home.

A home. A (gasp) family. College for the kiddies. Whatever. Without proper planning, these obligations simply enslave. I've started early so I don't have to scramble later. Like our good friends, the *baby boomers*, are doing.

Our needs can change, but so can our environment. Got a great career now? Cool, but *be careful*. The U.S. economy goes through periods of boom and bust—prosperity and recession. Interest rates, employment rates, they all climb and fall. Jobs are downsized and salaries can be cut. We may be transferred to another city or another country. We may have to take care a sick relative or, God forbid, may become ill ourselves. Keeping that in mind, return to your resources and think long term. Just scraping by with no financial cushion might work right now, but *expect the unexpected in years to come.* When disaster strikes, I personally want a fistful of cash to buy my way out of it. The future may be many things. But it's certainly unknown.

Shit happens, we know, but it just seems to happen more often when your finances are in a shambles. Worst-case scenario? Having to rely on someone else to take care of you—and if you want their money, you'll have to play by their rules. This includes your parents (who might make you move back in with them), your employer (who is free to make your life hell if he knows you can't afford to quit), and the good ol' government (which won't be putting you up in the Helmsley, I assure you).

When it comes to Social Security, *don't count on it*. Entitlement programs like this are, for all practical purposes, inconsequential. By the time we need them, chances are they won't be there. *Fine*. When your resources are in order, you won't need a handout from anyone.

So don't be a **Willy Loman**.

Start now to make some small changes that will ensure that you will always want for naught. The first change is to begin thinking in terms of resources and strategy. Your resources are your time and money. Your strategy will be your overall plan for allocating those resources. If you have invested your resources with a strategy that involves consistency, prudence, and care, you will be able to deal with life's challenges in your own way, on your own terms. You'll be able to get what you want.

Willy Loman: The main character of Arthur Miller's high-school standard *Death of a Salesman*. Loman, a small-time salesman, is eventually driven to suicide so that his family can collect insurance money.

This book is about investing your resources—in purchases large and small, and in financial "products," like stocks and bonds. This is not a book about getting rich quickly, or picking the one stock that will send you to Scarsdale. There is no such thing.

By the time you've finished this book, you'll have a plan to allocate a percentage of your current resources (or, if you're just now starting to save money, your future resources) to stock mutual funds. You'll understand financial investments, ranging from savings accounts and CDs to the risky world of options and futures. None of these financial "products" is terribly difficult to grasp, though each helps you to accomplish certain goals. Each boasts advantages and disadvantages that must be weighed against your goals. When you're aware of your goals, it's a lot easier to choose the right investments.

Greed is good. I want more of everything. More money. More space. More time. More love. Just more. My guess is that you do, too.

With money—*with resources*—you have choices. You have options. Being greedy is being able to get what you want. Being greedy for *money* is simply being able to pay for it.

You may not know jack about finance, but let me tell you: It's not that tough. Read on. I'll show you the way.

2 JUST SAY NO: DEBT

It is incumbent on every generation to pay its own debts as it goes. A principle which, if acted on, would save one-half the wars of the world.

—Thomas Jefferson

I call it being rich, although you might opt for the more politically correct incarnation, being "financially independent." That's what we all want, right? It only occurs, however, when we stop being dependent: on our parents, the government, or **"the kindness of strangers."**

It's *hard* not to be dependent. Since we were young, others have always been there to catch us when we fall. Parents, friends, lovers help us out of kindness, but ironically, it is this very kindness that can encourage us to remain dependent. As long as someone is willing to help us out, there's little incentive for us to become independent and succeed on our own.

One example of this sort of dependency is that which is fostered by Social Security. You probably already know that there's a good chance Social Security won't even exist by the time we're ready to retire, but understanding a bit more about this social program, its benefits and faults, will give us a little more insight into why dependency is something we just don't want to be a part of.

"I have always depended on **the kindness of strangers**.*" As many of you know, Blanche DuBois, the heroine of Tennessee William's* A Streetcar Named Desire, *eventually went insane.*

Here's a quick Cliff's Notes version to bring you up to speed: the Social Security system is one of the few surviving vestiges of President Franklin Roosevelt's New Deal. Created in the 1930s, it's a national pension plan for people who are retired, which is funded by people who are presently working. The money comes into the pool through payroll taxes and is paid out in benefits.

The logic behind Social Security was compelling in the 1930s and became even more compelling as the birth rate soared in the 1940s and 1950s. There was an enormous amount of people contributing to the system and very few taking out. The fund surpluses became huge as baby boomers entered the workplace and the relatively small numbers of people born in the 1930s and earlier entered retirement.

But look what's happened. The U.S. birth rate has leveled off, and the enormous numbers of individuals born in the forties and fifties are beginning to enter retirement. Simply, more money is starting to flow out than is flowing in. According to the Heritage Foundation, the system will begin paying out more in benefits than it takes in by the year 2010. By 2015 the shortfall will reach $90 billion dollars. By 2035, the shortfall will reach—gulp—$1 trillion dollars.

Social Security Deficit in Billions of Dollars

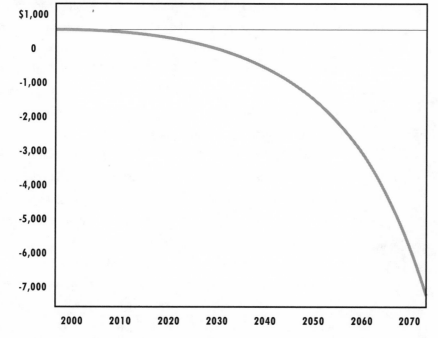

Source: The Heritage Foundation

Most people believe Social Security invests their contributions into an account that accrues interest and awaits their future retirement. Here's the real deal: Since 1939, the system has operated not as an investment program, but as a "pay-as-you-go" scheme. Our contributions today are immediately distributed to retirees. There is, in effect, no "savings" whatsoever. No special account in your name, no interest, no government employee looking out for your needs, no guarantee that, come your own retirement, the program will still be around.

You can see how being involved in Social Security fosters a sense of dependency. Because we're forced to make contributions to the program, we're depending on the prudence and sound judgment of people whom we've never even met on the disposition of our hard-earned dollars. Don't be lulled or fooled into feeling that someone else, the government in this case, is going to take care of you, no matter what promises have been made. Just as most of us know not to count on the government for Social Security (even as we continue to pay into the system), we don't want to have to depend on anyone—except ourselves—to help us fulfill our financial and personal goals. While we might know in the back of our minds that someone could help us out in crunch—whether it's our parents paying off our credit card debt or friends allowing us to crash at their pad for the night—the best course of action is to develop the independent mentality that having your own financial plan will bring. You'll appreciate knowing you can count on others in a crisis, but you'll appreciate even more the knowledge that most of the time you can count on yourself. So instead of relying on the government, we're going to rely on our own sound judgment in choosing prudent investments for our future.

While growing up and becoming independent doesn't mean that we cast aside all kindness and support directed toward us, it does necessitate an increased reliance on our own skills, abilities, and character. On the "Pacific Princess" of life, we are each our own Captain Stuebing. With a little planning and preparation, you can make almost anything happen.

So you need to identify your goals and come up with a plan to make them a reality. But we also have to keep our expectations realistic. While your heart is screaming "Porsche," your checkbook might be telling you "Pinto." **And that's . . . okay!**

Stuart Smalley: *Good enough? Smart enough? Wealthy enough?*

What will eventually allow you to park that Porsche 911 in your driveway is nailing down a plan and putting it into action. Realistic expectations foster achievable goals, while expectations of entitlement only foster dependency. So don't depend on your Great-aunt Toby to kick it anytime soon, leaving you countless millions. Depend on yourself.

GETTING PLANETARY

Neither hope nor luck should have any place in your financial plans. Hope rests on the workings of fate. Luck is unpredictable. Reaching our goals and getting what we want shouldn't depend on luck!

> *The public is out there throwing darts at a dart board. I don't throw darts. . . . I bet on sure things.*
>
> —Gordon Gekko

Sure, there are people who are always seem to be "lucky." But don't count on it. Count on being prepared. Opportunities present themselves all the time, and it is by no small coincidence that "lucky" people always seem to be those with enough cash to seize them. Having money is conducive to having luck. With apologies to members of the clergy: Praying don't help. *Planning does.*

If you were planning a road trip, you would never leave without a map, merely "hoping" to find Laguna Beach. You'd bring a map to ensure you'd reach your destination. The more precise the map, the better you followed the directions, the sooner you'd find your way to your destination. The same methodology applies to finances.

In Chapter 1, you started thinking about your goals, for now . . . and for the future. Now you need to take it a step further. Think critically about where you want to go . . . the "road trip" you are looking to take. Start crafting a plan that incorporates your destination and some of the steps along the way. While we know your plan is *subject to change* in a major way, think six months and one, five, and ten years into the future. Have a little fun with it.

Undoubtedly the shorter-term goals are easier to nail down. You might *know*, for example, that in six months you're going to want to go to Europe, or buy a new bike, or apply to graduate school. All of these work. Less specific but just as important to elucidate are the longer-term goals. You might *know* that in five years you don't want to still be living in a cramped one-bedroom studio, or still be having to hit your parents up for a few dollars here and there. You might know that you're going to want to save to start a business or an art collection. Even further out: I think most of us can look thirty years out and *know* we don't want to be working as hard as we are today.

Assets: Cash and tangible items of property that have a monetary value.

Liabilities: Amounts currently owed to others.

Assets	Liabilities

Wall Streeters call it the Balance Sheet. Big words. Simple concept. Subtract what you have from what you owe. Assets that are not easily transferable into cash, like your Star Wars *action figure collection, for example, don't count!*

Start with a reality check: How much money are you making? How much have you got saved? Any debts to pay off? Write it down if you must. Don't BS yourself. Be honest. Understanding the realities of your present financial situation is key; you can't change something until you know precisely what it is. Again, I'm not going to give you a third-grade form to fill out, just make a list of your total **assets** and **liabilities**. Subtract one from the other to get your "net worth."

I know this may seem simple, but the fact is you can't get to the good stuff: the saving, investing and yes . . . *speculating*, until your financial "house" is at least a bit more like *Little House on the Prairie* than *House Party*. Again, your plans will change. That's fine. But make some plans nevertheless, and begin to think in terms of using your two primary resources—money and time—to get you there. If you want to get into politics, sitting around your room, playing Sega, and smoking dope won't get you there. (Sitting around your office, playing the saxophone, and smoking dope, however . . . just might. . .)

DEBT: LOSERS ARE USERS AND USERS ARE LOSERS

If you want to be financially independent, you've got to get out of most, if not all, of your debts. Why? Because, in a word, debt sucks. When you owe someone else, you're simply not free to pursue your goals.

I'm not going to lecture you on having too many credit cards, or give you any frilly little "tips" on paying off the debts you might have already racked up. What you need to know is what debt is, and how it screws up your chances of accomplishing your financial goals.

We know now that money is a resource—there's just so much to go around. We invest our money to get the maximum return. Debt is the *opposite* of investing. Debt involves giving someone *else* a return. When we borrow money, we are paying for the privilege of spending money that we don't really have. That payment comes in the form of interest. We borrow X amount, and pay back X + interest. *It's that simple.*

Why would we borrow money? Why would we want to pay someone $1,100 later for the privilege of spending $1,000 now? You'd hope there would be a good reason, a very *timely* reason. For many, there isn't.

So why does *anyone* borrow money? Companies borrow money to finance their operations. Companies borrow money because they feel they can use it in a way that will actually make them even more money. They borrow money to *invest* it, knowing that the return on their investment, whether for parts for a plane or beef for a burger, will more than cover the cost of the loan. So when Boeing, for example, borrows money, they are doing it with a specific intent. They're not borrowing money so that the employees can go out drinking, but to make airplanes they are very sure they'll be able to sell at a profit later on. They're expecting the profit they make will be enough to repay the loan and interest, and still make the company money.

That's the only reason to go into debt: because the debt will actually allow you to make more money. Say you want to buy a house. You'll probably need a loan. That loan is called a mortgage. You get your mortgage, move the family in, and every month pay interest on your loan—but in return you get the benefit of having bought the house. Assuming real estate continues its slow upward climb in value, a house will escalate in value over the time it takes you to pay back the loan. With any luck, you will make a profit and, in the meantime, also have a place to live.

This is considered "good debt." It's important to make the distinction: You borrowed money, but for good reason: to invest in a home, a investment that historically has performed favorably over time. Borrowing money to fund one's music collection or penchant for fine dining is "bad debt." The money you're borrowing (presumably on a credit card) is not being directly invested to pay off the loan.

Think about this the next time you're glancing over your credit card bills. Is the stuff you've borrowed money to buy specifically going to make you enough money to repay the debt? Is it going to make you any money at all? More often than not, the answer is a resounding no.

During the massive bull market of the mid 1990s, there were reports of some individuals borrowing money (some even through their credit cards) to invest in the stock market. Without exception, these individuals got screwed. It's an asinine proposition: The stock market, on average, returns about 11 percent a year. So borrowing money at 17 percent through a credit card in order to invest in the stock market is simply ludicrous. When it comes to borrowing money to get into the market, don't do it. Don't even think about it.

THE CREDIT CARD CONUNDRUM

Because they are the single most debilitating force in preventing us from saving money, it's significant to note how much we use our credit cards, and how much they screw us out of achieving our financial goals.

The statistics are startling. The typical American family holds seven credit cards, has an average balance of $3,225, and pays an interest rate of approximately 18 percent. The average balance for students is $2,226, while graduate students average $5,800. Card-holding Americans pay an average of $1,000 a year in interest payments and fees alone. **This is lunacy.**

When you carry a balance on a credit card, you are borrowing money at the rate of interest usually given to white-collar criminals, bankrupt businesses, or Third World piss-poor countries.

Their strategies have worked. As young people we're ripe for targeting. Nearly 60 percent of all college students have at least one credit card. Twenty percent carry four or more. Most sign up before their sophomore year, responding to credit card issuers' offers of free concert tickets, computer software, or discount air fares in exchange for submitting an application. Credit card companies are not stupid: They target college kids in hopes of attracting the "brand loyalty" that prompts most to hold on to that first credit card for as long as 15 years. Though there are several smaller companies, Visa and MasterCard own the multi-trillion-dollar-a-year industry.

But whose fault is all this debt? It's not the card company's—it's ours. Nobody forces us to charge stuff. We must take responsibility for our own decisions. If we as a genera-

Account Number		Credit Line	Cash or Credit Available	Days in Billing Cycle	Closing Date	Total Minimum Payment Due	Payment Due Date
		$12,600.00	$10,389.68	30	11/05/98	$44.00	12/03/98

Posting Date	Transaction Date	Reference Number	Card Type	Category	Transactions		Charges	Credits (CR)
					NOVEMBER 1998 STATEMENT			
PURCHASES AND ADJUSTMENTS								
10/19	10/17	0795	VS	C	HYATT HOTELS HILL COUN SAN ANTONIO TX HOTEL FOLIO # 0019007910170 ARRIVAL DATE 10/18/98		51.39	
10/20	10/18	9320	VS	C	NEW JAPAN ORIENTAL CAF EVANSTON IL		25.06	
10/21	10/19	2602	VS	C	BLIND FAITH CAFE EVANSTON IL		13.77	
10/22	10/20	5835	VS	C	BLIND FAITH CAFE EVANSTON IL		13.77	
10/22	10/21	0162	VS	C	AMOCO STATION 1069509 CHICAGO IL		6.00	
10/23	10/21	4855	VS	C	ALLRIGHT PRKNG00302893 CHICAGO IL		5.50	
10/23	10/21	7923	VS	C	COPYCAT OF EVANSTONE I EVANSTON IL		4.50	
10/23	10/22	9691	VS	C	USPS 1615400204 EVANSTON IL		2.04	
10/24	10/22	2574	VS	C	KINKO'S COPIES SKOKIE IL		10.00	
10/24	10/22	0261	VS	C	BLIND FAITH CAFE EVANSTON IL		13.77	
10/24	10/23	2005	VS	C	SHELL NO.21215455441 CHICAGO IL		6.89	
10/26	10/23	1757	VS	C	ALLRIGHT PRKNG00302893 CHICAGO IL		14.50	
10/26	10/23	0795	VS	C	BLIND FAITH CAFE EVANSTON IL		13.77	
10/26	10/24	3581	VS	C	COPYCAT OF EVANSTONE I EVANSTON IL		8.40	
10/26	10/24	6724	VS	C	BLIND FAITH CAFE EVANSTON IL		13.77	
10/26	10/24	8106	VS	C	CHICAGO COMPACT DISC 847-328-2202 IL		10.79	

tion are intelligent enough to get into institutions of higher learning, surely we should be able to handle credit cards. All the pertinent disclosure information is federally mandated to accompany each card. Except we don't read it. We charge now and complain later. Learning to accept the responsibility and consequences of our actions is a major factor in fostering financial independence. The key is to stop charging and stop complaining.

I know. I know. Letting the credit card companies off the hook doesn't tow the "party line" as effectively as well as a good rhetorical ass-whooping, but let's be serious! Whether the card is green, silver, platinum, or gold, the frustrating truth is that we have only ourselves to blame for getting into debt. Simply put, we reap what we sow. To solve the trillion-dollar credit card conundrum, all that needs to change is our attitude.

Boss says, never carry a balance!

The fact is: There is no bigger waste of money in this world than carrying a balance on a credit card. *Don't talk to me about airline miles, Yahoo! points, or cash-back award bonuses.* When you carry a balance, *any balance*, on a credit card, you have instantly eliminated the usefulness of any other savings or investment whatsoever. **Tattoo** it on your chest if you must: *Carrying credit card debt is never, never, never an option.* If you're carrying a balance—even with a relatively low 13 percent interest rate—you're going to have to save 13 percent more, work 13 percent harder, or make 13 percent more on your investments just to keep up.

Let's say you charge $2,000 on a credit card at 18 percent. After two years of paying off $100 per month, you will have paid a total of $2,400—almost a quarter more than the original balance. This is assuming, of course, that you don't rack up any new debt on top of the old.

Even more disastrous would be paying only the "minimum balance" the card requires. Say you charge up $3,000 at 18 percent interest. Make the minimum monthly payment (usually 2 percent, or $60) and it will take over 33 years to pay the card off. Of course, the total dollar amount you'd be paying back on $3,000 would will have skyrocketed to over $6,500. So it doesn't matter if the item you bought was on sale, or discounted, or anything like that. When you finance your purchases through a credit card, you

Over 2.5 billion credit card solicitations were mailed to consumers last year, an average of 75 per household. Business owners receive on average three to four applications per week

aren't saving anything. You are simply paying 15 percent, 17 percent, up to 20 percent (per year) more for everything you buy.

The answer is simply to stop. Stop carrying a balance—any balance. Stop paying for some Visa executive's new BMW. *Stop buying things you can't afford.* If you don't buy things you can't afford, you will never have any problems with credit card debt.

Sounds so dreadfully simple, but it's no coincidence that those who can least afford high-interest payments are the ones with the highest credit card balances. If you can't afford to pay for it in cash, you simply can't afford it.

"I can't afford it." Say that out loud a few times. Get used to saying it. Capitalist Pigs say it a lot.

And don't be duped by the ol' "low-rate" trick, or by believing that consolidating your bills onto one card really materially changes anything. These are useful intermediate steps for people with serious credit card problems, but they're short-term splints, not long-term cures. "Low rates" are almost always short-term teasers—after a few months, you're back to the normal "screw-me" rate. And you're still paying more than you should.

So don't play these credit card games. Don't waste your time cruising the net every night looking for the lowest interest rate. *That's a hassle. That's annoying. And that's still costing you money.* If you make it a point and a practice never to carry a balance, all of this *michagais* becomes moot.

REMEDY RECIPE

Talk, talk, talk. The fact is: You still have a credit card balance. It might just be that a few weeks of prudent saving and scaling back your spending are enough to eradicate this scourge from your life. Excellent. Once you're free of credit card debt, you'll never want to go back to wasting your time, money, and energy on the cult of credit.

But let's say you're in trouble. Although you don't know how you did it (and don't have much to show for it), you've managed to rack up enough debt to make you eligible for a recurring role on *Sanford and Son*. Your debt is not the type of thing that just a little cutting back can fix. It's gotten to the point where when the phone rings, your heart pounds with the fear that it's a credit card agency looking to give you the "talking to" you *know* you so rightly

deserve. All is not lost, but you do need to take some more aggressive steps t
self on the road to righteousness.

Although transferring credit card balances is not always the answer, for pe
unfortunate situation, some consolidation is key. Check out Bank Rate Mor
bankrate.com) to find the card with the lowest interest rate. Many newspape
lists of cards with low rates. You might even find that some tough talk with y
credit card company will get you a rate competitive with the low ones you've re

Transfer all your balances to one card . . . yes, the one with the lowest interest rate.
This will become your credit card. *Your only credit card.* Get rid of the rest.

Then prepare for pain, because it's gonna hurt.

You are going to have to take drastic and substantial measures to eliminate your debt,
partly because of the sheer size of your debt, and partly because a
whopping amount of interest will continue to accrue even as you
actively work to pay off your balance.

Don't go out to dinner, don't go shopping, don't buy new
clothes, deny yourself anything and everything 'cept for the bare
essentials. Pay it off. Be done with it. Other books might give you
some giddy little chart about how to structure payments, *a little
here a little there*—kinda like getting a pair of pants shortened.
Homey, don't play that game. I go more for the "Wham bam thank
you ma'am" approach. *Pay it off!!!* I want you to make yourself as uncomfortable as possible to pay it off. I want you to remember that feeling the next time you buy something
you don't really need.

> Avoid taking out another loan just
> to pay off your previous ones.
> There's no weaseling your way
> around the inevitable discomfort
> of paying off what you owe.

It will hurt. It should. Deny yourself as much as possible for as long as it takes you
to pay off that credit card. If you drive to work and pay for parking, take a bus. If you
dine out, break out the rice cooker. If you see movies, it's library time. Do whatever you
have to do to pay off the debt.

Are you with me here? I'm serious! In fact, I'm so serious about the need to immediately pay off your credit card debt that I don't want you to read a *page more of this book until
you have*. I've dog-eared this page for you, so go ahead and flip it down. Don't worry about
creasing the pages; this book won't bring you much in the way of resale value anyway. So go
pay off your debt. Cause you can't start making money with investments until you stop giving it away with your consumer debt. Put this book up on the shelf until you do. It won't
move . . . I promise.

GIVE YOURSELF SOME CREDIT

You did it. Congrats. Welcome back.

It's not that you're not going to have a credit card.

I don't advocate the "cut 'em up and use cash" bullshit. For one, electronica is slowly but surely making inroads into our economy. It's quite likely that in the coming years, paper currency will be phased out altogether, replaced by a card or series of cards that will function as our means of payment for almost everything. When it comes to packin' plastic, get used to it. You'll just learn to be cautious and careful.

Most of the opportunities to get cash off a credit card—the "checks" they encourage you to use, for example—carry a minimum percentage service charge. If we could borrow CASH for free off a credit card, one could easily borrow $1,000, immediately invest it in a 30-day CD, and make money off the spread. God knows I've tried.

And credit cards can actually be of great use. They are excellent for purchasing expensive items like appliances, airline tickets, and computer equipment. You won't have to carry wads of cash through department store parking lots, and the credit card transaction will leave you with a highly visible record of your purchases. These paper trails come in handy if you need to return an item or have a problem with a purchase. (Credit card companies sometimes also offer protection against theft or damage for items purchased with their cards.) Paper trails can also help you out at tax time, when the government demands receipts for all the items you intend to write off. The key is to make sure you have the cash on hand in the bank *before* you make the purchase and to pay the credit card bill in full at the end of the month. *If you stick to this simple discipline, you'll never have a problem again.*

You'll actually *need* a credit card for certain purchases. Hotels and car rental agencies will almost always demand a credit card number to hold a reservation. *¡No problemo!* You won't be charging anything that you don't have the cash to pay.

A credit card is also handy in an emergency. Your car breaks down on a dark highway. Fine. Use the card. But use your head: The new Beastie Boys album does not qualify as an emergency.

Lastly, enjoy this tasty tidbit: When you charge money on a credit card and pay it back each month, you are actually screwing the credit card company. And as someone who does it every month, lemme say . . . it feels great!

Say what? That's right. When you charge something on a credit card, you are taking out a short-term loan. It's a loan on which you will pay absolutely no interest if you pay it off completely before the payment-due date (usually within 30 days of the billing date). You're getting to use the money, *for free*, as long as you pay it back within thirty days. Money has a time value—it's worth something every single second you have it. So by borrowing money from Visa, paying it back within 30 days, *and not paying any interest*, you are *screwing* them out of their return.

So here's the plan. First, you're going to have just *one* credit card. It'll streamline your bookkeeping, make you more aware of the total amount you're spending, and help you avoid the temptation that a wallet full of plastic can promote. If you haven't already consolidated your cards, do so immediately. Shop around for a good, basic card. Don't worry about the interest rate, because on the CP plan, you won't carry a balance and, hence, will never pay finance charges again. Instead, pick a widely accepted card, maybe one that has some nifty bonuses like free auto rental insurance, and make sure there's no annual fee, or ask the company to waive it.

Now that you've got your one credit card, I want you to revisualize it: Don't think of it as a line of credit, but merely as a convenient way of not having to carry cash— that's all. Whenever you make a purchase, you'll do it with the knowledge that your money is sitting in your checking or savings account, waiting until the bill comes so that you can pay it off . . . in full.

WEALTH: GETTING JIGGY WIT IT

Don't buy things you can't afford. Seems frightfully simple, doesn't it? It *is* simple: The debt dilemma is solved with a tangy dollop of discipline. But when that sort of discipline becomes a part of your life, you'll see how useful a practice it can become.

We want to be wealthy. But wealthy people, more often than not, have more discipline than dollars. The world's greatest investor, Warren Buffet, is worth an estimated $29 billion, but he still lives in the very modest Omaha, Nebraska, home in which he was raised. No Beverly Hills mansion, no motor pool of Porsches. Even Abby Joseph Cohen, chief equity strategist at Goldman, Sachs (a large investment bank), still relies on public transportation to get to work.

Lifelong financial independence is the result of habit. It's the by-product of consistently following a mundane routine of frugality. Wealthy people love money, and they're reluctant to part with it. Though we might associate them with ostentatious spending, the truth is that they are less likely to splurge than we might think. They don't eat out every night. They don't rack up a pile of parking tickets, and they don't tell 7-Eleven clerks to "just keep the change." Without question, the wealthy make wealth a habit, not a hobby. They are wealthy because they act wealthy all of the time, not just occasionally saving a few dollars here and there between spending splurges.

Failing to develop this sort of discipline can be disastrous, even for those who pull down the big bucks. This is why so many highly paid athletes and musicians blow their cash and get into trouble: They haven't learned that the quickest, easiest, and most effective way to have more money is to stop spending so much. M. C. Hammer is just one in the long, sad line of millionaire celebrities turned charity cases. Realistically looking even a few months into the future would have kept Hammer in parachute pants for years to come.

It's not about being a miser, merely about living beneath, rather than beyond, your means. Wealthy people don't deny themselves material pleasures; they spend money on items that they need and can afford. They *save* their money and invest it in products that make them more money. In fact, the easiest way to have more money is to save money, a topic to which Chapter 3 is entirely devoted.

3 STARTING WITH SAVING

I'm not good at math. I'm underpaid by corporate America. Budgets suck.

Yada yada yada.

Excuses abound when it comes to not saving our money. It's no coincidence that people with the most excuses seem to have to the least amount of money. I've had excuses. I've had money. *Money is better.*

Want more money? Of course! Even if we don't want the "stuff" money can buy, there are few people in this world who wouldn't relish the freedom, security, and safety a few extra hundred thou in the bank would bring. The "secret" to having more money is clear, and it has nothing to do with marrying a mogul or making magic in the markets. As old skool as it may sound, *the way to get money is to save it.* A skyrocketing salary won't do it; neither will picking a hot mutual fund or stock.

The bottom line: If you want to have more money, stop spending so much.

I know, I know . . . easier said than done. Okay. So you spend money with the recklessness of Robert Downey, Jr., on a Saturday night **coke binge** through east L.A. Even if you've made some financial faux pas in the past, you can get it together with a

> **Cash. I'm just not happy when I don't have it. The minute I have it, I have to spend it. And I just buy stupid things.**
>
> —Andy Warhol

Mick Fleetwood has said that he spent over $8 million in cocaine during Fleetwood Mac's heyday. If he had put even *half* that amount into the bank in 1977, when the album *Rumors* was released, he would have made an additional $420,000 (4 mil compounded over two years at 5 percent = $420,000) by the time *Tusk* came out in 1979.

Look at some of the possessions you bought in the last 12 months. How many of them do you actually use on a regular basis? How many are gone? Lost? Broken? Buying something and not using it regularly is just like giving the money away in the first place. In investment terms, it's a 100 percent loss on investment.

minimum of hassle. It just takes a concerted effort, some planning, and some patience.

I don't do budgets. They are the financial equivalent of those ridiculous Richard Simmons Deal-a-Meal plans, where each day you get to check off two carbohydrates, two fruits, and so on. Too much hassle . . . too much headache. When it comes to getting our finances in order, we're not looking to trim a bit here and a bit there. We're looking to make a comprehensive change in the way we treat our money. You won't have to count pennies like calories because you won't have the urge to splurge in the first place.

Flip to the back of this book. Unlike many of the wussy financial books on the market, you won't find a condescending series of forms and budgets for you to fill in, check off, and send away for a gold star. Like credit card games . . . *Homey don't play that either.*

So there won't be a strict set of rules. You don't need to buy a financial calculator. And trust me, it won't be cup-o-noodles from here on out. You're not going to starve . . . but save.

What I *will* do is show you how to make some long-term changes in the way you *think* about your money. You'll stop spending your money unconsciously and start getting real satisfaction from the purchases you do choose to make. Remember: *A dime is a terrible thing to waste!*

SWEAT THE SMALL STUFF

"Okay," you say, "but I'm *not* reckless. Every penny I make goes to things I really need!" Bullshit. Here's the deal: If you really want to have more money, you've got to make changes. Now. The longer you wait, the longer it will take to get things done. Moreover, the longer you wait to get started, the more you stand to lose in term of dollars later on. When it comes to saving, time can be your worst enemy or your best friend.

It's like working out at the gym. Merely *thinking* about going keeps your ass perpetually plump. Actually going, even a few times a week, begins the process of shipping you into shape. It's not magic—you just have to do it. Same goes for your finances.

Here's the problem: Most people, no matter what their income is, spend what they make. Money comes in and they shuffle it right on out. *Don't be one of them.* This is why we have banks in the first place. It's a place to store the money that we have no reason to spend. And there's plenty of reasons not to spend.

Here's you: "Oh, but I can't really save anything right now." I just don't buy it! Unless you've had a lung removed in the last few months or have taken in five orphaned siblings, you can find a way to save. Maybe it's only a few bucks a month. That's fine. The amount isn't important, the attitude is. You've got to change your attitude about spending.

But I'm pretty strapped as it is! Even if you're not living large doesn't mean that you actually *need* everything you buy. Where does the money go?

It's lost. All of it. And mostly on the small stuff. Most people who blow their money aren't buying big-ticket items like a car or a house. They spend it, ironically, on items of *no value, or items that lose their value immediately after purchase.* Like hair gel. Or coffee. Or concert tickets. Buy a magazine off the newsstand for $2.50. Before you even walk out of the *store* it's become worthless. You are investing your resources in items that offer no tangible return on investment.

WHAT DO YOU WANT?

Cable. Parking. Phone bills. Takeout. I call this stuff "gen. admin.," or "general administrative"—the everyday nickels and dimes that keep us going. A few bucks here and there never seem to cost that much at the time, but it's the small items that add up. I know it's difficult—these typical indulgences have come to simply seem like the cost of being alive. But beginning to cut down on even a few of the "necessities" will quickly put more money in your pocket or, better yet, in your bank account. Spend five dollars less every day, and after a year you'll have over $1,825. Put that dough in a risk-free CD and you'll have close to $2,000.

Cable me? Try clobber me! A $40 cable bill will run you almost $500 a year. I'm not telling you to skip *South Park*, merely to realize how much our "necessities" are really luxuries, and how much those suckers cost us in the long run.

I'm not asking you to live in a rat-infested room slurping gruel and shivering in front of an empty fireplace. The idea is this: Tiny changes in your routine can compound into a substantial impact on your bottom line. As insignificant as it seems at the time, a few bucks here and there can really add up.

Rochmonas (rach-MO-nes):
Yiddish word meaning
compassion, pity, or mercy.

Finally, forget about miracles. God doesn't pay your Visa bill—you do. And while he's never been on *Capitalist Pig*, I'm fairly certain that God has no **rochmonas** for the sordid spendthrift. So screw praying and stop paying. "Thou shalt have a parka from the J. Crew Christmas Catalog" can be found nowhere in the Old Testament, or *any* testament for that matter.

It all comes back to resources. Resources, as you know by now, are *time* and *money*. Everything—whether it's an education, a meal, a movie—is an investment of your time, money, or both. Being financially responsible means making sure that when you purchase something with your resources, you get back—in one form or another—more than you spend. Economists call it the "return on your investment." Whether you're buying T-bills or T-birds, stocks or sashimi, the question is simple: What is the return and was it worth my investment? Being aware of your return, on both every dollar and every hour, is, to quote GI Joe, "half the battle."

So monitor your expenses for a week or two. Write them down, paying close attention to the small stuff, the regular purchases you make and probably don't even think about. Add it up. Annualize it, or calculate what your costs are for an entire year. Ask yourself, is it worth it? It's a personal decision, of course. I'm not saying you shouldn't get coffee or smoke cigarettes. I just want you to be aware of how much you're spending, and **where** you are spending it. Also, you want to feel as if you are getting a good value in the purchases you do make: When you spend money you should enjoy it to the fullest extent.

So make sure that each dollar you spend comes back to you in a tangible way. In short, make sure that whatever spending you're doing is "worth it."

An example: As the consummate slopmeister, I generally let my cramped studio/office/living quarters acquire a vague resemblance to a Beirut bomb shelter. Every month, I hire a professional housekeeper to whip my little hovel into a state of sanitized, organized perfection. It takes her two hours and costs me thirty dollars. It's a lot of money—money I could be socking away into a mutual fund—but for me, thirty dollars spent on professional cleaning yields an excellent return on my investment. In fact, I consider it a bargain. For one thing, it saves me from having to buy an arsenal of cleaning supplies. *But the real reason?* It saves me an entire Saturday afternoon on my hands and knees picking up cigarette butts, crumpled papers, and empty cans of Diet Coke off the floor.

After taking a trip to Amsterdam last year, a friend ask me how in hell I got the money to pay for it. Interesting that she asked me that very question while sucking down a Winston and a latte. If she gave up even part of her tobacco and coffee habit, she'd have enough for "expensive" trips as well.

Investment	Frequency	$	Yearly cost (hours of work, based on a wage of $12/hour)
Cigarettes	1 pack/day	$3	$1,095 (91)
Latte	1/day	$2.50	$912.50 (76)
Trip to Europe	1/year	$1,500	$1,500 (125)
Cable TV	12 months	$50	$600 (50)
Movies	1/week	$7	$364 (30)
*69	once/week	75¢	$39 (3¼)
Takeout	2/week	$12.50	$1,300 (108)

Knowing my muted propensity toward *too* much physical labor, it would undoubtedly take me longer to accomplish the task than it takes the maid. It would also drive me crazy. Ultimately, having my apartment cleaned up improves my mental health and productivity. Compared to Prozac, a maid is cheap. For me and my priorities, *it's a good return on investment.*

On the other hand, I'd never spend three bucks for a bagel sandwich or seventy-five cents for a can of Coke. Are you *kidding?* We're talking about yeast, flour, water, and sugar here! For me, it's not worth it. I'll make my own sandwich and drink Kool-Aid for the proverbial pennies a glass. A year without the daily bagel and Coke saves me $675.25, quite a chunk of change. Again: It's knowing your priorities.

That's *my* personal approach to a couple of specific nonfinancial investments. You, however, might consciously appreciate the convenience of the same bagel and Coke but prefer to invest your Saturday afternoons into cleaning house. Or maybe you hire the help but bake the bagels yourself.

How can you determine if you are getting a good return on your investment? With financial products, such stocks, bonds, and mutual funds, it's simple. Fund A had a 10 percent return. Fund B's return was 15 percent. Duh.

But we compare. When you compare one investment to the other, especially non-financial, investments, it's a lot easier to see just how much of an investment you are making in just about anything. I've done a few samples on the chart.

Whether they run to Puccini or Poi Dog, our individual tastes and preferences are irrelevant here. *Greed Is Good* is about having the individual freedom to make choices about how you want to live your life and spend your resources. Often the hardest part about getting what you want, is knowing what you want.

So what are your priorities? *What do you want?* And do your actions correspond with what you want? Even more specifically, *are you doing what you need to do to get what you want?* Ask yourself that the next time you slap down $3.50 for a frappuccino while Visa is charging you 17 percent interest on an outstanding balance. You might "say" you want to get out of debt, but your actions aren't corresponding with your words.

Go back to the plans you listed in Chapter 2. Are you working toward your plans? Are you making them a priority? Whether it is getting out of debt, going back to school, whatever—your goals are not simply going to appear. You've got to make them happen.

Totally clichéd but totally true: Talk *is* cheap. And actions do speak louder than words. So don't talk about getting what you want; go ahead and get it. Your actions dictate the course.

SPENDING: THE ACT OF INVESTING IN STUFF

I've already promised that I won't put you on a budget. And if you want specific ideas for cutting back expenses, there are innumerable **tightwad** guides that can help you pinch pennies. You can clip the occasional coupon or make your own soap. To me, that's a hassle. The straightest and easiest road to *saving*—to having more money—is to change the way we think about spending and consumption.

The basics set you back very little. Two thousand calories of rice a day and a couple of feathers to sleep on at night won't stretch anyone's paycheck. There's a certain baseline liberation that comes with realizing that the true **necessities** are cheap. Everything else that we buy is fluff.

After securing food and shelter, you've got a lot left over at the end of the day. So where does it all go? Chances are you're not quite sure. That's because most of our spending is unconscious. It's automatic.

This is a book about investment. Though we don't think of investing as part of our day-to-day routine, in fact, every time you lay down a dollar, you are making an investment. We invest not only in stocks and securities but in parking spaces and sandwiches. Most of us know that investors work hard to get high returns on their money. They research stocks, study mutual fund reports, and double-check the numbers. But because we don't think of our spending as investing, we don't give it the same level of scrutiny and care. We spend automatically, without thinking. We're not really keeping an eye on whether we're getting a good return on our investment.

When you begin to see your spending as investing, you'll undoubtedly find, as I have, that you spend less, because you're aware that the return on most of what we buy isn't worth it in the first place. And when you spend less, you have money left over, money that can (and, I hope, will) be invested in much more lucrative ways, like the stocks, bonds, and mutual funds outlined later in the book.

In the paragraphs that follow I've outlined a few of the tips, tricks, and traps that screw us up by making us spend more and save less. More specifically, they encourage us to make bad investments in the things we buy. By becoming more aware of this process, of why we get hoodwinked into blowing our proverbial load on worthless junk, you will undoubtedly stop wasting so much cash.

Let me remind you . . . greed is good. What we want here is money, not merchandise. Freedom can't be bought with a copy of *Chicken Soup for the Soul, Part XV*, so don't waste your money on stuff that you don't need, that won't either appreciate or be used for several years to come.

Buying a Life (or a lifestyle)

You bought something. Why? Was it because you needed it? Did you want to make a statement about the type of person you are . . . or want to be? Was it an "impulse" buy inspired by an in-store display? Maybe the atmosphere was such that you just couldn't stop browsing? Was the purchase a "reward" for working late every night last week?

In the summer of 1998, the ultra-hip mail-order merchandiser Abercrombie & Fitch distributed a wildly popular magazine-cum-catalog aimed squarely at young people. The volume, a 200-pager, with a circulation of 700,000, was filled with the requisite A&F gear—parkas, pullovers, jeans—plus a whole lot more.

It was packed with treatises on dating, drinking, lounging, and living. The photographic layouts featured A&F's clothes as almost an afterthought; the rhetorical focus of text and visuals was obviously on the "typical" clan of well-scrubbed young people hanging out,

A&F
QUARTERLY

ON THE ROAD

BACK TO SCHOOL ISSUE #9 $5

going on road trips, lifting weights, socializing, and generally having a ball. The **catalog** was filled with page after page of images of a youthful, glamorous, carefree lifestyle.

Both the imagery and the preponderance of text pages with articles on cool restaurants and electronic gadgets led to the unavoidable question: Why would A&F fill the pages of their catalog with the description and imagery of a youthful lifestyle, rather than with even short descriptions of the products themselves? The reason is, they are selling the images: We don't buy A&F jeans, parkas, and turtlenecks because we need them—we buy them because of the attitude or lifestyle they represent. The catalog's message is clear: You too can have as much fun as our models. You too can look this darn sexy. Just buy our khakis for $49, thank you very much!

Lifestyle marketing is everywhere. We can't escape it. When we buy Nikes, for example, we don't merely buy a pair of shoes, but literally buy into the entire marketing fantasy that Nike has worked so hard to create. Buying Nike shoes is buying a piece of the "Just Do It" mentality: it's about commitment, it's about competitiveness, it's about being a winner. An entire lifestyle packed neatly into a simple pair of sneakers.

This is why many advertisements don't even feature the products that they're selling. In 1989, Nissan introduced a new line of car, the Infiniti, through a $60 million ad campaign that never showed the cars themselves. We saw seagulls. We saw nature. Not a fuel injector to be found. Buying an Infiniti became buying a way of thinking—a way of looking at the world. *C'mon!* It's a car, for chrissake! Just give me four wheels and styling that doesn't look like the Flintstone mobile.

Take a look at your stuff. Most of your material possessions are probably emblazoned with a logo, slogan, or identifying brand name. Besides the Golden Arches, sweeping swoosh, and other identifying marks, the "brands" consist of the million-dollar mythology that has been carefully created surrounding the particular products.

Let's talk about lip cream. My lips don't know the difference between bargain basement and the Body Shop. As a die-hard Chicagoan, I can attest that generic lip junk or Vaseline soothes just as well as the high-end variety that's putting tofu on Body Shop entrepreneur **Anita Roddick's** proverbial plate. The difference? Mostly mythology: Generic lip cream makes you feel cheap, whereas Body Shop brand makes you feel like a domesticated Dian Fossey, rescuing chapped lips and chimps in one simple purchase. The Body Shop "lifestyle" is environmentally friendly and socially liberal. The connection they are hoping we make is that if you care about the earth, you'll buy Body Shop. It sounds hilarious, but Body Shop sold $482 million worth of merchandise in 1998. Anita Roddick is laughing, all right, all the way to the bank.

Anita Roddick opened the first Body Shop in Brighton, England, in 1976. From there she expanded across England, into Europe, and finally into the United States.

Closer to home and ultimately more frightening is Martha Stewart. On her television show or in her magazine or series of expensive coffee-table books, Martha is the maternal McGuyver. Some women eat up the idea of living the Martha Stewart lifestyle. "A couscous-colored Kleenex cozy . . . it's a GOOD THING!" PUH-LEEZE!!! Don't buy into this bullshit. A Kleenex cozy alone won't turn your one-bedroom convertible into the Martha Stewart fantasy world of Waspy lawn parties, high tea, and dewy meadows. But Martha has mined a mint. It came not from hand labeling high-end honey (as featured in the February 1996 issue of her magazine) but by selling millions of the misguided on the lifestyle of "Stewarthood."

You're probably already aware of lifestyle marketing, simply because we are targeted more than any other demographic. It's almost to be expected. One postmodern move of marketing brilliance: Coca-Cola has effectively co-opted the "anti-image" vibe in their new campaign for **Sprite**. "Image is nothing. . . . Thirst is everything," the ads scream. The subtext is clear: People fed up with image marketing drink Sprite. The beverage of the independent thinker, right? Uh-huh. It's the same bubbly beverage from the

Please note: Real hipsters drink water. From the tap.

decidedly more silly "I like the Sprite in you" days. Don't be a lapdog to every marketing maven that comes along with a new slogan. Concentrate on the product. Buy what you like because you like it, not because it makes you anything or anyone else. Because it doesn't.

But what about quality? Don't we buy well-known brands because of the higher quality of the products themselves? Again, *I don't believe it.* Only God knows why my Sony cordless phone broke three times, while the Radio Shack special continues to connect. The truth is that most of the major labels, in terms of quality, are indistinguishable from their less hyped (and less expensive) counterparts. Despite the marketing, most products are basically generic commodities. Like plain white T-shirts. Like *salt*. Why do we consistently pony up for items whose only distinguishable benefit is the strength of the intangible brand? The armchair psychologist in all of us knows: We find the idea of a particular brand to be "cool" or appealing. Wanting to associate ourselves with said coolness, we surround ourselves with those brands, paying a premium in the process. This type of behavior, of which we are all guilty, can really break the bank. In the abstract, it's also kind of sad.

You can buy a lifestyle, but you can't buy a life.

A sound strategy for avoiding the lifestyle-purchase trap is to focus on the products you're buying rather than the folklore you're learning. Remember your priorities. What do you need? What do you want? If you need pants, then buy pants. If it's the model-laden A&F road trip adventure that your heart desires, then get a map, some models, and get going. *Know what you want*, because buying khakis isn't going to get you any closer to California, and popularity, friendship, or self-esteem just don't come out of a catalog.

Besides, being an individual, to some extent, is being different. In the *Dance Fever* of distinction, buying the same Gap **schmatte** as everyone else isn't going to score you points for originality. Set your own style. Be a shepherd, not a sheep.

Finally, realize that salable "lifestyles," no matter how exceedingly hip at the time, eventually fall prey to the next big thing. Remember Izod? The company's sales peaked in the eighties at $450 million. By the early nineties, consumers wanted to be perceived as more individualistic and rejected visible logos in general, and Izod sales fell dramatically—virtually disappeared after the yuppified 1980s. Lifestyle trends tend to follow the a natural cycle of popularity. Being on the cutting edge, as you probably now realize, is more work than it's actually worth. When it comes to both our time and money, it's a bad investment.

The Inflation of Expectations

"I'm entitled to the good life! Don't I deserve my three-dollar latte every afternoon? Don't I get to live in the two-thousand-dollar loft-style New York apartment a la *Friends*? Don't I get to drive a fuel-injected European sports car?"

Nope!

Shocking as it may seem, we're not entitled to these things just because we live in America. Our status as citizens of the world's greatest capitalist country merely gives us the passport to profit, not an annuity to affluence. Drunk on *Dynasty*, *Dallas*, and *90210* reruns, some foreigners think that all Americans are born abnormally affluent. That, of course, is a fantasy. Ironically, many of us are foolishly beginning to believe it as well.

Recent research at the University of Connecticut's Roper Center tells us that what people view as a "necessity of life"—what people think they're entitled to—has changed greatly over the last several years. In 1987, a poll showed that most Americans felt that an income of $50,000 a year would be enough to "fulfill all [their] dreams." Less than a decade later, the "fulfill all your dreams" number had more than doubled.

Even more shocking, a recently published study found that people living in households making $100,000 per year say they can't buy everything they need. *What gives?* These people can't make ends meet on a six-figure income? How much coke *are* they sniffing? As I see it, unless you have an *Eight Is Enough*–sized family (all with Dick Van Patten's appetite), most likely the problem is not your income but your **expectations**.

According to a 1998 survey conducted by Yankelovich Partners, 57 percent of students **expect** to be wealthier than their parents, up from 52 percent in 1997. Students expect an average annual starting salary of $36,000, and 18 percent expect to be making $50,000 or more.

Americans' expectations and corresponding spending have escalated over the past two decades. There's a reason for this shift. Once we compared ourselves to our neighbors, people in the same general income bracket. There was some "keeping up with the Joneses," perhaps lust for a new lawnmower or color TV, but because everyone on the block made about the same amount of money, it was not terribly difficult to keep up. But we don't know our neighbors anymore, and sitting on the front porch while sipping iced tea and gossiping about Esther's "purdy" new hat is for most of us, quite simply, a pipe dream. We've still got neighbors of a sort, but they're not on their front porches anymore. They're on television.

In case you've been comatose since *Cop Rock*, let me take this opportunity to remind you that television, hard as this may be to hear, *ain't real!* Television is chock full of the rich and beautiful, but totally devoid of the realistic and reasonable.

Most of the eighties shows we grew up watching, from *thirtysomething* to *Cosby*, presented highly affluent lifestyles as the norm. After spending our adolescence watching TV, most of us think Cosby's million-dollar Brooklyn brownstone looks like a downright reasonable residence. When Arnie on *L.A. Law* got a lap swimming pool, millions of us subconsciously adjusted our sense of normal adulthood consumption. More recently, we've tuned into *Melrose Place* and *Friends*, starring characters who supposedly hold jobs just like you and me, yet live in digs that are remarkably more affluent and never seem to spend any time working. The *Friends* apartment, for example, although undeniably cool, is by *no means* even a close approximation of the digs that entry-level New York twenty-somethings can afford. Kids who flock to New York City with the hopes of living the hip *Friends* life are shocked to discover that their pay will barely get them a one-bedroom share (usually with a stranger) in the armpit of town.

So the American Dream is no longer a modest house with a white picket fence. It's been inflated into a country estate with granite kitchen countertops, a Jacuzzi built into the bathroom, and tall cedar fencing to keep the neighbors from gawking at your $2,000 gas grill. And don't forget the extra-large garage for your two Jeeps and a Jag. This world exists—on television, that is.

What's a consumer to do? If you want to start saving and investing, it'll help to develop the sense of modest expectations and frugality that defined the pre–World War II mentality of our elders. A long time ago, pants were mended, not replaced. Books were borrowed, not bought. And people realized that cash was king and crap was crap. Try talking to your grandparents; get a sense of their Depression-era expectations. Let your **bubbie** tell you how she scrimped and saved, how she rationed during the war, and how amazingly happy it was possible to be without the newest, best, and brightest of everything. If your Bubbie is unavailable, call mine (www.capitalistpig.com).

Bubbie (Bŭ-be): Yiddish for "granny."

Our expectations have become so inflated, in fact, that even how we classify "poor" has become totally wacked. According to the Census Bureau, 30 million Americans are living in poverty. Not to sound cruel, but it's a misleading term. By almost any global standard, Americans who are classified as "poor" don't have it that bad. In 1995, over 41 percent of all poor households owned their own homes. Seventy percent own a car; 27 percent percent own two or more cars; 97 percent of poor households have a color television—nearly half own two or more; 75 percent have a VCR, 64 percent own a microwave, and 25 percent have an automatic dishwasher.

Impulse: Be, but Don't Buy

We are drawn to impulsive people. Fascinated by them. They are, as Kerouac put it, the "roman candles" of the world, exploding in God knows what direction; always surprising us with the unexpected.

In *Lethal Weapon* terminology, it's Mel Gibson's impulsive character to Danny Glover's more circumspect one. The level-headed one never seems to have as much fun as the impulsive, seemingly reckless, gunslinger.

Now, I'm a big believer in risk. As a commodities trader, I understand that taking risks, especially well-calculated risks, is the very essence of sound speculation. We'll unpack *that* tasty package later in the book, but for now, let's understand the relationship between impulse and risk as it relates to spending and saving.

Taking a risk is taking a chance. It's understanding the potential upsides and downsides of a particular action or situation, then deciding if the risk *parameters* are congruent with our own. Is skydiving risky? Depends on your own risk tolerance—are you afraid of heights? Speed? Or perhaps smashing into the ground at 200 mph?

Now, being *impulsive* is a much different animal from taking risks. Being impulsive means doing the unexpected and surprising everybody, perhaps even ourselves. Sometimes impulsive behavior can be fun, even rewarding. But if you think skydiving is risky, being impulsive with your money is downright dangerous.

In the retail realm, here's how impulse buying often occurs:

Imagine you're standing at the checkout line at the Piggly Wiggly, patiently holding a week's worth of chips, salsa, and Diet Coke. Your eyes scan the displays opposite the register. Cigarettes. Batteries. Altoids. "Gee," you think to yourself, "Altoids are only two ninety-nine . . . I've got that in my pocket right now." They weren't on your list, and you hadn't planned on buying them. You don't even really want them—but you somehow really want to *buy* them. Like a *Star Trek* tractor beam, they seem to be drawing you closer. And just as it's your turn to check out, you grab the Altoids and toss them in with your other groceries. Reveling in the excitement of the unexpected, you feel the adrenaline rush of a cheap high. One part guilty, one part glad, you justify the purchase in your mind: "I'll use them. Besides, it's only three dollars."

When you buy on **impulse** you, one, buy stuff you don't really need, and, two, buy stuff that quickly becomes worthless.

> *The only people for me are the mad ones, the ones who are mad to live, mad to talk, mad to be saved, desirous of everything at the same time, the ones who never yawn or say a commonplace thing, but burn, burn, burn, like fabulous yellow roman candles exploding like spiders across the stars.*
>
> —Jack Kerouac, *On the Road*

For most of us, just seeing how quickly **impulse** buys can add up is enough of a deterrent. If you still can't resist the urge to splurge, make it a point to stay out of harm's way. Don't browse through the magazine racks, stay away from the coffee cart, and, especially, avoid window shopping like a network showing of *Leonard, Part 6*. Window shopping is the impulse buy just waiting to happen.

It's almost as if you're giving your money away. When we buy something impulsively, we don't think very much about the consequences because they don't seem terribly significant. Three bucks on mints isn't going to put your in the poor house, right? Besides, what can you do with $2.99? Not much.

How'd you like to find $1,091.35? That's how much you'll have spent if you spend that $2.99 every day for a year, pretty much the cost of a daily double espresso. Now we're talking real money. With $1,091.35, you could go on vacation. And take me with you. Put it in the bank for a year (at a low interest rate) and now you've got even more. Now we're talking real money. Individually, impulse buys seem harmless; collectively, they clean you out like economic Ex-Lax.

Here's how buying *should* work. You need something specific. You go buy it. You come home and watch *Sports Center* on ESPN. End of story.

Here it comes, the unabridged guide to shopping: Make a list of what you need. Go buy it. Go home. Don't dawdle, dabble, or delay. Every minute you spend in the store is one more minute you might buy something you don't need or want.

The Reward Trap

The term "rat race" is shorthand for the day-to-day realities of work life. You get up. Lap up a latte. Work like a warhorse. Race home through rush hour. Sleep during *Seinfeld*.

The impulse buy in effect.

And do it all over the next day.

'Neath the veil of this regular routine, however, is the more disturbing cycle of self-nurturing "rewards" we create to relieve the stress of the strenuous effort of the race itself. It is this very vicious circle that leaves many of us overfatigued and underfinanced. *Fuhgeddaboudit.*

Here's how it happens: With most jobs, we work ourselves into a state of exhaustion, slaving away for a boss, teacher, or colleague who undoubtedly doesn't deserve the high position of authority to begin with. In a attempt to recharge our own internal batteries, we reward ourselves, most often with a purchase, justifying the expense as a "just reward" for a job well done.

Perhaps it's a vacation. Or a new CD. Or jeans. Or a nice meal. We get in the habit of buying ourselves "presents" to combat the fatigue, boredom, and bullshit of the relentless rat race. The unfortunate reality, however, is that most of our hard work goes into supporting these splurges. The harder we work, the bigger the rewards. We're running a race, not as rats, but dogs. Pavlovian pawns in a circle of consumerism.

While working at Starbucks, noontime brought the dilemma: What to do about lunch? At the time I was making just over five bucks an hour, before taxes. After bowing to baby boomers all morning long, lunchtime was a welcome respite. What I could never understand, however, was my coworkers' interest in ordering takeout Chinese as a midday reward for their morning's labors. The bill from Chin's Chop Suey invariably ended up costing about ten bucks a person, leaving me wondering why they didn't just skip lunch and leave two hours earlier. I, on the other hand, by bringing a sandwich from home, was essentially giving myself an automatic **bonus** of about 30 bucks a week over my caffeinated comrades. When you think about how much time one spends to make that money, it's just not worth the effort.

$30/week $\times$ 52 weeks = $1,560

When work sucks so bad that you are constantly needing rewards, something's got to change. Chances are, it's your job. If you can, get yourself to another work environment, one where every bit of effort isn't put forth merely for the short-lived chewbone of a material reward. A massage, dinner out, or vacation may provide instant gratification, but those purchases ultimately keep us truckin' on the same old track. We make it. Spend it. Buy it. And blow it.

Instead, get in the habit of rewarding yourself with a long-lasting investment . . . like extra cash later on, when you really need it. *Ah,* **dividends**! The gift that keeps on giving! Could there be a monetary reward better than more money? No way! The satisfaction of putting money away, seeing the interest accrue, and

Dividend: The portion of a company's after-tax earnings that is paid directly to stockholders.

garnering the freedom that goes along with the extra cash is the best reward imaginable. We're looking for satisfaction, we're looking to be able to accumulate enough money to have choices. When you free yourself from needing so many rewards, you free yourself from much of the work it takes to procure those rewards. Less stuff. More satisfaction.

Love for Sale

After receiving a gift, how many times have you thought "Gee . . . it's nice, but I'd rather have the money"? Adding insult to injury, if you try to return the gift, chances are the store won't give you a refund, just a credit toward more junk you don't really need.

Oy! We're supposed to be saving resources. But more often then not, the holiday gift exchange results in waste.

When you give someone an expensive gift, you are exchanging your resources (cash) for an item that may or may not be of similar value to the recipient. In buying a gift, we are in effect placing a "value" call on a particular piece of merchandise. While there's no question your friend will appreciate the thought, there's no telling if she will value the item, in dollar-denominated terms, as highly as you. A watch, for example, that costs us $50 won't necessarily be valued as highly by the recipient of the gift. So don't do it. It is the thought that counts, and thoughts, even the deeply personal ones, are free. Friends and family would prefer a honest, personal handwritten note (MSRP: $.59) more than almost anything you could find in the Brookstone catalog (backpack picnic set, MSRP: $150). Wouldn't you?

One classy way of giving gifts is to make a reasonable donation to a local charity. They will gladly notify your friends that you have given money to a worthy cause in their name. Even better, you'll be able to write off the gift as a charitable deduction on your income tax return—just be sure to keep the acknowledgment of your gift that the charity sends back to you.

Caught Up in Convenience

"Jane! Stop this crazy thing!"

—George Jetson

George Jetson's desperate cry for help, uttered from his automatic dog walker in the final moments of *The Jetsons* closing credits, pretty much sums up the conundrum of convenience.

Written with a wonderfully idealistic take on life in the twenty-first century, **The Jetsons** showcased how technological conveniences would supposedly replace labor with leisure. In the shadow of Sputnik and the space race, the show forecast a futuristic age where everything, from dreams to dinner, came at the touch of a button.

Okay, so you don't work at Spacely Sprockets, but there's no question that at every turn there are products, services, and items designed to make our lives more *convenient*. Convenience, while terribly . . . ummm . . . convenient, costs way too much. Unlike George, who was able to support an entire family (and one robot maid), most of us simply can't afford much of the conveniences we now take for granted.

The problem with convenience is that what we "save" in time we dole out in dollars. Nobody's going to argue that it's not *easier* to buy lunch rather then making it yourself. The difference, of course, is the premium price of what convenience actually costs.

Convenience is easy. Convenience saves time. And we pay for all of it. It's the difference between buying a six-pack of soda ($2.60) and bringing one can to work each day or buying one can from the soda machine each day ($.75 × 6 = $4.50). You are getting the same amount of "stuff" while paying roughly twice the price. It doesn't take a Harvard MBA to know that this hare-brained style of money management is nothing less then *totally retarded*.

ATM fees are the same deal. *Yes*, the cash station saves the hassle of going to the teller, but use another bank's network and you'll incur a fee of a dollar or so. What's one dollar? On the average $20 withdrawal, that's a full 5 percent gone . . . just given away in the name of "convenience." You'll have to work 5 percent more hours, or make 5 percent more in the market to cover the cost of that convenience. Constantly running to the ATM for a twenty here and there seems easy, but we are trading a lot of our hard work for a tiny kernel of convenience, paying a high price for what should be free. If you have $1,000 in the bank earning 3 percent interest, going to the ATM even every week, costing $52 yearly, completely wipes out the interest of $30. You are no longer getting paid for keeping your money in the bank, but are *paying* the bank for the privilege of withdrawing your money.

THE SIMPLEST SAVING STRATEGY: LIVING BENEATH YOUR MEANS

The highest order of greed, and the easiest way to combat many of the money maladies outlined above, is simply to live beneath your means. Kinda like "Gandhi does greed."

Living beneath your means sounds scary, although let me assure you, it has nothing to do with moving into a cardboard box or slurping up super-value meals for the rest of your days. It's simply about buying everything you need, some of what you want, and not feeling as if you've "missed out" on much of anything.

Living beneath your means starts out with establishing what means you have. Refer to the "assets and liabilities" sheet we mulled over in Chapter 2. It should all be there.

Okay. Chances are, you've got a job. If you don't, get one, you lazy-ass! At the time of this writing, the country is enjoying the lowest unemployment in over 25 years. It doesn't have to be *the* job, but *a* job. Work at a café, wash dishes, hell . . . even work at Starbucks if you must—it's a job, not a career choice. You don't need to read the *Wall Street Journal* to know that getting a steady income stream is vital, no matter what your lifestyle is to become.

Work is work. There's an unfounded elitism among some college-educated individuals who think that because they've got a piddly piece of parchment, they are forever exempt from manual labor, comparatively low pay, or the (gasp!) service sector. Now I abhor washing dishes as much as the next guy, but *any port in a storm*, as the saying goes. With a job, you can start to get *greedy*. Without, and you're simply stranded in squalor. So put down your attitude, pick up the want ads, and get a friggin' job!

With a job, you've got some cash coming in the door. Spend not! Start saving, little by little. Relish the feeling of watching your bank account grow. In the dark of night, when the J. Crew catalog beckons you with its new spring line, pull out your bank statements and see how the numbers have added up. That money—that $100 or $300 or $500 sitting in savings—is YOURS! You've worked for it! So be greedy! Be a stingy bastard and hold that urge to splurge.

Hobo no 'mo . . . You've got a job and savings. Excellent! Now how you treat that income, savings, and, yes, resources is everything. Don't treat it carelessly. Savor the power, the choices, and the opportunity a few bucks in the bank can bring! Living in luxury quickly puts you back in the poor house. It's time to learn to live beneath your means, and you'll have money in the bank.

The quickest way to illustrate how it works is simple: Add up everything you have, *then pretend to have half as much.* It sounds crazy, but it works.

Sound scary? Being aware of some of the buying traps discussed above can make the process much less painful. When you treat your spending as an investment and avoid blowing it on traps like convenience, impulse, and lifestyle buys, you'll find that living on half your means is much easier than you'd imagine.

Life will seem more simple, streamlined, and balanced. The question "Can I afford it?" becomes moot. When you live beneath you means, you can afford *everything* you choose, many times over. That's the beauty! You will find yourself living very comfortably, because the decisions you make regarding money will never compromise the less expensive life you've chosen. When you practice living beneath your means, the cramped studio seems superbly spacious, and the sale-rack sweaters seem like haute couture. Moreover, as you're enjoying your newfound frugality, you've got some serious peace of mind sitting in savings.

Think of it as a mental trick you're playing on yourself. You've got to convince yourself that you've saved half of what you actually have. Make it a game. Challenge yourself to buy only the necessities, forgoing buying crap "just because you can afford it." When you are living beneath your means . . . you can't afford it! It's a tremendous mental burden lifted from your shoulders.

A few years back, when I first started living beneath my means, I went a bit—shall we say—overboard. I lived in a half-sized studio (closet is more like it), ate most of my meals out of a can, and basically bought nothing at all. Instead of going shopping, I went to the library. Instead of going to the movies, I went to the beach. Normal? Nope. But I made a fortune.

You don't need to make that radical a lifestyle change. Because even living just slightly beneath your means will produce the tangible results we're looking for: Money in the bank.

Banks don't blow! The most sickening pleasure in living beneath your means is what happens to the "other half," the savings that you've excluded (at least mentally) from your day-to-day dollars. This is the ultimate kicker: As you work to live beneath you means, that money is going to begin to work as well . . . work for you. As you continue to work and live on one income, your savings, your other "income," will compound through a variety of investment products. You'll be a dual-income family without having to get married.

$1,000 Compounded at 11%

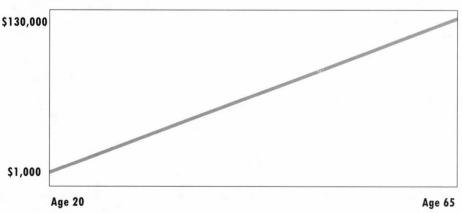

$130,000

$1,000

Age 20   **Age 65**

ONWARD AND UPWARD

The name of our game, my friends, is wealth creation. It comes in two decidedly different formats, active and passive. Active wealth creation is the job. It is the activity, or series of activities, with which we fill our days, providing goods and/or services in exchange for a wage. Passive wealth creation is when your money works for you through a variety of investment products or vehicles. Passive wealth creation takes longer, but yields substantially more beefy rewards. Stashing a mere $1,000 into an average mutual fund while in your early twenties will yield over $130,000 by the time you're ready to retire.

That's a hundred grand that you'll have had to do NO work for. Compounding doesn't take effort, just time. So get the money together by working, by not spending as much, and by not having debt. *Then start letting the money work for you.* Living beneath your means, basically living a little leaner *now,* is no big deal. Forgo a few of the luxuries you've come to take for granted. Take outrageous pleasure in knowing that the junk you would have bought now will be worthless later on, while the money you save (and invest) will have grown exponentially. You can work for the money. Or you can let your money work for you. It takes discipline and commitment. Ultimately, the choice to be wealthy or poor is up to you. Which is it going to be?

PART 2:
INVESTING

4 INVESTING IN SLOW MO

In Part 1, I talked about saving, and the importance of making every dollar count. In Part Two, which focuses on investing, I'm going to tell you how to begin using financial investments to reach your goals. I will be covering stocks, bonds, and mutual funds, and you'll be investing in all of 'em. But not before we do a little backtracking:

A large part of understanding what investing *is* involves understanding what it is *not*.

For most of us, investing seems kind of foreign. It's something that always occurs "over there," perhaps in the bowels of Wall Street or on the high-pressure trading floors of big-time investment banks. We learned this BS from the BS-box. Am I going to blame the media for our misunderstanding of money? *Hell, yeah!* Sown from the **Peter Arnett** school of responsible journalism, most of our misconceptions about the process of investing come from what we've seen on TV and in films.

TV shows are brimming with misleading professional stereotypes. For lawyers, it was *L.A. Law* and *The Practice*. Doctors were originally fictionalized on *M*A*S*H*, then *St. Elsewhere;* now it's *ER.* Most of the enlightened among us understand that these shows are entertainment, not documentaries. I mean, George Clooney is one hell of an actor, but I wouldn't want him taking out *my* appendix.

Hollywood loves Wall Street stereotypes. If you want to

The journalist **Peter Arnett** rose to stardom as a result of his reporting from Baghdad during the Gulf War, but after narrating the infamously irresponsible "Valley of Death" poison-gas story for CNN, he claimed he was ignorant of the story's details. CNN, which was forced to retract the story, has now issued a "no excuses" policy whereby all their correspondents are held accountable for the accuracy of the stories they narrate.

know what investing, isn't . . . let's go to the movies. Money is so undeniably *interesting*, so salaciously sexy, that it makes perfect fodder for filmmakers. Most of these finance fantasies boast more inaccuracies than your average Oliver Stone bio-pic. In fact, Stone himself directed 1987's *Wall Street*, arguably the greatest tour de force of fictitious finance.

Wall Street, as you might remember, stars Michael Douglas and Charlie Sheen in a modern-day morality play set during the height of the go-go 1980s. Michael Douglas won an Oscar (and my eternal admiration) for his brilliant portrayal of Gordon Gekko, the F-U financial mastermind loosely based on the real-life trader Ivan Boesky. The plot centers on Gekko's use of **insider information** to manipulate the markets. Gekko makes his millions using leverage—placing big, short-term bets on a small number of stocks. In a world of **big dogs** nobody is bigger than Gordon Gekko. Gekko's testosterone-laden personality personifies the Wall Street stereotype: he slams phones down Rambo style, spouts classic gunslinger dialog, and barely creases his Armani suit.

Insider information is information regarding a company's affairs and plans (say, a merger) that has not been publicly released. Insider trading is the illegal buying or selling of a security using this information, which, obviously, gives the trader an unfair advantage over other investors.

"Big dogs" is a term often used by the legendary bond trader Charlie DiFrancesca to describe large, well-capitalized traders. The best description of "big dog" trading can be found in the highly excellent *Charlie D,* by William D. Falloon (John Wiley).

While many of the terms and tactics portrayed, especially in *Wall Street*, are accurate, what's unrealistic is that these movies only show the high-stakes side of finance—a side that for most people just doesn't exist. I know, because I see it almost every morning. At age twenty-two I became a member of the Mid-America Commodities Exchange, a subsidiary of the world's largest futures exchange, the **Chicago Board of Trade**, where I trade futures and options on everything from bonds (U.S. Treasury) to beans (soy, that is). Yes . . . I've seen fortunes won and lost in a matter of moments, à la *Wall Street*. It does happen. But that side of the business has nothing to do with investment. It's trading. There's a difference: Traders make trades. Investors make money.

Photo credit: Britt Fohrman

So don't be lured into thinking that investing is something that takes dozens of frantic phone calls to a broker, or involves taking on huge risks like a sophomore-sized **Soros**. Trading, which is what we see in the movies, and investing, which is what the next three chapters focus on, are not one and the same. It's a important distinction to make, and is one of the reasons why this book distinguishes between "investing" and "speculation."

We'll talk about trading later, but first, let's investigate where we'll really make our millions . . . investing.

Trading Places *is worth repeat viewings as well.*

Procure yourself some pork rinds and have yourself a *Capitalist Pig* movie night! *Wall Street* is required viewing (by far my favorite movie). Other recommended favorites include *Other People's Money,* a comedy about a mom-and-pop business that tries to fight a hostile takeover by a corporate raider (played by Danny DeVito), and *Barbarians at the Gate,* based on the best-selling book by Bryan Burrough and John Helyar. It is a gripping account of the fight to control RJR Nabisco during the then-largest takeover in Wall Street history.

WHAT IT IS

With a nod to the high school teacher who warned me never to include denotative definitions in papers of importance, I thought I'd begin by pulling up a good old-fashioned dictionary definition of "invest." *Webster's Third New International Dictionary* gives the following definition: "*1a:* to commit (money) for a long period in order to earn a financial return *b:* to place (money) with a view to minimizing risk rather than speculating for large gains at greater hazard *2:* to make use of with particular thought of future benefits or advantages: to commit funds for future gain or purchase something of intrinsic value: make an investment."

After scouring the "Capitalist Pig" archives, I came up with an even more focused explanation. What is an investment? *An investment takes place whenever we commit limited resources (our money) to a product (securities, like stocks, bonds, or mutual funds) with the expectation of gaining probable returns.*

When we invest we choose to direct our resources into something for which we expect to garner a probable, demonstrable return at some point in the future. Two of the key words here are "probable" and "expect." Here's where the *Wall Street* movie malarkey falls apart: Unlike traders, investors aren't just *hoping* their securities will pay off . . . they're expecting it. Investors who have done their homework can actually *expect* a certain return based on the past performance of a particular type of security. All the investor is "hoping" for is that the investment of choice will continue to perform in the manner which it always has. There's no phone slamming or split-second decisions to contend with when you invest, because from moment to moment your game plan just doesn't change.

Is investing fun? Not especially. That is, unless you enjoy watching paint dry. Unlike trading, investing *should* be boring. There shouldn't be panicked decisions about buying or selling or wild hopes of instant fortune. When you invest, you choose the appropriate product that fits your investment goal, sit back, and wait for it to perform in the expected manner. It takes years.

Let's say you buy a stock mutual fund. Why would you do that? Because you know that over a long period of time, stocks have performed better than any other type of investment. Good decision. The market drops 3 percent, turning your $1,000 into $970 after just a few weeks. What are you going to do? *Sell?* C'mon! You're looking ten years out—not ten minutes. Investments fluctuate . . . they go up some and down some. Over time, you can expect them to perform how they always have—in the case of stocks, about 11 percent a year.

Investing takes patience. It takes prudence. It takes time.

WE GOT TIME, DAMMIT!

We have something **Alan Greenspan** and the millions of platinum card–carrying baby boomers don't. It's a commodity, a resource that is arguably more valuable than *gold*.

Alan Greenspan has been the chairman of the Board of Governors of the Federal Reserve System since Ronald Reagan first appointed him in 1987. As chairman, Greenspan helps set the country's monetary policy.

Cats, Andrew Lloyd Webber's
fur-ball fantasy gone awry, is
currently the longest-running show
on Broadway, having played
over 17 years and more than
6,200 performances.

Compound interest is the phenomenon of rapidly growing returns
you earn when you let money continually earn interest on itself.

It's time. O Time! How do I dig thee! Deliciously long, beautiful weeks . . . month after month, days line up and our lives stretch out into the future, into the vast unknown.

So I'm planning (tentatively) on spending another 50 or so years on this planet. Seeing the changes that have occurred over the previous 50, one can only imagine the wacky shit that'll be going down come 2050. *So much will change.* Who knows, maybe even **Cats** will close. Now I'm *really* talking crazy!

So expect the unexpected. Of this much, however, I am certain: Whatever happens, my money will work harder than I do. I take a sweetly sick satisfaction in knowing that somewhere in the world, every second of the day and night, my money is hard at work. That is investing.

That's also where the boring part comes in. It's my money that's doing all the work. I'm not actually *doing* anything. Nothing, that is, except watching my fortune compound over long periods of time.

Ben Franklin called this phenomenon "the eighth wonder of the world," but you and I can just call it compound interest. **Compound interest** is the exponential growth that occurs when you let even a small amount of money continually earn interest on itself. The return grows faster with each passing year.

For example, if you put $1,000 into an investment that earns 10 percent interest per year (which is actually a little less than the 11 percent return that large company stocks have historically produced, and significantly less than the 12.7 percent that small stocks have historically done), at the end of the year you'll have $1,100. Big whoop, right? Okay, get ready for magic. Don't spend that hundred dollars in interest! The compounding occurs when you don't touch the interest—when the interest itself begins earning interest. Let's say you don't touch your investment. After another year, you'll have earned that same 10 percent, except it won't be on just $1,000 as before, but $1,100. The upshot? In Year 2 you'll have $1,210. Year 3, you'll have $1,331. It's adding up! By Year 10 you will have more than doubled your money, to a staggering $2,594. This is compounding. And this is how you'll meet your goals.

While it's tempting to think that the 10 percent yearly return is the most important part of your investment, the key component here is the boring one—time. When you don't touch your investment, time works its groovy magic. No selling, no phone slamming, no throat

Power of Compounding

Hypothetical investment in stocks

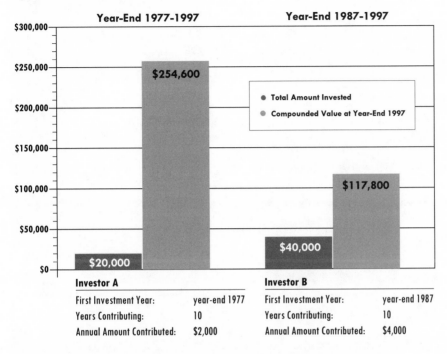

| Year-End 1977-1997 | Year-End 1987-1997 |

- ● Total Amount Invested
- ● Compounded Value at Year-End 1997

$254,600

$117,800

$20,000

$40,000

Investor A

First Investment Year:	year-end 1977
Years Contributing:	10
Annual Amount Contributed:	$2,000

Investor B

First Investment Year:	year-end 1987
Years Contributing:	10
Annual Amount Contributed:	$4,000

Dow Jones Industrial Average (Long-term)

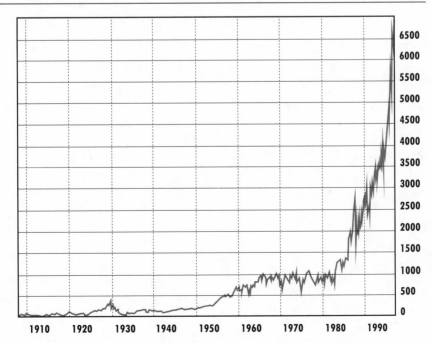

What's as good as gold? Almost any-thing, considering it's performance over the last few years. The price of the metal has been in a steady decline since the early 1980s when fears over inflation pushed the price of gold well over the $800/ounce market. For most of the latter half of the 1990s, the price has languished in the $300/ounce range. Why? Unlike stocks and bonds, which represent economic interests in productive companies, gold has no productive economic value. It doesn't pay an interest rate, doesn't provide an income stream, it doesn't do much of anything. So for long-term invest-ment, all that glitters is not gold.

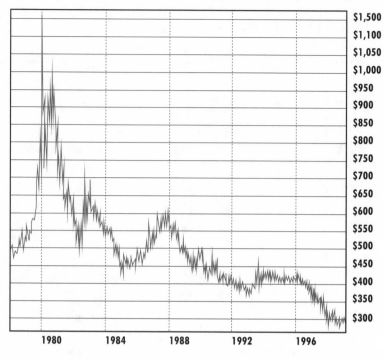

$1 COMPOUNDED AT 10 PERCENT PER YEAR	
Year 1	$1.10
Year 2	$1.21
Year 3	$1.33
Year 4	$1.46
Year 5	$1.61
Year 10	$2.59
Year 15	$4.17
Year 20	$6.72
Year 30	$17.44
Year 50	$117.39

grabbing. And compound interest is just as effective with lower rates of return. Invest $1,000 at 8 percent, (which is a very reasonable return for many bond, or "fixed income," funds), and after ten years your grand will have sky-rocketed to $2,159. Wait ten years more and you'll have $4,661. Ten more? Now you've got an amazing $10,063. You've just turned $1,000 into $10,000 . . . without even lifting a finger.

To get a better picture of how important time really is, consider this: If a 20-year-old puts $1,000 into a mutual fund that returns on average 12 per-cent a year, by the time he or she turns 50, that money will have grown to just over $30,000 ($35,949). If he or she waits until age 30 to begin, the return will amount to over $10,000 ($10,892) What a difference a decade of com-pounding makes!

Letting interest compound over time is, without a doubt, the most important way you'll make money. It works on any type of investment "product," not just mutual funds, as long you never touch the interest. The only action you *should* take is to add regularly to your initial stash. An example: Let's say you started at age 20 with $1,000 and added to it regularly. Even if you dumped an additional $25 a month into the fund, the price of dinner and a few drinks, your return would have compounded into— *are you ready for this?*—$123,323.74 by the time you are 50.

Yet another example. Let's take our first example, in which the $1,000 became $30,000 after 30 years. But say that from the very beginning you added just a bit more each month—$50. At the end of 30 years your money would compound to an astounding $210,000. Now here comes lazy-ass, who starts investing the same amount at 30. Catch-up boy who starts at 30 will have made only $60,000. Big difference.

A few disclaimers: Inflation keeps humming along, making our money worth less with each passing year, so keep in mind that in 30 years, for example, $100,000 won't buy as much as it does today. Also, taxes also cut into your profits: the government gets its share of every dollar we make. Unless you've got a penchant for prison (or buddies in the Bahamas), taxes are unavoidable.

GETTING YOUR GOALS

You invested. You added. You waited. You made a fortune. That's investing! Not exactly too tough, right? The process of investing is simpler than a *Scooby-Doo* storyline. You evaluate your particular goals, understanding *what you want,* choose an investment "product" or "vehicle" most appropriate to reach those goals (like stocks or bonds), and keep adding to your investment. Then you wait. And wait. And let compound interest do its thing. After a period of years, the investment will perform as expected, and you reach your goals.

So what do you want? A secure retirement? House in the suburbs? Money in the bank? Daytona in the driveway? You've got to THINK about exactly why you want to invest, in order to know exactly WHAT you'll be investing in. So know at least some of your long-term goals and be ready to prioritize, because any investing we do will directly support (and reflect) reaching those goals.

Here's you: "Okay . . . okay . . . hold the phone, Tyrone. Are you telling me that's all there is to investing??? But I want to make

Among nonprofessionals, it is estimated that some 80 percent of active traders lose money. This is especially true for those trading with options, commodities, or the more speculative securities.

Starting Now vs. Starting Later

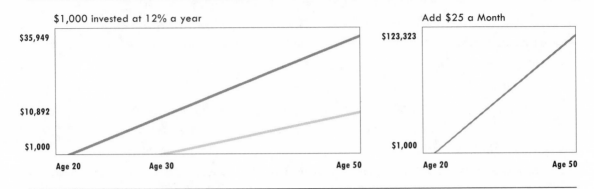

$1,000 invested at 12% a year

- $35,949
- $10,892
- $1,000

Age 20 — Age 30 — Age 50

Add $25 a Month

- $123,323
- $1,000

Age 20 — Age 50

more money now, not thirty years from now!" Here's me: "Then get a job!!!!" Investing is not a full-time profession!

While trading and other kinds of short-term speculation— things I'll discuss in depth in Part III—are exciting, educational, and a ton of fun, they won't bring you closer to your goals. Again, this is where the movie mythology turns to mush. The chances of your being able to make a LIVING off of buying and selling securities all day long are about as good as Tina Yothers's winning a postcancellation Emmy for her work on *Family Ties*. Even the quasi-professional "day traders" who outfit themselves with real-time quotes and the best charting system go *bust*.

It just ain't going to happen. Good investing is painfully unexciting—but it is the well-thought-out map that can bring you to the payoff of realizing your dreams.

RISKS OF INVESTING (AND NOT INVESTING)

But isn't investing risky?

Yes . . . and no. "Risk" is a pretty obscure term, so let's understand exactly what we're talking about. First things first. The world is chock full of risk. Will global warming melt the polar ice caps? With nuclear war annihilate us all? Will Chumbawamba ever release another song as annoying as "Tubthumping"? These are all risks that we live with—risks we are essentially *forced* to live with just by being alive. These are systematic risks—the type we can basically do nothing about.

Forget about money for a moment (*just for a moment, mind you!*). How do we deal with the risks that we face every day? The answer, of course, is that we are selective about the particular risks to which we expose ourselves. We take calculated risks—the type of risks where we are fairly certain of the outcomes. We take risks that make sense, where our potential "upside" is greater than the "downside," and where even the worse-case scenario is something we can live with.

Even doing *nothing* carries a risk. Think about it: You have been sniffling for weeks. By not going to the doctor to have it checked out, you are running the risk that it's something more serious. By waiting to take action, you end up treating not a runny nose . . . but pneumonia. So risk happens. Get used to it . . . it's just part of life.

Every investment, whether it's the market or supposedly "safe" bank accounts or certificates of deposit, carries some risk. How is a bank account risky? A bank account is insured, so you won't have the risk of loss of principal. But a bank account doesn't protect you against inflation risk, the risk that because our money is worth a bit less each year, our purchasing power will decline over time. Investors who choose to avoid risk by hiding their money under the mattress are in for shock a few years down the line: With inflation at 3.1 percent (an historical average), your $1,000 will be worth only $543 in 20 years. You've protected your principal, but lost purchasing power.

So investing has risk. This is true. But we're going to take reasonable risk—the type of risk that is appropriate for our individual goals.

Most people put off investing in the stock market, for example, because they think it's too "high."

They fear that they'll invest in the market and it will crash, immediately wiping them out. Could the market crash? Certainly! It did in 1929. It did in 1987. It even experienced a "mini" crash in 1997. But what happened? The market, of course, simply bounced back. It might have taken a few years, but after every major downturn in the stock market's value, it has continued to move higher. So while the "risk" of a market crash is always real, history has shown us that the risk is more of an emotional one than anything else. Time after time, the market has continued to move up.

So just what does taking reasonable risks mean? A reasonable risk is one that is appropriate for you and your goals. This simply means that you go into an investment having already considered all the possible scenarios—what you could lose, what you might

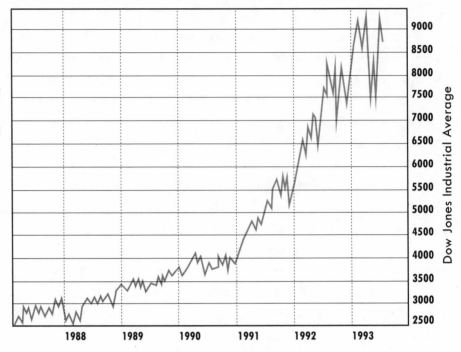

Too high? Is there such a thing? The problem with trying to "time" the market, trying to buy low and sell high, is that we really have no idea of how "high" is "high." When the Dow was at 4000, the market seemed high at 5000. When the market was at 6000, it 7000 seemed like the stratosphere.

gain. If you can't afford to lose one penny . . . meaning that you have an actual need for your investment capital in the short term, then you should not be in the market. Maybe you should be in a money market account or a CD. On the other hand, if you don't have an immediate need for your investment capital, then the risk of holding stocks is much less. There's a much greater chance that by the time you do need the money, the market will be higher than it was when you started, and you'll have made money on your investments.

So we can see how "risk" is a kinda personal thing. It directly relates back to each of our individual goals and particular set of circumstances. We can determine which financial products to invest in, or essentially how much "risk" to take on, because we know our goals. Taking on more risk than you should is reckless. At the same time, so is taking on less risk, because there is less of a chance you'll reach your goals.

INVESTING VS. SPECULATING: DIFFERENT AND UNEQUAL

Speculating is making short-term, informed predictions of price movement. Is IBM going to go up tomorrow? Perhaps. Is the price of soybeans heading toward a tumble? It might happen. We can make educated guesses on the basis of a number of factors, but nobody really knows. IBM just might be up tomorrow, but if it were obvious, then everyone would already have bought today. Speculating is mostly what we see in the movies: Gordon Gekko and the people in the trading pit are speculators. They try to jump into the market at low prices and get out at the highest, essentially predicting the very near future. They might be right . . . or wrong. But because short-term fluctuations in the price of anything are far from predictable, speculating this way carries a significantly higher level of risk. IBM might be up tomorrow, but what if it's not? What if it's not up for a week? For a month? For a year?

Speculating is fun. It's a rush. But it's risky. . . . Accurately predicting the future, especially in the short term, is just plain impossible.

And *then* there's investing. Investors don't lose sleep worrying whether or not IBM is going to go up tomorrow. Why? Because investors know that over *time*, common stocks like IBM have gone up . . . have consistently outpaced inflation and provided a high rate of return. So while IBM may or may not go up today, investors know that over the next several years its trajectory will most likely be upward.

Second, investors wouldn't put every damn dollar into IBM to begin with. They've spread their money around into other stocks, as well as into completely different types of investment products, such as bonds and CDs, so the risk of loss is further diminished by not "betting the farm" on just one horse. Investing is not gambling! It's not hoping for the quick buck, which is what speculating is. Investing is knowing your history. Knowing what types of investments have done well in the past, knowing what your goals are, and making a match—that is, matching your goals with the investments that have historically been able to meet those goals. Investing is also being a realist, having realistic expectations of an particular investment's performance, and having a long-term time horizon in order to let those expectations be realized.

IBM Stock Gets the Blues

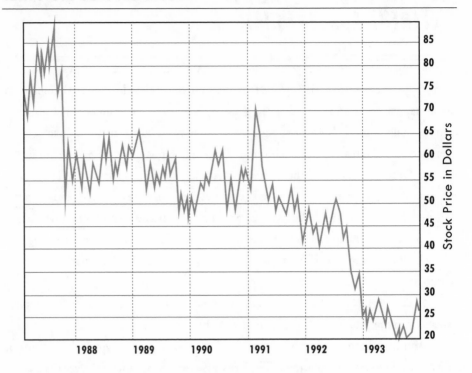

INVESTING: RISK, NOT RECKLESSNESS

Over the short term . . . truly anything can happen. Investments, especially the stock market, regularly fluctuate—often dramatically. How dramatically? When the market crashed on October 19, 1987, it lost 20 percent in one day. Wait: It gets worse. Several times during the past century, stocks have fallen into periods of declining prices, what economists call a **bear market**.

Conversely, we've had great periods of fluctuation to the upside. For example, just recently, between 1994 and 1997, the stock market rose an amazing 128.45 percent (the Standard and Poor's 500 Index). In our wildest wet dreams we are actually able to jump in and out—riding bull markets while blowing off the bears. That's definitely a dream, because this "timing" just doesn't work. On a short-term basis, it's absolutely impossible to predict the ups and downs of the market. Investors have it easy: They don't even try.

So while returns vary from day to day and year to year, this much we do know: Historically the stock market has gained an *average* of 11 percent each year.

That is, the "large caps," (capitalization) or stocks of the biggest companies, have over the past 67 years returned an average of 11 percent each year. "Small caps," or stocks of smaller companies, have done even better, returning an average of 12.7 percent per year over the same time period. It's been

WORST BEAR MARKETS IN RECENT HISTORY	
January 1973 to October 1974:	−48.2 percent
November 1968 to May 1970:	−36.1 percent
January 1987 to December 1987:	−33.5 percent

a rocky ride: Some years up, some years down, but the numbers don't lie. What this means is that investing your money in the stock market over a long period of time, say 30 to 40 years—through the good years and bad—you can reasonably expect, based on a long history of past performance, an average return of 11 percent for every year your money is in.

Is 11 percent good? Say you invested a hundred bucks. At 11 percent, after one year you've got $111. I know. . . . BFD. After 40 years, however, that same hundred bucks

Stocks, Bonds, Bills, and Inflation

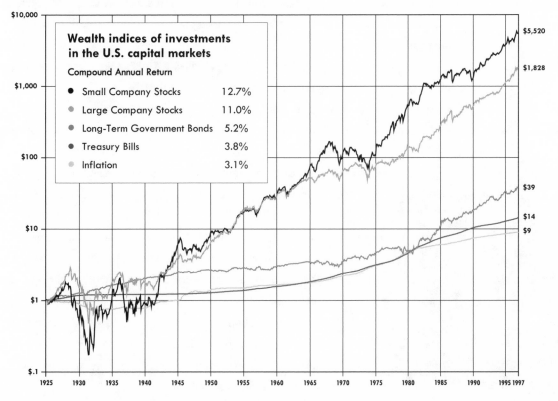

Wealth indices of investments in the U.S. capital markets

Compound Annual Return

●	Small Company Stocks	12.7%
●	Large Company Stocks	11.0%
●	Long-Term Government Bonds	5.2%
●	Treasury Bills	3.8%
●	Inflation	3.1%

Is 11% Good?
Active and Often Pays Off

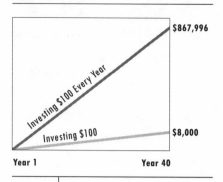

Investing $100 Every Year — $867,996

Investing $100 — $8,000

Year 1   Year 40

compounded at 11 percent becomes almost $8,000. And the pièce de résistance: Invest $100 in the stock market every year for 40 years—never touching a penny—and you will have accumulated an astounding $867,996.

Compound interest is a kind of magic even Doug Henning can't top.

This is why young people are specifically poised to make a hell of a lot of cash over their lifetimes. By investing early and often, we will be able to take advantage of compound interest for longer than any other age group. As young people, our "time horizon"—the amount of time before we actually need the money we are investing—is quite long. So we don't need to worry about predicting where the market will go from day to day, because we're simply letting stocks slowly continue moving upward, watching our money grow year after year.

So heed these words: Fluctuations, even wild and volatile ones, are normal for the stock market, hell for *any market*. Someone is always selling. Someone is always buying. When there are more buyers than sellers, the market goes up. When it's the opposite, the market goes down.

So despite the media's penchant for **Armageddon-style coverage** of even the most minor stock corrections the young person's best bet is to ride out the ups and downs, letting the law of averages make you more money than any Wall Street wizard ever could.

NOVEMBER 2, 1987 $2.00

TIME
THE
CRASH
After a wild week on Wall Street, the world is different

While I've used the stock market as the main example, I want to stress that the "magic" of compound interest works with any investment. Even the simple savings account, paying a paltry 3 percent a year, will turn $1,000 into $3,315 if untouched for 40 years. Again, compounding works even better if you add to your original investment. Stash $25 every month in that same savings account and you'll have well over $25,000 by the time you're ready to retire. As long as the interest is able to compound upon itself, you'll reap the benefits of compounding.

I'll talk more about the stock market and other investment products later in this part. For now, though, it's enough that you understand how letting compound interest work over time can minimize risk and maximize your return.

LEARNING CURVE

Investing is easy . . . but not effortless. There's no cookie-cutter answer as to how you should invest your money, meaning that as an investor, you do have some important decisions to make. Your investment decisions should be made with the same care as any other life choice, even more care, perhaps. So before you "toss" your money into anything, you've got to make sure you are aware not only of what you're doing, but why you're doing it in the first place.

"That Pig guy told me to put my money in mutual funds, so I did." For chrissake! Think for yourself for a moment. Taking anyone's advice without knowing the "why" relegates to you the status of a mere minion. Bought a mutual fund? Big whoop. Anyone can buy a mutual fund—the forms are so simple even friggin' Yackoff Smirnoff could find his way into some shares. But why did you buy the fund? What goals of yours will it meet? Who's the manager? What are the fees? "I heard about it in the newspaper" or "My friend says it's good" just don't fly. Sound investment decisions are ones where you can explain not only what you're invested in, but why you're invested to begin with.

Think about the prudence and thought you put into your nonmarket "investments." Your job, for example, is not only a means to some income, but also consumes a large investment of your time. You'll likely be spending 40 hours a week there—minimum. Thus, choosing where to work (where to invest your time) isn't a decision you make lightly. You research the company, try to pick up vibes about its corporate culture, ask about salary and benefits, and think about whether the position will help you reach your goals. You've got a *reason* for working there. If questioned, you could come up with a list of the specific reasons you choose to remain an employee. When it comes to your investments, you've got to have the same level of knowledge, insight, and confidence that the investment decisions you are making are the right ones.

A single individual can move the entire stock market with relative ease—that is, if the individual is a mutual fund or hedge fund manager with a few billion dollars under his or her management. After a particularly healthy recovery in the stock market one afternoon, *Forbes* magazine columnist Laszlo Birinyi explained how "the market recovered solely because an index fund bought huge amounts of stock late [that afternoon]. This 'buy program' took the market up 150 points in 15 minutes." So don't be freaked by a few hundred points. It might just be a mutual fund manager with an itchy trigger finger.

"Before and After"

Pud: *Hi, I bought the XYZ stock mutual fund. What do you think?*

Jonathan: *Why'd you buy it?*

Pud: *My cousin's brother's broker recommended it.*

Jonathan: *What can you tell me about it?*

Pud: *Not much. But I'm down a few hundred dollars.*

Don't be this! I have zero sympathy for the people who put more attention into deciding what to order at dinner than where they put their money. You've got to be informed as to *what* you're investing in and *why you're investing in it.*

Pig: *Hey, Jonathan, I bought the XYZ stock mutual fund. What do you think?*

Jonathan: *Why'd you buy it?*

Morningstar is the Chicago-based mutual fund ranking and tracking service. Their information, found both in print and on the Web, detail all the relevant characteristics of a particular fund, including fees, style, and management approach.

Pig: *Well, I'm not going to need the money for a long time, so I wanted a stock fund because stocks routinely provide the best return. The XYZ fund has five stars from* **Morningstar**, *low fees, and an experienced manager I feel I can trust. I'm down a few bucks, but I'm in it for the long haul.*

Oy! What a great explanation of the WHY of investing. This caller is obviously aware as to her investment decision, and even though she doesn't plan on making any changes, she is confident and informed. These are the types of responses the pig . . . ah, intelligent investor . . . is prepared to give.

TO THINE OWN SELF BE TRUE

Before you invest in anything, you've got lots of questions to ask and just as many to answer. *Think!* What's the money for? How soon do you need it? What's your tolerance for risk? Could you stand the thought of a **paper loss** for a few years? There are lots of different types of investments to choose from—the stock market is only one. Actually, it's one that could most likely head south at any moment, for any number of years. If you invest in it, are you prepared to wait a decade for it to bounce back?

What are your goals? If you're investing the money for retirement, the stock market is an ideal choice. But if you're planning on buying a house or starting a business in the near future, a good portion of your cash needs to reside in more conservative investment products, the kind that provide less return, but less potential for loss within the time frame in which you need the money. Deciding which investment product(s) to choose from comes *after* you've decided why you're investing in the first place.

Think about the returns you need to reach your goals, but also consider the risks you are willing to take. What's your personal tolerance for risk? If you put your money in the market, will you be able to sleep at night? Or will the **Dow**'s every dip send you into a terrible tizzy? For some wussies—umm, I mean investors—it's just too hard not to freak out when the market experiences the inevitable downturn or drop. It's true: When prices are going up, everybody's loving the "long term," but during bear markets, people get paranoid. When your investment is down 30 percent, will you still be able think long term? How much Xanax will it take to remind you just how long the long haul is?

I've seen it hundreds of times. The market takes a dive, and people who just a few weeks prior were long-term investors rush to sell out of their holdings. Panic sets in and people go nutty with the fear of losing any more of their money. These "intelligent" individuals invariably end up selling just as the market begins to rebound, successfully confirming individual investors' historical role as the biggest idiots on Wall Street.

So be honest with yourself and your tolerance for risk. If it takes getting a THINK LONG TERM tattoo to prevent you from panicking . . . do it.

But still, any investment that keeps you up all night is a bad one. Especially if you are new to the markets, even knowing the his-

When you buy a stock and sell it at a loss, you've "realized" the investment loss. When the value of a stock you have bought has gone down but you have not yet sold the stock, you have a **paper loss**, an investment loss that you have not yet "realized," i.e., not yet sold. Oftentimes, when held long enough, paper losses become paper gains.

The **Dow Jones Industrial Average** is the most well-known and widely followed index of U.S. stocks. It was invented in 1896 by Charles Dow, who also started the *Wall Street Journal*, and to this day, *Journal* editors have the authority to change the Dow's component stocks. The index tracks 30 large companies whose stocks trade on the New York Stock Exchange and includes the likes of AT&T, Disney, General Electric, and Phillip Morris. Because it only tracks 30 stocks, the index is often criticized as being too narrow a measure of the overall market.

torical facts might be cold comfort in periods of market decline. Nightmares of ending up in the po' house? The tossing and turning is your body's way of telling you that you've taken on too much risk, or, more likely, or don't understand the mechanics of the investments you've already made. I heartily believe, however, that if you know *what* you're doing and *why* you're doing it, there is less propensity to panic. Yes, you'll encounter risk, but it will be calculated risk. Investing CP style means choosing the investment products that suit your goals and your risk tolerance. It's having a realistic and educated awareness of particular investment products, so when downturns do come, they are expected—even welcomed—as reflections of the normal nature of markets.

BE WARY OF THE GURUS

I used to have a car that drove me . . . crazy, that is. When the greasy mechanic told me my wheels needed a piston pump, what the hell did I know about it? My game is stocks, not shocks. Another mechanic (just as greasy), another entirely different opinion. It sucked. I was powerless. Not knowing anything about engines, I was a sheep. I have since gotten rid of the car.

When you place that much trust in someone else, you put too much power in their hands. So don't bank on other people's smarts . . . use some of your own. There are shepherds and there are sheep. Sheep get slaughtered.

Everyone's got a scheme. Everyone's got an angle. Everyone thinks there's a shortcut. *There is no shortcut.* There's no great undiscovered way to investing riches, despite the junket of junk mail offers from charlatans claiming to have *the* secret system of success. It just doesn't exist. I mean . . . even if it did, why would anyone share it, much less send you unsolicited literature about it? Let's be serious!

On "Capitalist Pig," I get lots of calls from wonderfully arrogant listeners who like to reel off a million reasons why they've chosen a particular investment. They know the upside and downside potential of the investment, have modest, realistic expectations, and can explain how the investment fits into their overall portfolio and how it will meet their goals. I *love* these people. They're not relying on gurus, but their own research and self-knowledge. This level of awareness minimizes their risk and is a Capitalist Pig's wet dream. Well, one of them, anyway.

One of the most influential stock gurus doesn't even manage money—he reports on it. Gene Marcial writes a column for *Business Week*, a major publication that is read by almost everyone on "The Street." Marcial's column, entitled "Inside Wall Street," is supposed to give its readers the inside dirt on hot stock deals: takeovers, share buybacks, and other factors that would move stock prices. It seems, however, that Marcial's reporting, which almost always comes from unnamed sources, turns out to be more fantasy than reality. According to an excellent study by *Brill's Content* (November 1998), out of 42 big-money deals Marcial reported as being in the works, only three actually came to fruition. Overall, his stock picks trailed the market, meaning that you would have done better in an index fund than by rushing out, buying the mag, reading Marcial's tips, and immediately calling your broker.

Brokerage houses also make recommendations. They issue "buys" or "sells" on any number of stocks. The only problem being that many times, they have a vested interest in moving the price of the stock for their own purposes. If a brokerage house has a lot of stock on its books, or holds a great deal of, say, IBM in its own inventory, do you think they'll actually make a sell recommendation on IBM, knowing it will push the stock down further? As reported in the *New York Times* (July 25, 1998), Mark Hulbert, who writes the informative *Hulbert Financial Digest*, discovered that fewer than 1 percent of all the recommendations the brokerage houses makes are sells. One third are holds. The overwhelming majority, two thirds, are buys. Remember: Brokers are salespeople, and when it comes to the stock market it's not unusual to be sold a bag of goods that is just plain empty. So using a guru, or even an "esteemed" brokerage house's buy/sell/hold recommendations, just can't form the basis of your investing decisions.

Make your own decisions. Don't be some guru's devoted disciple. Understand the financial system: how it works, its products, and their risks. This book will show you the basics and get you started, but there's no shortcut to success. You simply have to learn this stuff and make your own decisions. Recommendations should be thought of as opinions, because, like everything else in the market, that's what they are.

GETTING DOWN WITH DIVERSITY

Take a look at your music collection. You've got your sturdy standards, the discs you've listened to for years, the ones that merit repeat spins at the Club de You. You've got your nostalgic favorites: Toto, J. Giles Band, Mr. Mister . . . perhaps something from Michael in his darker days. You've got the obligatory must-haves: Bob Marley's *Legend*, James Taylor's *Greatest Hits*, something from Zeppelin. Undoubtedly, the other genres are represented as well: You've probably got some **classical** lying around and perhaps even some Miles Davis, Charlie Parker, or other assorted jazz. Toss in a few minor mistakes (R.E.M.'s *Monster* comes to mind), a few greatest hits of the seventies, and you've got yourself a collection—a **portfolio** of music.

The point is that you are *diversified*. You have a wide assortment of options. Whatever you're in the mood for, chances are you've got a disc to fit the festivities. The same concept applies to our investments. Along with time, diversification is probably the single most important nook in the nook-and-cranny–laden labor of love we call investing.

Simply put, diversification means placing your resources in more than one investment, rather than betting the farm on a single solitary solution. By investing in a few different types of financial instruments, you make sure that if one goes sour, another picks up the slack. Not only does diversification smooth out your overall returns, but it also reduces the impact any one investment will have on your portfolio.

Let's see how this relates to your stocks, rather than your music collection. When you buy shares in a particular company, say Coca-Cola, you obviously run the risk that the value of your shares could decline. Yes . . . Coke is a great company that has been around for years, but over a period of months or even years, it's quite likely the Coke stock could take a tumble. It happens to the even the "bluest" of the **blue chips**.

Say you own shares of Coke. That's all. Nothing else. Coke takes a hit . . . and you get *hammered*. If your entire portfolio is made up of only one company, it leaves you way

A 1993 study conducted at the University of California demonstrated that listening to a **Mozart** piano sonata for ten minutes raised the measurable IQ of subjects by up to nine points.

Portfolio: An assortment of investments held by either an individual or an institution.

The term **blue chip** generally refers to large, stable companies with a history of steady revenues and dividend payments. Coca-Cola, IBM, and J. P. Morgan are all examples of "blue chip" companies.

too vulnerable to a serious decline. On the other hand, in a portfolio of several stocks, say, a bit of Coke, Nike, General Motors, and Microsoft, it would be much less likely that all of them would decline. *That is why we diversify.*

Diversification is one of the huge advantages of mutual funds, which I'll discuss in Chapter 8. A mutual fund allows you to buy a little piece of a lot of different companies, without having to pick the stocks themselves. So instead of owning just one stock, a mutual fund allows you to diversify your risk. Some mutual funds own hundreds of stocks. Some own thousands.

It's by no means foolproof. Just because you are diversified doesn't mean you can't lose money. Stocks tend to move in the same direction, so if the market drops dramatically, you can be pretty certain that your mutual funds, although diversified, will drop in value as well. The point is that you will likely lose less than you would have had you just bought one specific stock.

So you've got to diversify, but not just the stocks. You should diversify your investment styles. Because individual asset classes, or types of investments, tend to move in the same direction, we want to own several different types of these classes. This keeps us in sync with the diversity vibe of spreading the risk around, keeping our investment eggs in a variety of well-buffered baskets.

Bonds are a start. As you'll see in Chapter 6, bonds represent a company's debt, while stock represents a company's equity, or ownership. You'll want to own a bit of both—you'll see why in the next chapter. By venturing outside the stock market, bond investors are diversifying a stock portfolio into another asset class. Corporate bonds, bank certificates of deposit, and U.S. Treasury securities (all types of bonds) pay you interest. This interest, or "yield," can drastically boost your return, especially when the stock market sags. "Correlation" refers to the tendency of different asset classes to move (or not move) in the same direction. By owning asset classes of low correlation, you remain diversified enough to weather any market storm.

Are you with me? We want to be diversified. Although we know the stock market provides the highest overall return, we want to own some other investments besides just stocks, so that when the market does decline, our overall portfolio won't take too much of a tumble.

Diversification is vital—to a point. Spreading our dollars too thinly, over too many different investments, results in a mishmash of mediocrity. So it's not like you want to own "a little of this and a little of that." Making too many investments lends itself to a portfolio with average returns and above-average hassle. If you own an large-cap mutual fund, or a mutual fund that holds stocks of larger companies, you don't need to also buy an S&P 500 index fund, which *also* holds large-cap stocks. One of these would be redundant. The two funds will undoubtedly overlap, and you'll end up owning the same stocks in two different funds. This is especially troublesome if you are paying **loads** or **fees** for each individual investment. Most people who invest with mutual funds (as I hope you will) need between two and five different funds. Six, tops.

Wall Streeters often slap fancy names on plain, common-sense notions, and diversification is a perfect example. Almost instinctively, we know not to put all of our eggs in one basket. It comes almost naturally to everything we do: We diversify our information sources by subscribing to different magazines and watching different television programs. We diversify our social circle by hanging out with different types of people. The same notion is true for our investments. So you'll be sure to want to invest in a variety of different products, from cash to bonds, stocks and mutual funds—the whole shebang.

Again, the key is to structure your investment portfolio to fit your goals. For example, everyone should have some "cash" investments, such as CDs or money market accounts, but if you're investing for a goal 30 years out, cash shouldn't make up a huge part of your overall portfolio, because cash investments don't provide high long-term returns that beat inflation. Asset allocation—or choosing how much of your money to put into each type of investment—is what the craft of proper investing is all about.

PYRAMID SCHEME: THE INVESTMENT PYRAMID

Every time we spend money, we are making an investment. Some investments provide an intangible return, like the pleasure we might get from seeing a movie. Buying dinner might provide us nourishment, a "return" we also need to survive. When it comes to making money, however—getting a tangible return in the form of money—investing in a dinner and movie won't get you any dollars. It might however, get you a date.

So as investors we're looking to put our money in places that will provide monetary returns. There are several different types of investment products, and each one occupies a position on the "Pig Pyramid," a graphical representation of each product's investment risk and return characteristics. The pyramid shows us how each particular type of investment, or "asset class," ranks on a hierarchy of risk . . . and reward. Investments toward the bottom of the pyramid, like savings accounts and cash, provide small returns but little risk of loss of principle. Conversely, the assets toward the top of the pyramid can offer up big and beefy returns . . . at substantially more risk. The point is to structure a portfolio from the pyramid, choosing the types of investments that most directly reflect our particular investment goals. Because we're going to diversify, chances are we'll invest in something from almost every level of the pyramid.

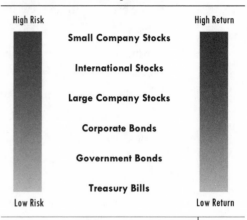

Risk Tolerance Spectrum

High Risk   **Small Company Stocks**   High Return

International Stocks

Large Company Stocks

Corporate Bonds

Government Bonds

Treasury Bills

Low Risk   Low Return

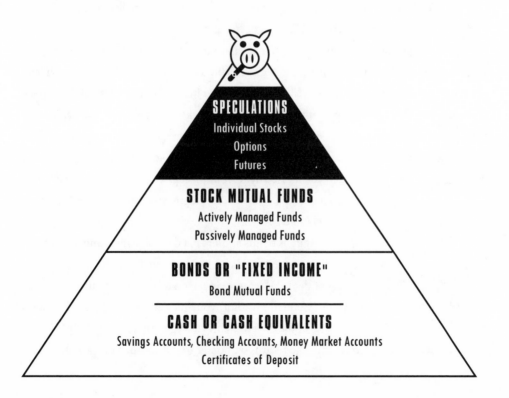

SPECULATIONS
Individual Stocks
Options
Futures

STOCK MUTUAL FUNDS
Actively Managed Funds
Passively Managed Funds

BONDS OR "FIXED INCOME"
Bond Mutual Funds

CASH OR CASH EQUIVALENTS
Savings Accounts, Checking Accounts, Money Market Accounts
Certificates of Deposit

Let's return to risk vs. reward for a moment. There is (or should be) a direct correlation between risk and reward. The more money you want to make, the more risk you must be willing to assume. There are no free rides, no investments that provide huge returns with no risk at all. So we'll use factors like time, compound interest, and diversification to reduce the risks we do choose to take. We'll also use some common sense, avoiding any reckless moves that might put us in the po' house *too* prematurely—or at all.

Another note: We call it the "investment pyramid" because it contains almost all of the different places we could conceivably put our money. As you can see, the "speculative products" reside toward the top of pyramid, meaning that while they provide higher returns than "investments," they also offer more risk . . . way more risk. You will notice that this upper section is a different color. This is to distinguish speculations from investments. "Speculation" is the term we use to describe what we'll do with our "fun" money, the money we may or may not want to use to take on more risk than necessary. The process of speculation, of which this book devotes an entire third, is fun, educational, exciting—and dangerous. Speculators, by definition, take on more risk than necessary. It's something you can do . . . if you want, but we'll only be speculating with a small part of our overall portfolio. That's why the pyramid is a pyramid, the smaller, more risky asset classes will make up only a tiny part of our overall portfolio.

Let's quickly run through the pyramid, starting at the bottom: Despite the move to modernize, credits cards will never be as undeniably F-U as a good old American greenback. Cash, and cash equivalents like money market funds, form the base of the investment pyramid because they offer the least amount of risk . . . and return. A dollar in your pocket won't return anything at all, while "cash equivalents" generally provide what Wall Street guys call the "risk-free rate," meaning that when you hold cash securities, there's no

chance you'll lose any of your principle. You also won't make jack shit in terms of a return. Cash might be "king" but offers a return decidedly more pawnish.

Next up is bonds and/or "fixed income investments." This is where things start to get a bit more . . . shall we say, saucy? Bonds represent debt. When you invest in a bond or in "fixed income" you are essentially lending your money to someone—a bank, a company, or the government—and getting paid an **interest rate** in return. The returns on bonds are bigger than on cash, but there

Interest refers to the time value of money. The amount it costs to borrow or lend money is generally referred to as an interest rate, or the rate of interest that is being paid on money itself.

is also more risk. Bond prices fluctuate when interest rates fluctu-ate, so despite their seemingly squeaky-clean reliability, it is possi-ble to lose money investing in bonds.

Stocks, or "**equity** investments," are still higher up the pyra-mid, and, as you can probably tell already, I'm a big fan of these suckers. What's not to like? Stocks have constantly provided high returns over time, outpacing inflation and every other asset class. Of course, you do run into more risk. Stocks are volatile; prices fluctuate wildly in short periods of time. In fact, stocks have regularly entered long periods of declining prices, what you know now as "bear markets." It can happen: During a period of the early 1970s, stocks lost over 45 percent of their value, meaning that your $1,000 would have been turned into $550 bucks in just a few months. Of course, your loss would have been a paper loss; you only actu-ally "lose" the money when you sell.

Some unique characteristics of the Pig Pyramid. I've broken down the "stocks" cat-egory into "stock mutual funds" and "stocks" for the following rea-son: Stock mutual funds own stocks, but usually more than one. In fact, the average stock mutual fund holds more than 123 individual stocks, so by investing in a fund you are automatically buying a diversified portfolio of individual stocks. Clearly, buying an individ-ual stock is unquestionably more risky because there is no diversity. Therefore, stock mutual funds should be considered investments, whereas we'll call individual stocks "speculations." Thus individual stocks deserve a higher (and riskier) spot on our pyramid.

Just bear in mind that stocks and stock mutual funds are the same thing, except funds offer a diversified portfolio while individual stocks are undiversified and way more risky for the smaller investor.

Finally, in the nosebleed section of our Mt. McKinley of money are the derivatives: options and futures. Ever been to Vegas, my friend? These supercharged speculations offer the opportunity for either outsized gains or a financial ass-whooping you'll never forget. As you can see, this asset class is at the top of the Pig Pyramid—it's the smallest, and should thus only make up a tiny bit of our overall portfolio, if at all. When gettin' down with derivatives, tread lightly, Kimo Sabe! Not for the poor, hungry, or faint of heart.

Equity: Refers to ownership. When you own stocks, you own a piece of a particular company.

Sure, you could assemble your own diversified portfolio of individual stocks, but it would take literally tens of thousands of dollars, something most young people just don't have. Mutual funds, however, offer immediate diversification and with very low minimums, and are a better description of what an investment (as opposed to a speculation) should be.

PACE YOURSELF

Remember: It's not all or nothing. We're going to own something from *every part* of the pyramid. We'll start with savings, but ultimately end up with a blend of investments that will include all categories on the pyramid (except maybe the derivatives). Again, this is what Wall Streeters call "asset allocation." It's dividing your cash among the different types of investment. The amount of money you have in a certain investment is usually expressed as a percentage of an entire portfolio: if you decided to put half your money in stocks and half in the bank, you would have a portfolio made up of 50 percent stocks and 50 percent cash. Really snooty show-offs tend to use the word "exposure," as in "I've got seventy-five percent exposure to the equity markets." CP Says: Snooty sounds savvy. "Exposure"—is a good way to conceptualize how you structure your portfolio.

Asset allocation is vital. It constitutes the decisions you make about where to invest your resources. During the bodacious bull market of the 1990s, it was widely publicized as fact that anyone under age 30 should be fully invested in the stock market. According to arrogant, overpaid money managers, young people with anything less than the full equity exposure are idiots. Don't buy this bullshit. The amount of money you put in the market should reflect your goals, not the overconfidence of a loudmouth fund manager looking to increase his **Assets Under Management**.

Assets Under Management

refers to the amount of money an equity fund manager has under his/her direction. Since fund managers get compensated as a percentage of AUM, it's in their best interests to convince you to invest as much as possible.

When I first started hosting "Capitalist Pig," I often overheard brokers recommend an old "rule of thumb" with regard to asset allocation. Subtract your age from 100, they'd say, and *that's* the percentage of your investable assets that should be in the stock market.

But I don't do "rules of thumb." Much of the "stocks for the long run" routine has been funded by the parade of financial service providers who, through millions of dollars of marketing, regularly proclaim equities as the next great messiah. Of course, they get 1 percent or so of every dollar you invest, every year you remain invested!

But be aware: If your goal is making any kind of serious money, you'll need to have some exposure to the stock market. You also need to be comfortable. If your tolerance for risk is low—if you get queasy with every mild drop in the Dow, you'll want to adjust your asset allocation accordingly. Fewer stocks, more bonds and cash. It's perfectly coolio, as they say, for people new to investing to start slowly. Take the time to move up the investment pyramid at a rate that's comfortable for you. You might start with 50 percent in stocks, moving more into the market once you get more comfortable with the zigs and zags that will undoubtedly occur.

Speaking of asset allocation, I'd also recommend, very highly, in fact, that you keep a cash reserve of at least two months' living expenses in a safe place (not a sock . . .). Good places for your "emergency cash" include savings accounts, money market accounts, or certificates of deposit. Then, if Armageddon ever breaks out, you'll have a few thousand dollars to go down with the party. More realistically, if you lose your job or get sick or some other unforeseen malady occurs, you've got your emergency fund to bail you out. A note: If they can swing it, parents *do* qualify as an emergency fund, although by relying on them you are subjecting yourself to what might be the ultimate in embarrassment: asking them for money.

More than just for the maladies, cash stashed on the sidelines is an effective psychological buffer when the market drops. It's a comfort to know that no matter what happens in the markets, something is safe.

Unlike the Arch Deluxe, risk is here to stay. We can manage risk—specifically, our investment risk—through a variety of techniques, most notably time, diversification, and common sense. A long-term time horizon reduces the short-term risk that almost every investment faces, while diversification will help smooth out our portfolio's return, so that all of our investment eggs are not in one seemingly benign basket. Finally, there's common sense. We'll make sure that the risks we do take are well calculated.

Reckless investing is when you take on a level of risk that is inappropriate, unsuitable, or just plain stupid. For example, it's risky to own stocks, but it's not reckless. Stock prices fluctuate—and you could lose money—but history tells the tale: Over a long period of time, the risks of stock ownership are drastically reduced compared to the risk over a short time frame. Owning just *one* stock, however, or investing in stocks with money you need in the short term, could be described as reckless. Or just plain stupid.

There is another, less obvious type of recklessness. You understand that taking on too much risk is reckless, but so is taking on too little risk. This is because of inflation, or the economic tendency for prices of goods and services to rise over time. It's usually expressed as a numerical percentage, like, say, 3 percent. This means that over the course of one year, our money is worth 3 percent less. At 3 percent, $100, even safely stuffed into your mattress, is worth a mere $97 at the end of a year. This is why we must take on the right level of risk. Not too much, not to little, but *just right*.

The rate of inflation isn't set in stone. In the early 1980s, for example, it was running at about 12 percent. At the time of this writing, inflation was clicking along at about 2.5 percent a year.

Are you with me on this one? For a young person with a long investment horizon, not taking on enough risk is totally reckless. If you think you'll retire comfortably by putting most of your money in a savings account, you're just plain wrong. You'll simply be screwed when you find that you can't meet your goals later on.

Inflation causes our money to be worth less, reducing our purchasing power. We get fewer goods and services for the same amount of money. The "inflation risk," therefore, is the risk that our investments won't keep up with inflation.

To illustrate the recklessness of not taking enough risk, let's talk percentages. Say you can't stand the thought of losing a cent, so you put your entire portfolio into a savings account. At 3 percent a year, after 40 years your $1,000 will turn into $3,315.15. Not bad, right? Wrong. If inflation averages 2.5 percent over the same 40 years (which would be historically very low), the purchase power of the $3,315 will have eroded significantly: It will buy only about $1,220 worth of stuff (i.e., $1,220 stuff bought with today's preinflation dollars). Even worse, you'll still have to pay taxes on your return. Instead of a "safe" 3 percent, you've actually lost money after 40 years of waiting.

So if you want to beat inflation, build wealth, and maintain your purchasing power, you've got to pick investments that meet those goals. Over the long term, that simply means stocks.

For the next three chapters, I'll outline the three major types of investment products. We'll start at the bottom of the pyramid, with cash and cash equivalents, eventually pulling a George Jefferson and movin' on up.

So start slowly, but *start*. Time is money, and money never sleeps, so the sooner you get started the better off you will be.

5 CASH IS KING

"**C**ash" and "cash equivalents" are the general terms used to describe the variety of instruments that make up the foundation of the investment pyramid. In the Pig's "Wide World of Money," cash wouldn't qualify to garner you either the thrill of victory *or* the agony of defeat. Cash investments are the safest and least volatile of investments; the cash portion of your overall portfolio is essentially as good as gold. Actually, even better. That's the point. Cash offers us safety of principle and high liquidity, or the ability to get at our money when we need it.

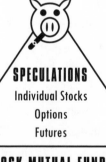

SPECULATIONS
Individual Stocks
Options
Futures

STOCK MUTUAL FUNDS
Actively Managed Funds
Passively Managed Funds

BONDS OR "FIXED INCOME"
Bond Mutual Funds

CASH OR CASH EQUIVALENTS
Savings Accounts, Checking Accounts, Money Market Accounts
Certificates of Deposit

Elvis is king? Not a chance. *Cash* is king, and although technology has begun to replace the need for actual coinage, the concept remains: You can't buy breakfast with a bond. You can't shop for a sofa with stocks. Money talks. Cash is the simply language of money.

WHAT IS IT?

Myron Kandel has been an instrumental part of CNN's business news team since he helped create the network in 1980. Currently he serves as financial editor and commentator for the network's popular *Moneyline News Hour.*

Cash is boring. You don't hear a lot about it, especially from members of the financial press, who obviously find its stability less than newsworthy. Put your money in the bank and it ain't going nowhere. You're not going to find **Myron Kandel** standing outside your neighborhood savings and loan anytime soon. Alas, it's true: There's not a whole hell of a lot of entertainment value to be squeezed out of a savings account.

Cash provides a guaranteed, albeit dismal, rate of return.

It's stable. It's safe. And therefore it makes an ideal investment for short-term goals up to about one year in the future.

One of the big benefits of cash is the liquidity, meaning that when you invest in cash you can get your hands on it in a hurry, if necessary. Compare this to, say, a piece of art. The most magnificent Matisse, while it might be highly valued, is terribly illiquid. If you need the money quickly, you can't just cash in your Cézanne at the local Citibank.

A car is another example: Say you own a car but need money in a hurry and go to sell your wheels. Because the car market is less liquid, meaning that there are fewer buyers and sellers at any given moment, there is a significant chance you'll be forced to sell at a lower price than you paid. So even though your car might be worth $10,000, you'll be forced to sell at the best price available, which could very well be below 10K. Real estate, heavy equipment, antiques, and collectibles are a few other examples of potentially prized but horribly illiquid investments.

And then there's cash. Cash, in its various forms, is considered the most liquid investment asset in existence. Accepted the world over, it truly is "everywhere you want to be." C'mon . . . you've seen *Miami Vice!* From landlords to drug lords, the U.S. dollar is the benchmark currency for the entire world.

Let's learn some lexicon: What we call "cash" actually refers to several types of investment products. Cash products include:

- The good old checking account, which usually pays no interest, unless you have Milkenesque millions on deposit.

- The savings account, same as always, an investment "classic" if there ever was one. It pays . . . a pittance. Savings accounts usually offer the lowest rate of any interest-bearing cash investment.

- The money market account, which is essentially a juiced-up checking account that pays a higher rate of interest but may or may not be FDIC-insured.

- The certificate of deposit, or **CD**, which requires you to lock up your money for a limited period of time for a slightly higher rate of interest.

I'll explain each in more detail later in this chapter.

I should also mention another cash equivalent, a very popular one, in fact, which is the U.S. Treasury Bill. The U.S. Government is constantly borrowing money from investors, and the Treasury Department issues short-term IOUs to those investors in the form of **Treasury Bills**. T-Bills have the shortest maturity the government offers: They are issued for periods of one year or less. They are marketable, meaning that you can buy and sell them at any time, and the interest earned on T-Bills is not subject to state and local income taxes. But you can't write checks against a T-Bill, and you need at least $1,000 to buy them. Plus, they're still more of a hassle to trade than money market accounts.

For an excellent discussion of investing in **Treasury Bills,** you might want to check out Michael O'Higgins's *Beating the Dow with Bonds* (HarperCollins).

CASH AIN'T TRASH

How high is a high rate of interest on a savings product? In lieu of a cheap-shot Cheech and Chong joke, let me first say that the interest rates on cash investments will fluctuate. Interest rates reflect the cost of money, so they tend to move moderately with the rate of inflation. Interest on savings accounts, the cash investment least susceptible to changes

The 1998 average interest rate
on passbook savings accounts was
2.17 percent.

in interest rates, has in recent years been around 2 percent, while a five-year certificate of deposit, a cash investment that fluctuates significantly more, usually ranges from 5 to 8 percent. Of course, these numbers can and will change: In 1980, for example, the United States experienced a huge rise in inflation. Many certificates of deposit were yielding over *10 percent*.

By investing in cash, we're not looking to make a mother lode of money. Cash investments offer safety and stability of principal. They also offer a return that will outpace inflation, but just barely: From 1926–1997, the average annual rate of return on cash (T-Bills) was 3.8 percent, compared with an average inflation rate of 3.1 percent.

Advantages of cash: Liquidity is a big plus. You can take money out of a checking account from almost anywhere in the world at any time of the day or night. You can have cash electronically wired across the ocean or quickly converted into a foreign currency. Unlike other, more illiquid assets, like precious metals and real estate, cash can be easily stored for safekeeping. There's not a bank in the world that wouldn't gladly hold on to your dollars for you. Give some props to the U.S. dollar!

Another advantage: safety of **principal**. "Principal" is the term we use to describe your initial, or original, investment. When it comes to safety, cash is *all that*. Make a deposit in a federally insured bank and you can be sure that, come hell, high water, or another Police Academy movie, you'll get your money back.

Principal is the money you initially invest.

Let's go to goals: Why invest in cash? It's an investment "product" that offers safety, stability . . . and shitty returns. For a portion of our portfolio, however, we *want* that very safety. Remember our discussion of the "emergency fund" at the beginning of Part II? The emergency fund is two months' worth of living expenses, enough for all the major expenditures like rent, car, food, and coffee. *Two months?* Yup. Life tends to be the story of "Plan B"—and the most unfortunate, annoying and expensive of crises have the tendency to occur at the most inopportune time. We need to know that if we need some cash in a hurry, it will be there. So keeping two months' worth of basic living expenses in cash will keep you liquid for a while, in case you get fired, fed up, or (God forbid) hurt. Everybody needs a portion of their investment portfolio in cash.

A second advantage: Cash functions as a short-term holding tank for the day-to-day minutia it takes to keep us going. You have bills to pay! Rent, credit cards, school, utilities . . . most bills require payment by *check*. So we need to have a place to store the money we'll need over the next few weeks. Got a job, **J.J**? When you get paid, where are you going to put it? The mattress, I'm sorry to say, just ain't going to cut it! A cash account, like checking or savings, suits this need quite well.

Another case for cash: Wall Streeters call it powder . . . as in gunpowder. Let's say the stock market crashes and there are investment bargains galore. With a little cash on the side, you can jump into quality investments just when everyone else is jumping out.

Even apart from financial investments, having some money in cash allows you to take advantage of unexpected opportunities. Airline fares on sale? One-day-only half-price sale at your favorite store? It's not like you want to run to sell stocks to raise money when you're dry. With cash: You the man. Without: You a gimp.

It's a "good news/bad news" type of thing. The good news about cash investments is that they don't really fluctuate that much in price. The bad news? They really don't fluctuate that much in price! Keeping your money in cash is the investment equivalent of sitting on the sidelines. You get to wear the uniform but don't really get to play. This is why the interest rate paid on cash investments is often referred to as the "risk-free" rate: by investing in cash you are exposing yourself to no risk of losing your principal. Remember the Pig Pyramid! Because there is so little risk, the return you receive is quite meager. Like Richard Simmons circa *Sweatin' to the Oldies*, it's no pain, no gain! Looking for safety? Cash. Looking to make money on your money? Keep looking.

Let's run some numbers: According to Ibbotson and Associates, a Chicago-based research company, if you had invested $1 in large-cap stocks, that is, the stocks of the largest companies in America, in 1926, you would have received an average annual return of 11 percent, turning your $1 into $1,828.33 by 1997. Had you kept it in cash investments (let's say T-bills), however, your $1 would earn an average return of 3.8 percent, making you a total of $14.25 dollars by 1997. *Ouch*. Comparing returns, you can see how over the long term, cash really loses its luster.

But what you sacrifice in return you soak up in safety. Investing in cash and cash equivalents is very appropriate for warehousing money you know you'll need for a particular purpose within a few months or years. I don't care how hot the stock market is, there's no better way of keeping your money safe over the short term than keeping it in cash. Even conservative stocks, the so-called "blue chips," can dabble in disaster. Even General Electric, one of the largest and most well-known companies in the world. In the fall of 1998, the stock declined more than 20 points. Will it bounce back? Over the short term, who the hell knows? So if you've *got to keep it* . . . keep it in cash.

CASH: WHAT IT IS AND WHERE IT LIVES

Most cash investments can be had at your local bank—the traditional stalwart of safety. So safe, actually, that I'm experiencing a brief Frosted Mini-Wheats Moment: The kid in me says that banks are boring . . . that we should just skip ahead to stocks. *Agggg!* Can't do it. Banks serve a investment purpose, so it's important to understand some of the basics of bank accounts.

Before we had Banana Republic, we had barter. Centuries ago, if you wanted, say, . . . a latte (they did have Starbucks back then, right?), you didn't pay in cash, but exchanged the goods for something else of similar value—say, an iced latte. More likely, it would have been cream in exchange for corn, lumber for lettuce, and so on. Then came currency, a standardized medium of exchangeable coinage. It wasn't until 1863 that we had an actual national currency. Before that, individual banks would regularly issue their own notes of exchange.

Banks make their money by lending out what you've given them. When they make loans, they charge the borrower an interest rate. In return for letting them lend out your money, they pay *you* interest. The difference between the interest they're paying you (usually pretty low) and what they're getting from the borrower (usually high) is the bank's profit.

In the midst of Depression, President Franklin Roosevelt, in an effort to restore confidence in the banking system, established the Federal Deposit Insurance Corporation (FDIC). This federal agency now guarantees deposits up to $100,000 per account against bank failure, meaning that in the *highly* unlikely event that your bank should fail (run out of money), the U.S. government intervenes in your defense.

So putting your money in the bank won't make you rich, but everyone needs a "banking relationship." Before renting an apartment, for example, many landlords will require a bank reference. With thousands of 'em out there, there are plenty of banks to choose from, so here are some of the "cash equivalents" that can be found at your local bank.

CHECKING ACCOUNTS. Checking accounts generally don't pay interest, so the potential for investment return is somewhere between zip and zilch. That's okay, because you're primarily going to use your checking account for making transactions, like paying bills, and holding money for short periods of time. With a checking account, there's no risk to your principal and the money is highly liquid. No matter how far you are from a bank, all you have to do is write a check.

Use checking accounts for paying bills. For "transactions." Don't keep thousands of dollars sitting in checking, especially if your account is wired up to an ATM card. Another $20 withdrawal doesn't seem so significant when there's a beefy balance on the screen. As little money as possible should be kept in checking—if you find that you have extra cash just sitting there month after month, it should be moved into something else . . . something that pays.

Of course, you DO NOT want to bounce a check—you'll be slapped with ridiculous fees and embarrassed to hell. Don't act like a ten-year-old, and your bank won't treat you like one. It's a lot harder to get them to budge on stuff like lower ATM fees when they see you've been bouncing checks.

With the exception of perhaps a *Blossom* marathon on USA, there are few things so tiresome as keeping one's checkbook balanced. This is especially true when your checking account has an ATM feature. Take out $20 without making a note, and you might find yourself mistakenly overdrawn. So every time you write a check, write it down in your records. You don't need to keep it to the penny—I tend to like to "round down," when estimating how much money is in my account. So if I deposit $123.40 . . . maybe I just write down that I deposited $120. Keeps the math simple, and keeps the account "padded" with a few extra bucks . . . just in case. Of course, you'll see the actual numbers each month when the bank sends you a statement of your account activity, plus all your canceled checks, which you should plan on actually looking at and keeping for at least a decade.

If trying to cram a "ballpark balance" in your already crowded cranium is killing you, use a computer. Most personal finance software programs have a checkbook register component. So even if you only update it monthly (when you get your statement), it'll still help you track where your capital is flowing. (Of course, good old-fashioned pencil and paper will still do the trick for you Luddites out there.)

High-rollers with more money might qualify for an interest-paying NOW (Negotiable Order of Withdrawal) account, which is a checking account that pays interest but restricts the number of checks you can write without penalty. Frankly, I think the fees and restrictions make NOWs less than WOWs.

Most banks charge for checking, so shop around. The business of banking is growing more competitive every day, and pressure from brokerages, mutual fund companies, and the like is prompting most banks to offer a bigger variety of products at even lower prices. Free checking can be had if you look hard enough; often a new bank will offer free checking for a short while . . . kind of a loss leader to gain new customers. Take advantage of offers like these, and, if you're eligible, any **student discounts** they might offer.

Almost every bank offers reduced fees if you maintain a high enough balance. Currently, the trend among national banks is to charge a low monthly fee and a nominal per-check charge. This stuff is always negotiable, so I strongly urge you to argue, annoy, bitch, and berate your local bank manager until she gives you free checking, or at least reduces the fees. If she doesn't meet your demands, find another bank. In an increasingly competitive era of bank consolidation, there's no reason to pay someone for the privilege of holding on to your cash.

If you *must* maintain a minimum balance, find out how the bank calculates "minimum." Some banks use a "daily minimum," meaning that if you dip below the minimum balance for even *one day* this could mean you lose your free checking for the whole month. A better choice is the "average daily balance" method. Here, the bank calculates your minimum by figuring the average amount in your account over a month. So if your minimum balance is $500, and you dip below $500 for a day or two but have an average of, say, $700 in the account for the month, you're okay and won't be subject to fees from "the man."

Incidentally, I have found "direct deposit" (having your paycheck automatically deposited into your checking account) very convenient. For one thing, the money is immediately posted into your account, allowing you to forgo waiting in line at your local branch or ATM. It also enforces some discipline on your spending habits, as there's less temptation to cash it and jet over to Tower Records when there's not an actual check in your hand. Your employer should be able to set this up with no hassle whatsoever.

Again, the ultimate use of a checking account is transactional. You'll need it for getting money into your life (cashing checks) and out of your life (writing checks). Any type of "storage" should occur in a savings account, money market account, or any of the other cash equivalents that pay higher rates of interest.

SAVINGS ACCOUNTS. The simple savings account has been much maligned in our capitalist culture . . . and for good reason. Savings accounts pay a very low interest rate—the lowest on any savings product besides checking—making it an okay choice for "saving" but poor one for storing. When your savings account starts to add up, it's time to move out—that is, move your money into a higher-paying investment vehicle, like a money market account, CD, or perhaps something more aggressive and long term, like the stock market. Still, a savings account does function in much the same way as checking, as a convenient "storage tank" for the short term.

Next time you go to your bank, check out the "wall o' interest rates" most banks have posted somewhere in the lobby. Look for the lowest interest rate—chances are, it's for a savings account. These days, savings accounts pay somewhere between 1 and 3 percent, an anemic return that makes these accounts unsuitable for real wealth creation. Why so low? In return for giving up high interest rates, you get lotsa liquidity. There's usually no minimum balance to maintain, and you have immediate access to all of your money. Savings accounts can be wired up to an ATM card, allowing you to get at your money anywhere, anytime, and they are insured by the FDIC. More than anything, savings accounts offer safety. There's just no way you'll lose any principal.

If you're just starting to save and don't yet have enough money to invest in a higher-yielding instrument, a savings account

SAVINGS ACCOUNT DATA BANK

Where: **Bank.**

Investment return: **Very low.**

Safety of principal: **Total.**

Purpose: **Offers high liquidity (access to your money) and stability of principal.**

Tip: **Savings accounts are for the short-term storage of your money and are more suited for people who need the ability to get at their cash at any time without restrictions. Longer-term savings should be kept in other products, most notably a money market account or certificate of deposit.**

is perfect place to begin erecting your empire. You can usually open a savings account with literally $1. Also, just like a checking account, a savings account is appropriate if you're planning on making a specific purchase in the near future. If you want to buy a car in the next few months, for example, that money can't be sitting in stocks. Park it in savings, make the meager 1 to 3 percent interest, buy the car, and be done with it.

The interest rate paid on savings accounts can vary from bank to bank, so it does make sense to look around for the highest rate before opening an account. Keep in mind, however, that the chances of one rate being *drastically* better than another are slim to none. The savings sticklers will want to check out the excellent and very user-friendly Bank Rate Monitor, found on the Web at www.bankrate.com. There you'll find a comparative listing of savings accounts from all across the nation.

MONEY MARKET ACCOUNTS. Like many of the other savings products, money market accounts come in a variety of incarnations, but the idea is always the same. These accounts pay higher rates of interest than checking or savings, although you'll need to maintain a more substantial balance. You can often write checks against a money market account, but again, these can be limited as to the size and frequency of your withdrawals, so read the statement and ask questions before you sign up. You can often use the teller or ATM with these types of accounts as well.

So what is a money market account? Well, the money market encompasses everything from short-term IOUs from the government to debt obligations from many of the nation's most stable companies. Money market accounts allow individuals to get the higher rate of interest the securities provide without having to cough up the millions of dollars it takes to directly participate in the money market itself. For our purposes, money market accounts act like savings accounts that pay slightly higher rates of interest. The rates change weekly, and, as with other savings products, generally track the direction of overall interest rates. While most money market accounts offer you the ability to write checks, again, these privileges are limited. Money market accounts (also called MMDAs or money market deposit accounts) therefore don't take the place of your normal checking account.

BANK-OFFERED MMDA ACCOUNTS. Bank-offered money market deposit accounts are insured by the FDIC, so you won't lose any sleep wondering if your savings will be safe. You will, however, want to be aware of the mountain of maintenance fees, penalties, and restrictions your bank might seek to impose. The most common is the minimum balance requirement: many banks won't pay any interest if your balance falls below a certain level.

MUTUAL FUND MONEY MARKET ACCOUNTS. If you have enough cash to open a money market account, I frankly think a bank isn't the place to do it. Get ready for fun, my friends, because the mutual fund money market is a savings product that you're definitely going to want to understand.

First of all . . . they're everywhere. Almost every mutual fund company offers a money market account; they are often called simply "cash funds." Like their bank-offered brethren, they too invest in short-term debt obligations from the federal government, large corporations, and the like. The kicker: With a mutual fund money market (say that ten times fast!) you'll get even higher rates than money markets offered though your bank. For example, while an MMDA might pay 2.5 percent interest, mutual fund money markets regularly pay two percentage points higher. Again, the rates are subject to change and do tend to move with the overall direction of interest rates, but mutual fund money markets will always offer higher returns than bank-offered MMDAs because of one fundamental difference: unlike MMDAs you get at a bank, money market mutual funds are not FDIC-insured.

Here's you: Then forget it. Here's me: Don't worry. It doesn't really even matter. That's right. They invest in the exactly the same risk-free instruments that bank-offered money market funds do, 'cept that because they are offered by private mutual fund companies, they just don't have the FDIC kiss of approval. Don't freak. It's the same damn thing.

Here's the setup: When you open a mutual fund money market account for, say, $1,000, you are actually buying 1,000 shares priced at $1 each. The interest you make in a money market is paid in the form of more shares, so the value of the shares themselves always stays at $1. A money market having to "break the buck" is practically unheard of—for all practical purposes, it just does not happen.

I like mutual fund money market accounts more than any other cash investment, for a few reasons. First, you can't beat the yield. No other cash product offers as much interest for the liquidity. Some even offer the same check-writing privileges as bank-offered money market accounts. Another plus is that mutual fund money market accounts kinda force you to set up an account with a mutual fund company, which will be helpful once we get into other, more aggressive, investments a little later in the book. The fund companies make it quite easy to transfer assets between your various accounts, so moving money from "cash" (mutual fund

Money market mutual funds, like other mutual funds, also will issue "fractional" shares, so don't worry about investing round numbers or being able to "afford" certain numbers of shares when putting your money in money market mutual funds.

money market account) into stocks (stock mutual funds) can easily be done on the phone or even online. Finally, though most funds insist that you have a minimum balance to open the account (usually $1,000), there's usually no penalty for falling below that level.

CERTIFICATES OF DEPOSIT. They're called CDs, but they've got nothing to do with music. Here's the deal: Certificates of deposit can best be thought of as a loan that you make to the bank. You give up access to your cash for a specified period of time in exchange for a correspondingly higher interest rate, depending on the length and amount you decide to deposit.

What's the big difference between CDs and all the other cash equivalents we've talked about? Lack of liquidity. When you invest your money in a certificate of deposit, you don't have easy access to it as you do with savings, checking, or money market accounts. You can't write checks against a CD—your money is "locked up" for a fixed amount of time, which can be anywhere from one month to five years.

You will be unable to retrieve your money until your CD matures, that is, until its predetermined term is up. Because you give up the liquidity, CDs pay a higher interest rate, currently ranging from about 4 percent for a one-month CD all the way up to 6 percent for a five-year CD. Again, the disadvantage is that, unlike money markets or savings or checking accounts, you do not have access to your money. Unless you want to incur a substantial penalty, you must wait until the CD matures before withdrawing funds.

Are we clear on this? *You don't have access to the cash.* The penalties aren't the chump change variety, either. Withdraw money from a CD before maturity and the bank will levy a substantial **penalty** that would most likely cause you to lose all of the interest that had accrued up to that point and perhaps even some of the principal. This is one of the major risks of investing in CDs. You have to be certain that you won't need the cash before maturity. If there's a chance you might need the money, better to keep it in checking, savings, or any of the more liquid cash equivalents.

The minimum deposit required on CDs varies from bank to bank, but generally you need at least $1,000. Generally, the longer the maturity, the higher the interest rate. By investing in a CD with a longer maturity, you are taking a certain risk that interest

Citibank, for example, will levy 90 days of interest **penalty** on a one-year CD, meaning that it will deduct 90 days' worth of interest if you need to withdraw money from your CD before it matures. If you need to withdraw money less than 90 days after you opened the account, they will take the interest equivalent out of your principal, and you will have lost money on the deal.

rates overall might change during the interim and you might miss an opportunity to "lend" your money at a higher interest rate. Unless the difference between, say, a two-year CD and a five-year CD is drastically different (like 3 or 4 percent), I don't really see the sense in locking your money up for too long a period of time.

If you don't need the liquidity, CDs offer a few distinct advantages. As previously noted, they come in several different maturities, so if you have a target date for when you'll need the money, you can open a CD of corresponding length. You'll have the certainty of a known interest rate, pay no commission, and sleep well at night knowing that no matter which way the financial markets move, your money is superbly safe.

Weirdly enough, you might also find, as I have, that the lack of liquidity of a CD can actually *save* you some money. If it's harder to get at your money, it's harder to spend it. If you know there's a beefy penalty for early withdrawal, you'll be less tempted to splurge on the unexpected.

Although they are FDIC-insured, there are two minor risks you run when investing in CDs. One is the same inflation risk you run with all the other cash equivalents discussed in this chapter. At 4 to 6 percent, the returns on CDs won't handily beat inflation in the long run as stocks will, so investing in them is not a good move if you're looking for long-term growth. Second, and less important, there's an interest-rate risk with CDs: Because you lock in an interest rate when you open a CD, there is the realistic chance that interest rates could change before your CD matures. Open a one-year CD at 5.5 percent and you might find the same investment yielding 6 percent just a few months later. While this doesn't make a huge hell of a difference, think about if we were talking about $100,000 rather than just $1,000. You'll have that kind of money. One day.

6 percent of $1,000 = $60;

5.5 percent = $55

6 percent of $100,000 = $6,000;

5.5 percent = $5,500

Here's a tip when you do get that kind of dough (as we all know you will): The best way to avoid interest-rate risk is to stick with shorter-term maturities (between six months and two years) or to "ladder" the maturities. Laddering the maturities means that instead of opening a three-year CD for, say, $3,000, you'll open three $1,000 CDs with, say, one-, three-, and five-year maturities. The idea is that when these CDs do mature, you'll be able to reinvest the money for a highter rate, if interest rates have risen. This laddering strategy is most appropriate for the retiree looking to live off interest income, not the young person looking to invest long term.

CDs vary dramatically from bank to bank, so it really pays to shop around for the highest interest rate. You can, to some extent, negotiate better rates. If the bank across the street is offering a better deal, talk to your bank and threaten to switch. In my experience, the bank will match the higher rates to keep your business.

Remember to check out Bank Rate Monitor on the Web (www.bankratemonitor.com). You can easily open CDs at a bank anywhere in the country, so don't be skittish about putting money into another state, if the interest rate makes it worth it. For example, in October of 1998, my local bank was offering a one-year CD for 5.1 percent, while a bank in New York was offering the same one-year CD for 5.7 percent. On a $1,000 investment, we're talking about making $51 bucks vs. $57. So spend 33 cents to make six bucks more. Not a big hassle.

A final thought or two: When your CD matures, the bank will give you the option of closing your account, that is, getting your money back, or "rolling over" your account: automatically opening up a new CD with the same maturity at whatever the interest rate happens to be at that time. Many people are content to let their savings continually compound in certificates of deposit: the interest you earn will simply be reinvested into the new CD.

Second, and this is very important: When comparing the interest rates paid on CDs, you'll

Treasury Plus Investment Account

	How Indexed T-Bill	Interest Rate %	Current APY
$0 - $9,999		2.75%	2.78%
$10,000 - $24,999		4.44%	4.53%
$25,000 - $49,999		4.44%	4.53%
$50,000 - $99,999	+.05%	4.49%	4.58%
$100,000 and over	+.10%	4.54%	4.64%

Certificates of Deposit

	Minimum Balance	Interest Rate %	Annual Percentage Yield %	Founder Rate	Annual Percentage Yield %
3-month	$1,000	4.40	4.49	4.53	4.62
6-month	$1,000	4.45	4.54	4.58	4.67
12-month	$1,000	4.50	4.59	4.63	4.72
18-month	$1,000	4.50	4.59	4.63	4.72
24-month	$1,000	4.55	4.65	4.68	4.78

CERTIFICATE OF DEPOSIT DATA BANK

Where: **Bank**

Investment return: **Varies depending on the length of the CDs maturity, which can vary from one month to five years. CDs with longer maturities pay higher rates of interest.**

Safety of principal: **Total. FDIC-insured when bought through a bank.**

Purpose: **CDs offer higher interest rates but no liquidity, or access to your money. Thus, they are perfect for longer-term savings, or if you need the discipline of not being able to get at (and spend) your cash.**

Tip: **Shop around for the best rates and don't be afraid to send your money out of state. Be sure to have the interest compounded and not sent to you each month. This will give you a higher overall yield.**

see two different numbers, one slightly higher than the other. The annual interest rate is the amount of interest they'll pay on a particular CD, assuming you choose to have the interest sent to you each month. This is what retirees who need investment income do. They open up CDs and have the interest sent to them each month. When the CD matures, their principal is returned.

The annual compounded yield, on the other hand, is the effective return you'll get if you have your interest compounded over the CD's entire maturity. The compounded yield is going to be higher than the stated interest rate, because your interest is earning interest. This is the option you should choose. On a $1,000 CD at 4.6 percent, the monthly interest would be $3.83, or interest of $46.00 for the year. What the hell is the point of getting a check for $3.83 sent to you each month? By letting your interest compound over the life of the CD, you'll make significantly more—namely, $47.00 (compounded monthly, interest accrues daily)—than you will having it sent to you each month. So when you open up a CD, be sure you specify you want the interest compounded. They'll know exactly what you're talking about.

In his 1991 smash hit "New Jack Hustler," Ice-T busted the following rhyme:

> *Got my crew in effect, I bought 'em new Jags,*
> *So much cash, gotta keep it in Hefty bags.*
> *All I think about is keys and Gs.*
> *Imagine that, me workin' at Mickey D's!*

What's wrong with this guy? As you now know, the Hefty bag is *not* an acceptable cash equivalent. In fact, if you're looking to store cash for more than a few years, then cash itself isn't even that good of a deal.

So while you will undoubtedly want to keep a portion of your portfolio in cash equivalents, it's just not an ideal choice for long-term investments. Think of cash equivalents as a launching pad. As you are able to save and accumulate cash, you'll want to begin taking a bit more risk, achieving higher returns with more aggressive investment instruments, namely, stock and bond mutual funds. Though the access and liquidity of cash are definite pluses, you'll be better off keeping the majority of your investable money in these other products, which will be outlined in the chapters to come.

But still . . . cash is a place to start. Open up one of the accounts above and get comfortable with the idea of keeping closer track of your money. Get used to reading statements, talking to bank officials, understanding interest rates, and watching your money grow. Remember: You'll need to keep that emergency fund—the two months' worth of living expenses—somewhere—so get started with savings accounts or, better still, a money market fund or six-month CD.

And Ice-T: You ain't no Puffy, but you've sold a hell of a lot of records. If your money is *still* in that Hefty bag, call me. We can probably work something out.

6 BRING ON THE BONDS

To quote Weezy Jefferson:

"We're movin' on up." The investment pyramid, that is. Next up comes bonds, or what Wall Streeters generally refer to as "fixed-income" investments. Bonds are called this because (1) they provide a stream of income, and (2) that level of income is fixed. Duh!

SPECULATIONS
Individual Stocks
Options
Futures

STOCK MUTUAL FUNDS
Actively Managed Funds
Passively Managed Funds

BONDS OR "FIXED INCOME"
Bond Mutual Funds

CASH OR CASH EQUIVALENTS
Savings Accounts, Checking Accounts, Money Market Accounts
Certificates of Deposit

Now riddle me this: If a 7-Eleven is open 24 hours a day, 7 days a week, 365 days a year . . . then why do the doors have locks?

It's an old joke but a good question. If the store is never closed . . . why would there be a need for the doors to have locks?

Okay, Mr. Wizard . . . a different, yet strikingly similar, brain twister: We know that out of any other investment class, the stock market has provided the highest long-term return over time (see graph on page 109). So if we're looking for the highest return on our investment, why even bother with bonds? That is, why even bother including bonds as part of your overall investment portfolio?

You'll know . . . in just a few pages. Can you feel the excitement as much as I do?

WHAT IS A BOND?

First things first: What is it? A bond is an I.O.U. It represents debt. When you invest in bonds, you are lending someone, usually a corporation or the U.S. government, your money. The government needs money to fund its ongoing operations, while large corporations routinely need money to help bring their products to market. When you buy bonds, you are going to lend them some of that money.

Creditor: Someone who lends money to another.

As the bond buyer, you are the creditor. The bond issuer is the person or entity that borrowed money by selling the bonds in the first place. As a **creditor** you are entitled to receive regular interest payments on your money. That's one of the benefits of investing in bonds: getting investment income. Historically, bonds don't return nearly as much as stocks, but neither do they entail the same level of risk.

Who needs bonds? Well, the elderly rely on bonds because they need a safe, dependable place to park their principal while they live off the interest. Old folk can't risk putting the money they need to live on in the stock market, because as we know, over a short span of years, anything can happen in the stock market. So retirees who frankly are planning on dying in a few years just don't have the time to ride out a downturn in equities. They need to protect their principal, so they buy bonds instead of stocks. This gets back to the whole notion of why asset allocation has to reflect your personal circumstances. For example, many people who have spent their lifetimes making money in the market move their money (or at least a portion of it) into bonds once they retire. They are then able to support themselves and live off the interest payments they receive from their bond holdings. How much dough are we talking about? Well, if you have a million bucks invested in a bond that pays you 6 percent, you'll make 60,000 a year without even getting out of bed in the morning. Yowza!

But unless you've got millions at work, you'll only get a few bucks from bonds. That's why for most of us, thinking of bonds as a source of "income" is a huge 'n' mighty misnomer. For example, if we invest $1,000 in a bond that pays 6 percent, we'll make $60 bucks a year in interest income. Personally, I need a bit more than that to keep me hot and happy.

That's the point. As young people, we don't need to live off our investments just yet, because we're still actively creating wealth at our jobs. I remind you that while investing in the financial markets is joyous, it's not a substitute for a job. So while I salute any piggish fantasies you might have of retiring at 25 (Christ knows I have 'em every day), I'll bring you back down to earth by saying that there's no way to live off your investments, either stocks or bonds, when you've got anything less than monster money. So unless Mommy and Daddy have bequeathed to you the big bucks, let's quickly dispel the notion that you'll be investing in bonds to live off the interest income they provide.

Are you with me? A bond is a loan. You lend someone money, they promise to pay you back . . . with interest. The interest part is key. We're not going to lend money for free . . . I mean, our resources are too valuable to be just given away, or lent without some form of payment. Greed is good, remember? So the interest is the payment we receive for allowing someone else the privilege of borrowing our money.

Again, when you own a bond, you are a creditor, and the debtor, or bond issuer, owes you . . . big time. As I mentioned before, they promise to pay you back the money you've lent. They also promise to pay you interest, which is generally set at a fixed rate, allowing you to count on the "fixed income" a bond will provide. This is the general 411 on bonds.

You lend. They pay. *Capiche?* But *when* they pay you, *how* they pay you—hell, *if* they pay you—are entirely different matters altogether. These specifics depend on a few factors, namely, the **maturity**, the **coupon**, the **face value**, and the **credit quality**.

Say WHAT???? Now listen, Rubin . . . take your Ritalin! Before these wacky terms prompt you to exchange this book for one with the word "morons" or "idiots" in the title, allow me to

Maturity: The date the bond expires

Coupon: The interest rate

Face value: The dollar amount the bondholder will receive at the bond's maturity

Credit quality: The creditworthiness of the borrower

John Maynard Keynes

(1883–1946) was an influential
economist in the early part of this
the twentieth century. Among his
accomplishments was the landmark
book, *The General Theory of
Employment, Interest and Money*,
which revolutionized economics and
created the new subfield of
"macroeconomics."

preface my discussion of the intricacies of fixed-income investment with a little caveat: It's not that important to know this stuff.

Keynesians might have me drawn and quartered . . . but it's
true. Unlike that professor who assigns busy work that you know
won't be on the final, I feel obligated to start off by saying that most
of this bond stuff you won't be using on a daily or even monthly
basis. In fact, you might not even use it at all.

Here's why: Bonds and fixed-income investments do deserve a
place in almost everyone's portfolio, even those of younger investors
without the Mac Daddy millions. But the bond market, alas, deals in
denominations that normally trump the gross national product of
many small countries, let alone our more pauperlike pockets.

Now, when you need to borrow money, how much does it
take to tide you over? Is a ten-spot from a friend enough, or does it take a full Franklin to
quench your financial thirst?

Or do you need to borrow more . . . say, $100 million? In the bond market, that's
chump change. The fixed-income market is enormous, and Uncle Sam is a main culprit:
The U.S. government is one the world's largest borrowers, with over $5.5 trillion of debt
outstanding. I guess size does matter.

Governments and companies need to borrow money. But because the numbers are
so astronomically obtuse, it's too difficult for a company or the government to borrow a
few hundred bucks here and there. They want moolah in the millions—more than you
and I will ever be able to lend. Don't take it personally, but large corporations don't want
to be bothered with the hassle of a zillion little loans. That's why most bonds are sold in
minimum denominations of $1,000, called the "face value."

Here's you: "I can swing that." Here's me: "Not a chance." Here's you: "But why
not?" Here's me: "Read Chapter Four." Here's you: "Which part?" Here's me: "Diversification."

The need to diversify is why we won't need to know a lot of the bond BS—the
tedious terminology I started to outline above. Diversification, as you undoubtedly
remember from Chapter 4, is one of the defining characteristics of a smart investment
strategy. You've got to diversify your investments . . . always and forever.

You remember that we need to spread our investment money around to several of
the different asset classes on the Pig Pyramid, right? Even if we want to be mostly in

stocks, we'll want to invest at least some of our assets in the other levels of the pyramid, diversifying among asset classes. That's one element of the big "D": investing in different types of assets. But we also need to make sure that within each level, or asset class, of the pyramid, our money isn't sitting all in one single investment. For example, we want to own stocks . . . but not just one stock, right? Same is true for bonds. So even though the bond issuer promises to pay you back, owning just one bond, or even two or three, isn't diversified enough.

Put it together: We need to be diversified and we don't have the big-time bucks it takes to really be a player in the bond market. Assembling a truly diversified portfolio of bonds—a portfolio that's actually going to be worth your while, might take $25,000—or more.

And if you've got that kind of monster cash lying around, the book for you isn't *Greed Is Good* but *Life Is Good*.

I'm oversimplifying, but it's true. YES, you could conceivably buy one corporate bond for, say, $1,000. But CP says you just wouldn't want to do it. Think about it: You buy a bond for $1,000 that pays 6 percent until maturity, or $60 per year. You'll pay a commission to your broker (commissions on bonds tend to start around $50 a trade, so buying and selling one bond would cost you about $100 in commissions). Then of course there's the fact that because corporate bonds are traded **OTC**, they tend to be less liquid than stocks—so while 3 million shares of AT&T stock might trade in a day, there may be only 400 trades in a day of a particular AT&T bond. Because it's less liquid, there's a bigger spread between the "bid" and "offer." The bid is the highest price someone is willing to sell; the offer is the lowest price at which someone is willing to sell. If you ever need to sell your bond before it matures, you'll have to "eat the spread," or pay the difference between the bid and offer, which could easily be 3 percent or more of the face value of the bond. Not to mention the fact that you still own only *one* bond, a totally undiversified portfolio. You see, bond interest rates are fixed, but bond prices fluctuate—so if you need to sell your bond before it matures, there's a very real chance you could get less than what you paid for it. Add up all this *michagais* and it's obvious that trying to buy bonds for a pint-sized portfolio is— um, what's the word?—oh yeah, stupid.

This does not mean, however, that you're excluded from buying bonds . . . no, no, no! Get ready for nonstop hilarity and high jinks, my piggish pals, because you'll be

Once "issued," or initially sold to the public, most bonds trade freely between brokers through a process called "**OTC**," or over the counter. Thus, unlike stocks, which trade on centralized exchanges, the "bond market" refers to the huge network of brokers and dealers who trade bonds among themselves on behalf of investors worldwide.

A **mutual fund** is a type of investment in which investors pool their
money in one large, centralized
fund. A bond mutual fund invests
its assets primarily in bonds or
fixed income instruments.

investing in a diversified portfolio of bonds just like the big boys.
You'll be doing it, however, via **bond mutual funds**—large pools
of money from smaller investors like yourself. You'll get all of the
benefits of bonds with none of the hassles I described above.

Even though you won't need to know all the nuances of how
individual bonds are sold, priced and traded, I'd still recommend
that you read the relatively short and painless explanation of same.
Not only will it give you a better understanding of how bond
mutual funds work, but at some point in the future you'll undoubtedly have the big-shot cash needed to buy individual bonds.

GETTING BONDED

Okay, so let's start over: From man's earliest days he was borrowing money and scram-
bling to pay it back. Bonds are among the oldest types of financial instruments, and to
this day, issuing bonds remains a effective way of raising money. "Issuing bonds" is simply Wall Street talk for borrowing money and promising to pay it back. The bond market plays a vital role in the creation of capital and the overall health of the economy.

Who has been borrowing all this money? Governments, corporations, but also you
and me. Mortgages, school loans, and credit card bills all make up the mammoth bond
market. People borrow money to buy houses. Idiots borrow money on credit cards. Students take out student loans for a diploma—I mean an education. Companies borrow
money to build widgets (or whatever). The government borrows money to finance the
ongoing operations of the entire country. In some form or another, almost all of us are on
someone's hook.

An example: A company needs money to expand its business or to finance its operations. How's it going to get the money? Well, there are two basic ways a company can
raise cash: (1) It can issue equity, or ownership in itself, by actually selling pieces of the
company to investors as "stock." (More about stock in Chapters 7 and 8.) Or (2), it can
borrow money by issuing bonds. A bond represents not ownership but loanership. It's
debt. The company promises to pay the loan back at some agreed-upon date in the future
(this date is known as the bond's "maturity"), plus interest. The interest may be paid
periodically, like every quarter or year. Or it may be tacked on at maturity, meaning that

you'll get the interest payments when you get your principal, or the "face value" of the loan, repaid when the bond finally matures. The idea is that the company will invest the money it borrows to make enough money to pay back the loan and the interest and still come out with some profit.

Bond holders are not owners of a company, but creditors to it. This has a few distinct advantages . . . and disadvantages. Bondholders don't get to stick their noses in the company's affairs the way stockholders do. They have no right to get involved with the decisions a company might be making on how to run its business. On the other hand, if the company goes bankrupt, bond-holders will get first dibs on the company's assets. In a bankruptcy, bondholders' claims are superior to stock holders', so if a company needs to be liquidated, that is, completely sold off piecemeal in the event of a bankruptcy, bondholders will get paid back the money they are owed before anyone else. Stockholders, on the other hand, are left holding the bag, which in the event of a bankruptcy is usually either empty or full of shit.

If you want to buy individual bonds, you'll need a broker, which is an individual or institution licensed to sell and trade investment securities. Most stockbrokers also trade bonds, or have connections with more established bond dealers who specialize in the various types of bonds available. Brokers can also buy and sell U.S. bonds, Treasury securities (like the T-Bills we talked about in Chapter 5), or they can be bought directly from the federal government through a system called Treasury Direct, where the feds maintain a pretty good Web site about all types of public debt (www.publicdebt. treas.gov).

TYPES OF BONDS

U.S. GOVERNMENT BONDS. Ted Kaczinsky and other conspiracy theorists might not trust the government, but the bond market does. The largest borrower of money is the federal government, which regularly issues bonds with a variety of maturities. Shorter-term U.S. bonds, ones that mature within 90 days to a year, are called Treasury bills or "T-Bills." They aren't really relevant here: The reason we discussed them in the "cash equivalent" section is because T-Bills are tremendously liquid and safe and

If you've ever had a Bar Mitzvah or been confirmed, you probably already have some experience in the fixed-income market. Savings bonds, originally created to help fund our wartime activities, are now commonly given to young people as gifts for special occasions. Savings bonds are issued by the Treasury in a few denominations, starting at $50. Savings bonds are safe, 'tis true, but laughably illiquid. Unlike most other bonds, there's no active secondary market in which the bonds are traded. This means you can't cash out early without paying a penalty. That measure of illiquidity combined with the fact that savings bonds pay very low interest makes them shitty investments for your portfolio.

When the savings bonds you might already own do mature, you'll want to quickly transfer that cash into a higher-yielding investment. A money market fund like the one we discussed last chapter gives you more of an interest bang for your investment buck than does a savings bond, plus the added liquidity of cash.

don't really fluctuate that much in yield on a week-to-week basis. So while they are technically a type of bond, T-Bills are essentially considered cash. Longer-term U.S. bonds, the ones relevant here, are called Treasury notes (mature in ten years or less) and Treasury bonds (mature in over ten years). Among their many attributes is a bit of a tax break: The interest is not subject to state or local income taxes.

Credit risk is the chance that a borrower will not be able to pay back the lender.

These bonds are safe, meaning that they have no **credit risk**. They are backed by the full "faith and credit" of the U.S. government; although we might have little or no faith in our leaders, we can count on the country's never running out of money. Worst-case scenario? They'll just print more. It is important to mention, however, that if you don't hold bonds to maturity, it's very possible to lose money investing in bonds . . . even U.S. government bonds. The risk you take is not a credit risk, but an interest-rate risk. If interest rates move, the value of U.S. government bonds (especially the longer maturities) can rise or fall in a big way. (More about this later.)

STATE AND LOCAL GOVERNMENT BONDS. State and local governments also borrow money, mostly for infrastructure investments like buildings, highways, and schools. These municipal bonds pay a lower rate of interest because the bondholder gets a tax break. Buy a muni, and you don't have to pay federal tax on the interest. If you live in the city or town that issued the bond, you don't have to pay state or local tax, either. One common type of muni bond is the general obligation bond, or "GO," which is backed by the taxing power of the issuer. Another type is revenue bonds; these are issued to raise money for things like toll roads that will provide a revenue stream to pay back the bond.

GOVERNMENTAL AGENCY BONDS. Other big borrowers are quasi-governmental agencies, like Fannie Mae (the Federal National Mortgage Association) or Ginnie Mae (the Government National Mortgage Association). Idiotic names but important entities. These agencies help people get mortgages to buy homes, or in the case of the Student Loan Marketing Association (SLMA), assist students to fund their education by lending them money.

CORPORATE BONDS. Corporate bonds are those issued by the private sector and are used for acquiring everything from new equipment to new companies. These are more risky than bonds issued by the government simply because they are not guaranteed, leaving you more exposed to a potential risk that the borrower (the company) won't be able to repay the loan. Because they lack the guarantee and are higher risk, corporate bonds will always pay a higher rate of interest than government bonds.

Let's talk returns. Returns can vary dramatically, depending on the company. High-quality corporate bonds—the type issued by solid, proven companies with a long history of borrowing money and paying it back—are less risky than bonds issued by junky corporations that don't have a dime to their name. Consequently, high-quality corporations don't have to pay as much interest as these junky companies, whose bonds, ironically enough, are called junk bonds. Who wants to lend money to these unproven long shots? Lots of people: Sometimes called "high-yield bonds," **junk bonds** (see following page) pay a much higher interest rate than corporate bonds of better quality, but the risk is correspondingly greater. With a junk bond, there's more of a chance for default, that is, more of a chance the company won't be able to repay the loan.

WHAT'S THE RATING?

As you know, the rate of return on an investment is based on the amount of risk one is willing to assume. The higher the risk, the higher the return. U.S. government bonds are guaranteed by the U.S. Treasury. The government has never defaulted on a bond, and these investments are considered the world's safest place to put your money. Corporate bonds, on the other hand, have definitely been known to default. Junk bonds default all the time.

THE MICHAEL MILKEN STORY

We can't even mention junk bonds without talking about one of the most illustrious financiers of the twentieth century: Michael Milken.

Milken, the high priest of **junk bonds**, presided over the bond department of Drexel Burnham Lambert, which became the premiere high-risk bond investment banking house. By 1984, Drexel Burnham began raising large sums of capital by issuing large quantities of junk bonds and aiding a new class of entrepreneurs called corporate raiders.

Raiders are those who masterminded unfriendly takeovers by convincing shareholders to sell, or "tender," their shares. When a raider sets his sights on a target company, he makes an offer for its shares and that offer is usually significantly higher than the current market price. If the raider can get enough shares to control the target company, it takes it over and then issues junk bonds to raise enough money to pay for the shares it has just purchased.

Transactions using Milken's junk bonds included—in addition to hostile takeovers—corporate mergers, acquisitions, and the aforementioned leveraged buyouts. By the late 1980s, the junk bond business had grown to $150 billion a year and Drexel Burnham Lambert had become one of the leading financial companies in America. Milken's own operations produced at least half of his firm's profits and Milken's compensation went from $25,000 a year in 1979 to $550 million in 1987.

However, the bubble burst for Milken when one of his clients, Ivan Boesky, was convicted of insider trading in 1986. During the investigation and the trial, Boesky implicated Milken and Drexel Burnham. The government charged both Milken and his firm with securities fraud in 1988, and Milken soon left the firm. Drexel Burnham reached a settlement with the government and agreed to pay a fine of $650 million. Milken ended up paying more than a billion dollars in fines, was sentenced to ten years in prison, and barred from engaging in the securities business.

So how do we know what's quality and what's crap? There are two major credit rating organizations: Moody's and Standard and Poor (S&P). They are the Siskel and Ebert of the bond market, independently evaluating the risk represented by each borrower. They maintain staffs of economists, accountants, and number crunchers who examine the company's books—trying to get a handle on the company's ability to pay back its loans. They provide a great service in the sense that they allow us a get a quick fix of a company's creditworthiness, so we won't inadvertently lend our cash to a company with no intention (or ability) to pay it back. Plus—they save us the hassle of having to go through the books ourselves, which can be an mind-numbing experience, to say the least.

How do ratings agencies come up with their ratings? It's largely based on the company's reputation and financial stability. An example: If a stranger you meet on the street asks to borrow $100 from you, would you lend it to him? Probably not. Let's say it was someone you knew, or knew of, say, Willie Ames, who played Buddy on **Charles in Charge**. Now, I know what you're thinking: This guy has been out of work for a long time. How do I know Willie

What's his credit rating?

will pay me back? You'd probably need some details: What's the money going to be used for? When does Willie plan on returning it? Has he ever borrowed money and not paid it back before? Worst-case scenario: Will Scott Baio bail him out?

Another example: You'd probably sooner lend money to a doctor than a druggie, simply because you'd expect the doctor would be better able to pay back the loan. As the creditor, you'd be taking less risk in lending your cash to the doctor. Remember the Pig Pyramid: *less risk = less return.*

Therefore, the interest rate you'd charge the doctor would be less than the one you'd charge the druggie. This is why credit card companies give their lowest rates to customers who pay their bills. They represent a lower credit risk and are deserving of a better rate.

Companies with better reputations are able to borrow money at lower interest rates, because there is less risk that the company will default on the loan.

The government, corporations, and individuals with the best credit ratings are able to borrow money at lower interest rates for longer periods of time. The same principle holds true for you and me: When we bounce a check or don't pay off our credit card bills, it's almost as if we're saying "Don't trust me" to the world. Food for thought.

BONDS: SOME INTRICACIES OF INVESTING

At this point, you're probably thinking that high-quality bonds, especially Treasuries that are guaranteed by the government, are safe—that when you invest in quality bonds, you don't have to worry about losing money. Not true.

Vast fortunes can be made—and lost—in the bond market. Unless you buy and hold a bond until maturity, it's quite likely your bond investment will fluctuate in value, causing you to lose or gain money if you sell it. Here's how that can happen:

Although the interest rate of a bond is fixed, the actual price of the individual bond itself can and will fluctuate. Movements in interest rates, the real or perceived quality of a particular bond issuer, or a host of other factors can all affect the price of individual bonds.

So actually, there are two ways you can make (or lose) money investing in bonds: The interest and the capital gain (or loss).

The interest payments you receive are fixed. How much interest will you receive? You'll receive the bond's yield, or the percentage return it pays based on the current price of the bonds. So if a bond yields 8 percent and you made a $1,000 investment, you would earn $80 on your investment.

The other factor is the capital return, which is the appreciation or depreciation of the price of the actual bond. Remember when I said that most bonds are issued in denominations of $1,000 a pop? That's what will fluctuate. Let's say you own a corporate bond which you bought for $1,000. Say everybody wants to buy your bond. The price—not the yield or interest rate, but the actual price of the bond—will therefore go up. If the price of your bond increases from, say, $1,000 to $1,030, you would make 3 percent in capital gains if you sold the bond prior to maturity. Of course, you are still receiving interest payments on the bond. We combine the capital gain and the yield the bond pays to get the investment's total return. So to finish off our example, if the price of your bond increases by 3 percent and you get an 8 percent yield, your total return would then be 11 percent.

The prices of bonds change when interest rates change, and if you know nothing else hard-core about bonds, know this: When interest rates rise, bond prices go down and vice-versa. Think about it: Interest rates are humming along at 6 percent. You buy a bond that pays you 6 percent on your money. All of a sudden, the interest-rate environment changes and rates go up to, say, 7 percent. Who's going to want your bond that pays 6 percent? Someone will buy it if you want to sell it, but it will likely be worth less than you paid because new bonds are now being issued at the higher rate.

Now you'll still get the 6 percent interest if you hold your bond until maturity. But if you need to sell the bond before maturity, and interest rates have risen between the time you bought and the time you want to sell, you will receive less than your original principal in return.

Got it? Holding just one bond is more risky than giving Marion Barry his car keys after a New Year's Eve party. This is why we need to be diversified. This is why we need bond mutual funds. More about that later.

An example will show us how holding an individual bond exposes us to too much risk. Looking to diversify a hefty stock portfolio, an investor (we'll call him Morty) decides to buy an individual bond. But since our Boesky-to-be doesn't have *too* much money, Morty can only afford to buy one bond. With the cash in his brokerage account, Morty calls his broker and buys a ten-year bond with a $1,000 face value, a 7 percent coupon rate, and a maturity date of November 1, 2007, ten years in the future. The $1,000 is the dollar amount, or the principal, that he'll receive back when the bond matures. Seven percent is the coupon rate, or the interest rate that Morty will receive on his money. This bond pays interest yearly, and since 7 percent of $1,000 is 70 bucks (duh), Morty can expect to receive 70 dollars every year until the bond matures in November 2007, or a total of $700. The face amount, the coupon rate, and the maturity date are set in stone—they won't change. What will change, however, are interest rates in general.

When Morty bought the bond it traded at face value, meaning that it was being traded for and thus was worth exactly the $1,000 he paid for it. Just six months after he bought it, however, inflation ticked up and interest rates began to rise. They went to 7 percent . . . then 8 percent.

At the same time, Morty needs money. He wants out of fixed income and decides to sell his bond at the current market price. Here's the problem: Who wants to buy a bond for $1,000 that pays $70 when new ones are being issued at 8 percent, paying $80 per thou-

---

BOND DATA BANK

Where: Your stockbroker. Bonds are traded through a network of dealers.

Investment return and safety of principal: Both vary according to several factors, including the bond's duration and the creditworthiness of its issuer. Long-term corporate bonds have had a 67-year annual average rate of return of 5.7 percent.

Purpose: To diversify a stock portfolio and provide interest income.

Tip: Because it takes several thousand dollars to assemble a diversified bond portfolio, beginning investors are usually better off with bond mutual funds, which require less money.

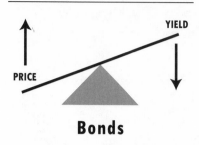

Bonds

sand? Interest rates have changed, and 7 percent just isn't that good when bonds are now being issued a full percentage point higher. Because the price of bonds falls when interest rates rise, Morty will be paid less than his original $1,000 investment for his bond.

Get it? No? Don't worry. As I said, most of this minutia applies only to those buying and selling individual bonds, which most of us simply won't be doing. Not because we're not da bomb wit bonds, but simply because we don't have enough money to assemble a diversified portfolio of individual bonds. Again—we're going to use bond mutual funds—and we're almost there. Once we are on the subject of bond mutual funds, much of the juicy jargon will become pointless trivia. Something to swill next time you have to make nice—nice with a Wall Street hotshot before a Bar Mitzvah, or something of that sort.

PUT ME IN BOND(AGE)

Okay—so back to the earlier question: If stocks have historically outperformed bonds (which they have), why bother making bonds a part of your portfolio?

I'll give you a hint. You'll find it in almost every McDonald's commercial. You'll find it in the cute and lovable kids from *Fame*. You'll find some of it on the Supreme Court but none of it at a Klan meeting. You'll also find it in Chapter 4, and even at the beginning of this chapter.

Of course, I'm talking about *diversity*.

Buying bonds diversifies a portfolio across asset classes. By putting some of our money outside the stock market and into the bond market, we're getting into investments that aren't all directly correlated. Remember, "correlated" means that the members of one asset class all tend to move the same way in price at the same time. It's the opposite with members of different asset classes. The expectation is that if stocks are sagging, the interest you are receiving on your bond investments can make up some of the slack, helping to improve performance and smooth out your overall portfolio's return. While it's not going to prevent your portfolio from experiencing the inevitable paper loss, it will make for a less bumpy ride on the road trip toward your goals.

Also, while I'm assuming most of us will be aiming at long-term goals many years down the line (necessitating mainly stock investments), there's the very real chance that even though we're young investors, we're going to have a genuine need for our investment *dinero* sooner rather than later. For example, if you're thinking about buying a car or a house in five years, you're not going to want to put that money in stocks. At the same time, cash is almost too conservative for that type of time horizon. A bond fund, on the other hand, might be the peg that fits perfectly into that hole, giving you a bigger return than cash but with less risk than stocks. Again, it's all about your goals.

MUTUAL FUNDS

"Mutual" means "together, shared," and "funds" means "money." A mutual fund is a shared pool of money. Hundreds or even thousands of investors pool their money, throwing it into a proverbial pot, and allow a central fund manager to make decisions about which securities to buy. So a mutual fund isn't actually an asset class but is, rather, an investment vehicle that allows investors to easily participate in almost any asset class—even ones they normally wouldn't be able to afford.

Gee, Jonathan, do you mean like fixed-income investments?

Ding! Ding! Ding! We have a winner! Bonds and fixed-income investments are a delish example of one of the many benefits of using mutual funds. As you know, one of the most important aspects of investment is diversification. We never want to have too many eggs in one basket. Mutual funds provide an easy way to invest in hundreds of eggs, even hundreds of baskets, with one swift transaction. A bond mutual fund won't just hold *a* bond, but dozens, even hundreds of individual bonds. As an investor in a bond mutual fund, you will thus own a tiny piece of each of those bonds.

This is one of the major advantages of using mutual funds. They allow you to invest relatively small amounts of cash at a time. Most mutual funds will let you open an account with about $1,000, and you can add to your investment in increments as low as $50. You could never get into bonds with such a puny amount of money, and you could certainly *never* get the diversified exposure that most mutual funds offer. Also, a mutual fund gives you some seriously simplified bookkeeping. The mutual fund company will send you regular statements plus confirmations whenever you add or withdraw money from your account.

Stock mutual funds invest in—you guessed it—stocks. Bond mutual funds invest in—bonds. Got it, Corky? You see, mutual funds are giant pools of cash that can be used for investments in any number of different financial instruments. There are tons of types. There are stock mutual funds (which buy and hold individual stocks), real estate mutual funds (which buy real estate securities), and, that's right, bond mutual funds. For now, let's stick with those.

So you want bond exposure, but you probably can't afford a diversified portfolio of several individual bonds. So you invest in a bond mutual fund. Your small cadre of cash is pooled together with that of thousands of other investors into a giant pot. The mutual fund manager, a professional who works for the mutual fund company you choose, will research and buy the individual bonds, and you won't need to know face value from the A-Team's **Faceman**.

What do you get?

For one thing, you'll be given shares. Not shares of stock, mind you, but shares of the mutual fund. These represent your portion of the pie, how much of the fund's overall assets are actually yours. The shares of a mutual fund are each given a price, which is called the **N.A.V.**, or net asset value. This is the fund's share price. But unlike with a stock, you don't need to worry about how many shares of a mutual fund you are buying. They will gladly issue you fractional shares. Most people find it easier to refer to the dollar amount they have in a particular fund than the number of shares.

MUTUAL FUNDS

Continued From Preceding Page

Fund Family / Fund Name	NAV	Dly % Ret.	YTD % Ret.	4-Wk. % Ret.
Henlopen	18.21	−0.4	+ 5.4	+ 2.8
Heritage				
CapApr A m	25.29	−1.1	+ 1.1	− 0.4
EagIntlEa b	27.32	−0.4	− 0.8	− 4.8
GrowEq A m	34.70	−2.4	+ 2.7	− 0.6
GrowEq C m	33.86	−2.4	+ 2.6	− 0.7
HighYldA m	9.78	...	+ 1.5	+ 0.8
IncGrowA m	15.23	−0.6	− 0.8	− 2.1
IncGrowC m	15.06	−0.5	− 0.9	− 2.2
SmCapStkA m	24.36	−2.2	− 2.9	− 3.6
SmCapStkC m	23.65	−2.2	− 3.0	− 3.7
Hibernia				
CapAprA m	24.86	−2.2	+ 1.6	− 1.0
LAMuInc m	11.43	−0.2	+ 1.0	+ 1.0
TotRtBd m	10.19	−0.3	+ 0.2	+ 0.4
USGovInc m	10.27	−0.2	+ 0.1	+ 0.3
HighMark				
BalFid	16.70	−0.6	+ 3.2	− 1.9

Fund Family / Fund Name	NAV	Dly % Ret.	YTD % Ret.	4-Wk. % Ret.
RegBankB m	49.00	−1.9	− 6.1	− 8.1
ShTmStr A m	7.90	−0.2	− 0.7	− 0.8
SovBal A m	13.84	−0.4	− 1.6	− 2.2
SovBal B m	13.83	−0.4	− 1.6	− 2.3
SovInv A m	23.77	−0.5	− 1.9	− 3.1
SovInv B m	23.72	−0.5	− 2.0	− 3.2
SpecEq A m	23.35	−2.1	− 3.1	− 3.5
SpecEq B m	22.41	−2.1	− 3.2	− 3.5
SpecEq C m	23.95	−2.2	− 3.1	− 3.5
SpecOppA m	10.49	−2.1	− 1.1	− 2.1
SpecOppB m	10.03	−2.1	− 1.1	− 2.1
SpecValB m	12.13	−0.8	+ 3.3	+ 0.4
StrInc A m	7.59	...	+ 0.8	+ 0.8
StrInc B m	7.59	...	+ 0.8	+ 0.8
TaxFBd A m	10.97	−0.2	+ 0.6	+ 0.6
TaxFBd B m	10.97	−0.2	+ 0.5	+ 0.5
John Hancock Inst				
IndDivIl	15.74	−1.7	+ 0.2	− 2.5
JB IntlEq b	17.79	−0.2	+ 4.0	− 1.5
IundtGrol f	17.82	−1.2	+ 6.1	+ 4.3

Fund Family / Fund Name	NAV	Dly % Ret.	YTD % Ret.
GrowInc m	9.68	−1.6	+ 0.3
ResSmCap m	14.54	−1.0	− 3.5
TaxFNatl m	11.69	−0.2	+ 0.6
USGovt m	2.63	...	+ 0.6
Lutheran Brother A			
HiYield f	8.42	+0.1	+ 1.9
Income f	8.76	−0.3	− 0.1
Lutheran f	28.82	−1.9	+ 3.0
MidCapGr f	11.08	−2.0	+ 1.6
MuniBd f	9.10	−0.2	+ 0.7
OppGrow f	10.58	−1.6	− 3.9
WorldGro f	11.27	...	− 0.9
Lutheran Brother B			
Lutheran m	28.67	−1.9	+ 2.9
MAPEquity f	24.00	−0.5	− 2.4
MAS			
DomFixIn	11.00	−0.3	+ 0.1
FixIn II	11.25	−0.2	+ 0.4
GloFixIn	10.79	−0.2	− 0.6

*If you wanted to invest $1,000 in the CP fund, you wouldn't ask to buy 65.7 shares. Rather, you'd just buy $1,000 worth of the fund at the current **N.A.V.**, 15.22 per share. The fund company will promptly issue you the correct number of shares, which very well may be a fractional amount.*

52 WEEK HI/LO	FUND NAME	NAV	CHANGE+
10.25 - 16.22	CP Grwth. Fund	15.22	+.21

Let's use a Sherwood-Schwartzian example: *Happy Days*.

The gang is at Arnold's (this is before, of course, it burns to the ground). Ralph Malph has just unscrewed the top to the salt shaker and Fonzie's holding court in his "office."

Richie has been talking about investing in the bond market, and after some selling (and necking) he has finally convinced Pinky Tuscadero to invest as well. Joanie wants in. So does Potsie. And Al. And Pat Morita. . . . Knowing they want diversified exposure, the gang decides to pool their money. Each chips in a few bucks and the entire stash of cash is handed over to Fonzie to invest. This is the basic idea behind a mutual fund. It's a lot of smaller investors getting together to invest for a common goal or purpose.

Sure, he lives in a rented room above the Cunninghams. It doesn't change the fact that Fonzie, in this scenario, is the fund manager. He'll make the individual buy/sell decisions about what bonds are held in the fund. While the gang won't know exactly what bonds are held in their mutual fund at all times, they will know what overall types of bonds that The Fonz will be holding. As the fund manager, Fonzie has already furnished them with a **prospectus** about what types of investments he plans to make. Let's say Fonzie decides to buy only the bonds of large U.S. corporations, which, depending on the maturity, carry a moderate degree of risk.

Prospectus: The document given to investors of a particular fund that spells out information about that fund's investment goals, past performance, fees, and risk.

So how will little Joanie pay for her college education? Or, more directly, how do you make money in mutual funds? When you invest in a bond mutual fund, you don't actually own the bonds themselves. You own a small share of the overall pool of money that (in the case of a bond fund) happens to be invested in bonds. As I said before, the mutual fund itself has a price per share, the *N.A.V.* So when the bonds or investments in the fund go up in price, so does the N.A.V. Your expectation is that Fonzie will choose good investments that will appreciate over time, causing the N.A.V. to rise in price along with the investments in the fund. You'll know what bonds Fonzie is buying

T. Rowe Price Spectrum Fund, Inc.

Prospectus
May 1, 1998

This prospectus contains information you should know before investing. Please keep it for future reference. A Statement of Additional Information about the funds, dated May 1, 1998, has been filed with the Securities and Exchange Commission and is incorporated by reference in this prospectus. To obtain a free copy, call 1-800-638-5660.

Mutual fund shares are not deposits or obligations of, or guaranteed by, any depository institution. Shares are not insured by the FDIC, Federal Reserve, or any other agency, and are subject to investment risks, including possible loss of the principal amount invested.

CONTENTS

THESE SECURITIES HAVE NOT BEEN APPROVED OR DISAPPROVED BY THE SECURITIES AND EXCHANGE COMMISSION, NOR HAS THE SECURITIES AND EXCHANGE COMMISSION PASSED UPON THE ACCURACY OR ADEQUACY OF THIS PROSPECTUS. ANY REPRESENTATION TO THE CONTRARY IS A CRIMINAL OFFENSE.

Table of Contents from a sample prospectus.

Top sites for researching mutual funds include: Morningstar (www.morningstar.net) and Lipper Analytical Services (www.lipperweb.com), which provides mutual fund data to news organizations and institutions worldwide.

because each quarter you'll get a mutual funds statement which will list each of the individual investments that make up the fund

And this, my friend, is how you make money in mutual funds. By letting them appreciate over time. You buy when you're young, sell when you're old(er), and trust that the N.A.V. of your fund will have appreciated significantly within that time. Mutual funds are just a vehicle for buying a particular asset class, like stocks or, in this case, bonds.

HAVING FUN(D) YET?

There are two major ways to buy mutual funds. One is to "go direct." Unlike stocks or bonds, which must be bought through a broker, you can buy shares of mutual funds yourself. Mutual fund companies will allow you to open an account directly with them. Almost all have 800 numbers where you can ask questions, get information, and, you guessed it: request a prospectus. The major disadvantage of going direct is that you are on your own. The mutual fund company representatives can answer questions about the fund itself, but they can't make specific recommendations about which fund you should invest in.

The other way to get into mutual funds is to open an account with any of the major full-service brokerage houses, where you will be able to talk to a salesperson—I mean broker (same thing!)—who will undoubtedly suggest any number of mutual funds. The salesperson will get compensated by either taking a yearly percentage of your account or by receiving the load, or commission, on the mutual funds they sell you. Sometimes they'll get both.

The fees on funds have a serious impact on your overall return. So as investors, we're going to be super-stingy, sticking to low-cost funds and attempting to minimize commissions wherever possible.

THE PROSPECTUS

Whether you're buying directly or through a broker, make sure you prospect the prospectus. A prospectus is Wall Street talk for a very important document issued by the mutual fund that outlines the goals, strategy, and risks of a particular fund. Fund managers can't just buy anything they feel like; they are restricted by the fund's "charter," which specifies exactly the types of investments the fund is allowed to make. If the fund's charter dictates it should buy large-cap technology stocks, you won't have to worry about the manager putting your money into mining companies, or anything else of that ilk. In order to know what you're investing in, you need to read the prospectus. Everyone does.

The prospectus also contains all the pertinent information regarding the fees that the mutual fund will be charging. That's right . . . mutual funds aren't free. You'll be paying management fees and fund expenses directly to the mutual fund company. They are calculated as a percentage of your overall investment, generally ranging from 0.5 up to about 1.5 percent. Fees make a huge difference in your overall return. Think about it: The market does about 11 percent a year, if you pay 1 percent to the fund company every single year, you're giving up a hefty slice of return, especially when the subtracted amount is compounded over time. Thanks to strict regulation, all of the information regarding fees is clearly marked in every mutual fund prospectus, so read it!

LOAD VS. NO-LOAD FUNDS

Can you drop a load? Before you even begin to wonder what that means, let me say that "load" is just Wall Street talk for a fee, or commission. Load funds, therefore, are mutual funds that charge a fee, usually expressed as a percentage of your overall investment. For example, if you invest $1,000 in a fund with an 4 percent load, only $960 of your cash actually gets invested. The fee goes directly to the salesperson or broker who sold you the fund in the first place.

Personally, I think load mutual funds suck. The main argument is that you're paying for the broker's "expertise" in recommending the fund, but truth be told, brokers push certain funds just like used-car salesmen selling Chevys. Mutual fund companies will offer incentives to brokers who sell their funds, or should I say, sell their funds to clients like you and me. Besides, with over 12,000 mutual funds out there, I just can't justify giving somebody an immediate percentage of my money just to make a choice for me—a choice that with a bit of education and understanding, all of us will be able to make ourselves. Loads really become troublesome with bond funds: Because of their lower historical return than stock funds, fees, loads, and commissions eat up even more of the overall return.

If a fund has no load, then it's called—you guessed it—a "no-load fund." These funds do not charge an initial sales fee, although, as with all mutual funds, you will pay a yearly management fee directly to the mutual fund company, as discussed above, which will be a straight percentage of your investment calculated annually. Again, they get this fee no matter how well or poorly the fund does. No-load funds are among the most popular and there are no-load funds for every different type of investment goal. From short-term bonds to dividend-paying stocks, there's a no-load fund for almost any type of investment goal you'd ever want to make. The main idea is to match your investment goals with the goals of the particular fund. If you're looking for long-term growth, a short-term bond fund just ain't going to cut it. At the same time, if you need to protect your principal, a stock fund just isn't the right choice. This is why it's so important to read the prospectus: to better understand exactly what the fund is trying to accomplish.

A quick example: One type of fund, called a sector fund, seeks only to invest in certain areas or sectors of the market, say, telecommunications stocks. Even if if natural resources stocks gain 20 percent and were the top performers in one year, don't expect your telecommunications sector fund to have bought any natural resource stocks. In this case, the fund's goals was to pick not just the best stocks, but the best stocks from a particular industry. You've got to know this stuff before you invest.

So read the prospectus, understand your investment needs, and pick funds that suit those needs.

REINVEST YOUR INCOME

No matter which type of mutual fund you choose, make sure your interest, dividends, and capital gains are being reinvested into the fund as shares and not sent to you as cash. Many mutual funds earn income in the form of interest (bonds) and dividends (stocks). The fund company will either send this to you as cash or simply reinvest the money directly into your account. Your grandparents might need the income to live on, but you've got some years of working ahead, so having this cash reinvested will allow your investment pot to grow and compound that much quicker. Plus, having the money reinvested will save you from the inevitable temptation of cashing and spending that check on crap, rather then investing it for your more important goals even further on down the line.

AUTOMATIC REINVESTMENT PROGRAMS.
I'd also recommend investigating an "automatic investment program," which is offered by almost every major mutual fund company. Basically, you authorize them to regularly withdraw a certain amount of money from your checking or savings account to be invested in the fund. This instills a doctrine of discipline into your investing account, so that each month you'll invest a small amount (as low as 25 bucks) without even having to think about it.

Also, you'll be employing a strategy known as "dollar-cost averaging." This is a souped-up term for a simple concept: Suppose you invest $50 in a bond fund every month. Thus, you are investing a fixed amount of money at regular intervals, no matter what the fund or market is doing. When prices are low, your Ulysses S. Grant will buy more shares of the mutual fund than when prices are higher. Over time, this will lower your average cost per share, for you will be buying more shares when prices are low, less shares when prices are higher. This is dollar-cost averaging.

The most important thing is to stick with your plan. Even when the market is down, you've got to continue investing regularly to make dollar-cost averaging work. CP consensus: Do it! Automatic dollar-cost averaging programs take the paperwork, hassle, and emotion out of investing. It becomes so automatic, you'll probably forget you're even doing it.

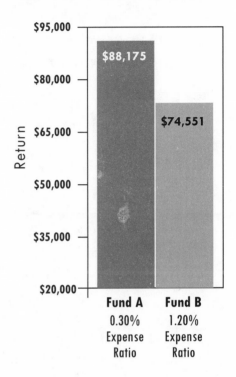

How Costs Affect Returns

Investment expenses can have a major impact on investment returns. For example, over 20 years an investment of $20,000 in Fund A, with an annual expense ratio of 0.30%, grew to $88,175. Meanwhile, a $20,000 investment in Fund B, with an annual expense ratio of 1.20% grew to only $74,551. The difference between the two amounts is more than two-thirds of the value of the original $20,000 investment.

The example assumes an average annual return of 8% before expenses in a tax-deffered account. All dividends and distributions were reinvested. This is a hypothetical illustration only and should not be considered indicative of the return on any investment.

ACTIVELY VS. PASSIVELY MANAGED FUNDS

One of the reasons I'm so negative about load mutual funds is because the "professional" whose service matters most is not the one who helps me choose a fund, but the person who actually manages the money in the fund. Remember, the broker just sells the fund—he or she doesn't actually decide what securities the fund will be buying, selling, and holding. As an investor, I want to know the individual who is actually going to be managing my money. It's not the broker, but the fund manager.

So who is it? What individual is making the decisions about which securities to buy and sell? Who is the fund manager? What type of investment strategy is he or she actively seeking to employ? Is the fund managed by one person or is there a team approach? These answers are found in the prospectus.

This brings up another advantage of mutual funds, that of professional management. Sure, The Fonz can start the jukebox with a karate kick, but can he pick bonds that will make us some money? Mutual fund managers are trained professionals whose entire job is to pick securities they are convinced will appreciate, or go up, in value. So these types of funds are said to be actively managed, because a fund manager is actively buying and selling securities on the basis of his or her experience, technique, and expectations. As a mutual fund investor, you are able to employ these experts to manage your money for just pennies on the dollar. The fund's expense ratio is the total percentage you will be charged annually for participating in the fund it is used to pay the fund company (and the fund manager). So if you've got $1,000 invested in a fund with a 1 percent annual expenses ratio, think of that $10 as buying you the expertise of a licensed and trained professional. That's one of the advantages of mutual funds: professional management.

From 1995 to 1998, only 4 percent of actively managed funds beat Vanguard's Index Trust 500 Portfolio.

Problem is, when it comes to returns, it's not always that much of an advantage. Despite their college degrees, computer networking models, and armies of researchers constantly watching the markets, mutual fund managers have a hard time consistently beating the benchmarks, or indexes, of a particular type of security.

An index is a specific group of investments that's designed to give an indication of a particular area of the capital markets. You remember the index called the Dow Jones Industrial Average from our discussion of stocks? Bonds also have indexes. The Lehman Brothers Aggregate Bond Index, for example, tracks the overall bond market. Fund managers whose picks don't do better than the unmanaged index are said to be "underperforming the index" or "trailing their benchmarks." Surprisingly, year after year most do just that. Just as it's difficult for the average investor to "beat the market," so it is for most professionals. I know it sounds strange—that a group of pros can't beat an unmanaged basket of stocks, but the statistics support this.

This has led to the development of passively managed, or index, funds. "Explosion" might be a better word than "development," because these types of mutual funds have gained an enormous amount of popularity in recent years. Passively managed funds don't try to beat the index: they merely try to match it. Whatever the market does, that's what the mutual fund does. Passively managed funds buy and hold the securities in the index. That's all.

Talk about an easy gig! The manager of an S&P 500 index fund, for example, doesn't try to find good stocks on the basis of earnings or valuations or anything that sort. He or she simply buys the 500 stocks that make up the S&P 500. They don't dump the losers or seek out the winners—they're goal is simply to match the return of the index itself, in this case the S&P 500. As an investor, you know exactly what you are getting because whatever the index does, you'll return will be almost the same. When you buy an index fund—you simply buy the index.

I'm a big, big, big, monster fan of passively managed funds, index funds especially. The biggest reason is that they have very low expenses, the lowest of any type of mutual fund. While an actively managed fund might charge 1.5 percent a year, the passively managed fund usually charges less than half that. Over long periods of time (mutual funds are long term, remember) it can really add up.

Another reason I like passively managed funds is that they have less **turnover**, giving you less of a tax bite at the end of the year. A quick note here on taxes. Taxes suck. Taxes are unavoidable. Taxes matter. You don't see H&R BLOCK tattooed across my chest, and it's beyond the scope of this book to delve too deeply into the tax ramifications of your investment decisions, but let me say that a once you get an investment program in place, it would totally behoove you to talk with a tax professional about ways of making your investing less taxing. As they say on the street, it's not

Vanguard charges just .20 percent in expenses for most of its index funds, compared to the average actively managed fund, which charges 1.44 percent. Obviously, you can save a bundle in fees.

Turnover: Turnover refers to the rate, expressed as a percentage, at which a mutual fund buys and sells securities each year. For example, if a fund has $500 million under management, and the manager bought and sold $500 million worth of stock in one year, the fund's turnover rate would be 100 percent.

how much you take, but how much you take home. As a mutual fund shareholder, you pay taxes on your **capital gains** for each security the fund trades. The more securities are bought and sold, the bigger your **capital gains tax**, and the less money you make. Passively managed funds, which typically buy and sell very few securities, are said to be "tax-efficient."

The final reason to be jazzed about index funds is that they allow you to fine-tune your investment portfolio down to the dime. Actively managed funds will often jump in and out of the market, based on the managers particular sense of where prices are headed. With actively managed funds, at any given time you don't know what the hell is in the portfolio. Is the manager expecting prices to rise or fall? Did he buy Intel or not? We don't know! As investors in actively managed funds, all we get is a quarterly statement of what's in the fund at that particular moment. In terms of the day-to-day buying and selling . . . who knows what the manager has been doing?

To me, this is problematic. Enter the index fund! Let's say you've got a 10K windfall to invest. Knowing that you won't need the cash soon, you decide you want a significant amount of stock exposure, with some bond exposure thrown in for diversity. You decide on an asset allocation of 70 percent to stocks, 30 percent to bonds. Put 7K in a **Russell 3000** index fund On the bond side, you feel comfortable that you can withstand some volatility, so you throw the remaining 3K into an intermediate-term corporate bond fund. Gee. That was tough.

In two simple transactions, you have invested in over 3,000 stocks and a broad selection of corporate bonds. You know exactly what your asset allocation is (70/30) and are paying rock-bottom expenses. Someone get your high school econ teacher on the phone; he/she would never believe just how far you've come!

While I'm not going to recommend a particular mutual fund, I will say that many CP listeners have had great experiences with a mutual fund company called Vanguard, known as the "index leaders," whose funds have among the lowest expenses in the business.

A final word on index funds: Because passively managed index funds are always (in fact, they are required) to stay fully invested in the index at all times, you'll have to make your own changes in your asset allocation that you feel are necessary. For example, in a bear market or period of falling prices, an active manager might choose to put a portion of a fund's money into cash as a defensive measure. He or she is making an active choice about how to respond to conditions. You're paying him or her to do just that: make some judgment calls about the state of the market. But index funds hold very little **cash**; they're always fully invested in their specific index. So if you sleep better knowing you've got some cash on the sidelines, then you'll have to take some resources out of the index fund and allocate them to cash investments.

I think this is the best way to invest. It allows you to be the "fund manager" and keeps you more aware of which stocks you're invested in.

Actually, index funds *do* hold a small percent of their assets, usually between 2 and 5 percent, in **cash**. This money is held in reserve so that when people want to sell their shares the fund doesn't have to sell securities to meet their redemptions. This "cash cushion" explains why most index mutual funds trail their benchmarks by a small margin.

TYPES OF BOND MUTUAL FUNDS

Now that you're sold on mutual funds, let's look at the different types of bond mutual funds available for you to buy. Bond mutual funds invest in certain types of (you guessed it) bonds. And bonds are generally classified by three major characteristics:

BY ISSUER. First, bond funds are classified by whose bonds it buys. A particular bond fund might buy only U.S. Treasury bonds, or only corporate bonds, for example. A type of bond fund might buy only municipal bonds, seeking to provide income exempt from federal income taxes.

BY CREDIT QUALITY OF ISSUER. Another classification is by the credit quality of the issuer. A "high-yield" fund would invest only in junk bonds, while an "investment-grade corporate" fund might invest only in corporate bonds that are given an A rating or higher by any one of the major ratings agencies.

BY AVERAGE MATURITY OF SECURITIES. Finally, bond funds are usually classified by the average maturity of the securities within the fund. An intermediate bond fund would invest only in bonds that mature in five to ten years; a short-term bond fund would invest in bonds that mature in five years or less; and a long-term fund would invest in bonds that mature in over ten years. This maturity question marks an important difference between investing in individual bonds and bond mutual funds: Individual bonds "mature" and repay your entire principal, whereas a bond mutual fund never matures; it doesn't ever "come due." It just seeks to hold bonds that will maintain a constant average maturity of five to ten years.

I should also mention that some bond funds, often called international or global, invest in the bonds of countries or corporations all over the world. These suckers, especially the ones that invest in **emerging markets**, are among the most volatile types of mutual funds there are. It's mainly because investing overseas carries an additional type of risk. Currency risk is the distinct possibility that the drachmas or sheckels or ringgits or whatever currency the bonds are issued in could fluctuate relative to the good old U.S. dollar. These funds are more speculative and should be approached with a higher degree of caution than domestic funds. Again, the prospectus will outline the particular risks so make sure to check it out.

Stock markets in countries that are moving from socialist or agrarian economies to capitalist systems (such as Malaysia, Turkey, and Mexico) are called emerging markets. Emerging markets are usually quite volatile.

Classifying bond funds: It's like pop (or "soda," depending on your regional lexicon). You have Coke. And Diet Coke. And Caffeine-Free Diet Coke. And Caffeine-Free Diet Cherry Coke. The combos keep on coming. Same goes for bond funds. In fact, most bond funds carry one or more of the above classifications, so it's not unlikely to see bond funds described as "short-term Treasury bond funds" or "high-yield intermediate corporate bond funds." Depending on the flavor you choose, bond funds can run from the boringly benign to the voraciously volatile. When you choose a bond fund, make sure it jives with your own investment goals, but also your tolerance for risk.

The longer the maturity of a bond fund's holding, the more susceptible the bond is to fluctuations in interest rates. For example, when interest rates go down, a long-term bond fund will rise in price much more than a short-term bond fund. Of course, if interest rates go up, the long-term bond fund's price will fall more.

In terms of credit quality, government bond funds have no credit risk, or no risk that the issuer won't pay back the money. Corporate bond funds, especially those described as junk or high-yield, are more susceptible to this risk.

CHOOSING A BOND FUND

Now you know the vocabulary, but do you know what bond funds mean to you? How do you go about making choices?

Although bonds are commonly thought to be less risky than the stock market, they do carry some unique types of risk that you should definitely be aware of. The most prominent is interest-rate risk. As I mentioned before, when interest rates move dramatically, bond mutual funds—especially those of longer maturities—can experience some hefty swings in their net asset value. Thus, longer-term bond funds, even those that invest in supersafe U.S. Treasury bonds, can fluctuate in value and even lose money. Even if you plan to hold on to the fund shares for many years to come, there's a good chance that some point you'll see the N.A.V. drop.

Another risk factor with bond funds is that of the credit risk of the bond issuer. Junk bond funds, which buy the bonds of low-rated, often bankrupt, and just plain shitty companies can rack up high returns, or lousy losses. If you're looking for supreme safety, a junk bond fund is not a wise choice.

So what is? How do you go about choosing a bond mutual fund?

Slow down, Tiger! Let's make sure we're kosher on a few minor details here. Okay, you want some bond exposure to your portfolio, yeah? Knowing that you want to be diversified, and that you don't have tons of cash, you decide to use bond mutual funds in lieu of buying individual bonds.

What types of returns to expect from your bond investments? It's not eye-popping, that's for sure. Check out the graph on page 57: According to Ibbotson and Associates, a dollar invested in long-term government bonds in 1925 would have grown to $39.07 by 1997, producing a compound annual return of 5.2 percent. Even long-term corporate bonds, which carry a higher risk premium then government bonds, returned a measly 5.7 percent over the same time period, turning a $1 investment into $55.38.

Compare that to the stock market, where returns average more in the 10 to 12 percent range, and it will be obvious to you that in the long run, stock investments will sorely kick the ass of any bonds or bond funds you might buy.

But we want to be diversified across asset classes, which will help smooth out our overall return. When the stock market underperforms or even (gasp) goes down for a few years, that steady 5 percent from a bond fund will taste oh so good, making your portfo-

GREED IS GOOD

115

BOND MUTUAL FUND DATA BANK

Where: Mutual fund companies.

Investment return: Varies. Generally bond funds do not outperform stock funds, although some of the more speculative bond funds—namely, junk bond funds—have posted double-digit returns.

Safety of principal: While not guaranteed, bond funds that invest in U.S. government Treasury bills carry virtually no credit risk; that is, there's virtually no chance the debt won't be repaid. The safety of corporate bond funds varies with the creditworthiness of the issuer, from very stable to very speculative.

Purpose: To diversify a portfolio and provide interest income. Well-suited for reaching financial goals one to ten years in the future.

Tip: The yields on bond funds, especially those of higher quality, generally don't vary that dramatically, so concentrate on finding low-cost funds with expense ratios below .5 percent to help maximize returns.

lio less volatile and letting you sleep better at night. Because bond funds don't generally post the higher numbers of other investments like stock funds, choosing the best bond fund often comes down to choosing the bond fund that (1) costs the least and (2) suits your individual investment needs and tolerance for risk.

As with stock mutual funds, concentrate on finding low-cost bond funds. This is especially important when we're talking about shorter-term bond funds, which carry less risk and correspondingly less return. For example, Treasury bills have returned about 3.8 percent a year from 1926 to 1997. How much value (return) can a manager juice out of those suckers without taking on too much additional risk? Not that much. So I'd be hard-pressed to recommend any bond mutual fund whose expense ratio is more than a few tenths of a percent. Information on fees can, of course, be found in the fund's prospectus. You'll also want to check out the fund's Morningstar report, which can be found at www.morningstar.net.

In the final analysis, deciding how much money to allocate to a bond fund has less to do with performance, more to do with personality. Yours. *You work hard for your money. So hard for it, honey!* How much money you choose to put in bonds should reflect your investment objectives, your time horizon, and your tolerance for risk. If you are serious about meeting certain financial goals, like a comfortable retirement, for example, there's not a great chance that bonds will alone get you where you are going. You'll need stocks to make that kind of return. But bonds should play a role in your portfolio now and later. Later you'll need them as income—when you're sucking food through a tube, your bonds will be providing you with fixed income. Now, bond mutual funds will diversify your portfolio away from being all in stocks. Chances are, you'll sleep better at night, knowing that when the markets dive your bond fund is grooving right along, kicking in with more steady, less spectacular returns.

A final thought: For those looking for the ultimate in simplicity, you might consider a balanced fund, which is a type of mutual fund that holds a portion of its assets in bonds and another portion of its assets in stocks. These funds, also called "growth and income funds," offer one-stop shopping, giving you an immediate diverse portfolio of bonds and stocks in one simple fund. The funds vary in terms of what percentages they hold in stock and bonds, Some offer a 50/50 split, others are more aggressive putting 60 percent in stock and 40 percent in bonds.

Bonds offer more volatility than cash, but also more return. Because your long-term goals can afford that volatility, you'll want to make bonds a part of your portfolio. The majority of your portfolio, however, should probably made up of stocks and stock mutual funds, a topic we'll chew on in the next chapter.

7 STOCKS AS AN INVESTMENT

Cash? Been there . . . done that. Bonds and fixed income? *Yawn. It's time to party.* Want to kick butt and

take names with your money? The stock market, also called the "equity market," is the place you'll administer that very *toochus*-whooping. It's not because stocks are inherently that special. Look on the Pig Pyramid. Stocks are just another step on the ladder—just another place to park your pesos, store your shekels, or direct your dollars. But stocks do hold the distinction of giving the highest return of any asset class over time. That's why, for most of us, they'll make up the majority of our investment portfolios.

Peter Lynch was the fund manager of Fidelity Investment's flagship Magellan fund from 1977 to 1990. Utilizing his "buy what you know" approach—buying stocks of companies whose products one uses and is familiar with, Lynch achieved an amazing 2700 percent return during his tenure. He has written several best-sellers, including *Beating the Street, One Up on Wall Street,* and *Learn to Earn.*

Peter Lynch would never admit it, but investing in the stock market is like masturbation: It's quick, convenient, and helps you sleep better at night. Thankfully, the fiscal benefits of investing far outweigh the lustful pleasures of sexual solitaire. While masturbation might satisfy one's libido, it does little to help one plan for retirement.

Ah yes! Retirement. You know, that thing you'll do once you're too useless to do anything else. Cruises, nurses, and Depends aren't cheap; better save now and avoid malnutrition later. Social Security: A joke. Corporate pensions: All but eliminated. Job security: Gone. Hell, even the Domino's 30-Minute guarantee has already been abolished. With such an uncertain future, you'd best be prepared.

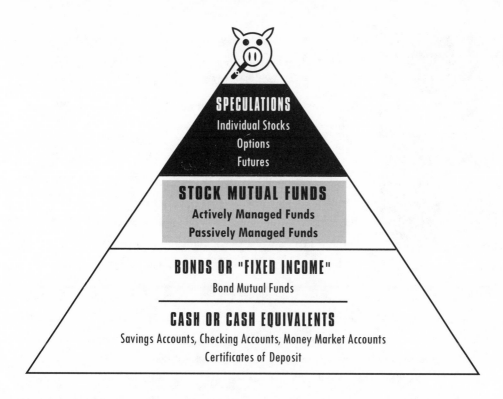

SPECULATIONS
Individual Stocks
Options
Futures

STOCK MUTUAL FUNDS
Actively Managed Funds
Passively Managed Funds

BONDS OR "FIXED INCOME"
Bond Mutual Funds

CASH OR CASH EQUIVALENTS
Savings Accounts, Checking Accounts, Money Market Accounts
Certificates of Deposit

WE ALL NEED A REASON (TO INVEST)

Your individual goals will determine how much you invest and where you invest it, but be forewarned: If your goals are ten or more years into the future and involve having, like, *money*, I believe the stock market is the best vehicle to make that happen.

Besides the monetary returns, there are less obvious reasons for starting to invest. While you won't find these listed in Fidelity's breezy brochures for prospective investors, I will now outline a few of the less-publicized perks of becoming a "Master of the Universe":

■ Chicks dig it. A well-funded 401(k) more than compensates for whatever else might be lacking. What girl doesn't get queasy when you whisper "Oh baby, you make my long bond even longer" in her ear? Don't be afraid to dress the part: Eighties power suits and red suspenders à la *Wall Street* tell the ladies that you can plot moving averages with the best of them.

Dear Jonathan
thanks
so much
for
watching!
Can't
wait to
come on!
Best Regards
Maria Bartiromo

- Guys dig it. Woman who can talk money are even more attractive than those who can talk sports. Witness the popularity of CNBC's "money honey" **Maria Bartiromo**. A saucy wuzzle of finance and femininity, Maria is going to make me the happiest guy in the world (she just doesn't know it yet).

- Parents dig it. When your Ps complain that you'll never amount to anything, feel free to wave your fund's top ten holdings in their face. While your father's greatest accomplishment was being the ten thousandth customer at the Sizzler, *you* have become part owner of America's greatest companies. General Electric, AT&T, and Boeing are but a few of the trinkets in your empire of wealth.

- Another plus to investing is the bumper crop of mail you'll receive. Buy into a fund, and with your first confirmation will come the proverbial investment "welcome wagon" of *junk mail*. In no time you'll be paging through two free weeks of *Investor's Business Daily* and contemplating the philosophical dilemma posed by our friends at the **Kaufmann Fund**: "Do tough guys *really* finish first?"

Of course, this stuff is secondary. *The primary reason to invest is that you're looking to make money,* and with a long-term horizon, investing is safe, easy, and relatively hassle-free. Mutual funds have made stock ownership more convenient than getting a dime bag in Central Park (not that I would know, of course). Just like bond mutual funds, stock mutual

funds offer automatic investment plans whereby as little as $25 or $50 is deducted from your bank account or paycheck. Put $50 a month into the stock market and you'll have over 78,000 bucks before your first midlife crisis. Keep it up until your second, and you'll have accumulated over $246,000, more than enough to pay for intensive therapy and a week in Boca. All of this on 50 bucks a month!

STARTING WITH STOCKS

Ever think about starting a business? Turning that part-time passion into everyday employment? You'll need some cash, no doubt. There's inventory to build and Xerox paper to buy. Unless you've got ROCKE-FELLER tattooed across your forehead, you'll need to raise some money. Your burgeoning business basically has two choices: You can issue bonds. Of course, now (*ahem*) we all know what bonds are: I.O.U.s that the company will repay in the future . . . with interest. This type of financing, or raising money, is called **issuing debt**.

One of the ways a company can raise money is by **issuing debt**, usually in the form of bonds that will be repaid with interest at a future date.

The other way companies can raise money is by issuing equity in the company itself through shares of stock. "Equity" means *ownership*, so these shares represent actual ownership in the company. When companies "go public," or decide to sell themselves to public shareholders, they hold what is called an IPO, or "initial public offering." As the name says, this is the first, or initial, time the company is selling the shares. That's when the company gets the money they were hoping to receive by issuing stock in the first place. After a company "goes public" its shares trade freely on an exchange between investors. Unless the company decides to sell **additional shares** of the company (called a dilution), after the IPO, they're out of the game.

When a company issues **additional shares** of stock, they effectively "dilute" the value of the stock that has been already issued. Imagine if an artist issues a "limited edition" number of signed prints. Then he issues another edition. The value of all the prints would immediately go down. The more he issues, the less each one is worth.

When you own stock, even one measly share, you truly own a piece of a particular company. It's a tiny piece, no doubt, but you do become an *owner*. To give you an idea of just how small a piece shareholders own, let's take McDonald's an as example. It has 676,559,000 shares outstanding, in the hands of the public. So 10, 50, or even 100 shares is only a minuscule percentage of the entire company.

But you are an owner. It's perfectly keeping in the Capitalist Pig style to buy a few shares of McDonald's and then immediately run down to your nearest Golden Arches and demand a meeting with the Hamburglar to discuss some company business.

The main reason you should want to own stock—hell, the *only* reason—is that its value generally keeps going up. Over time, stocks have consistently outperformed every other major

Stocks, Bonds, Bills, and Inflation

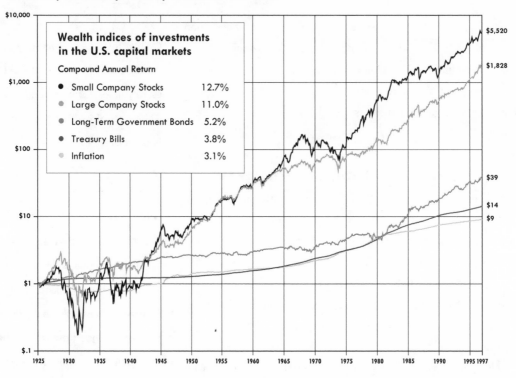

Wealth indices of investments in the U.S. capital markets

Compound Annual Return

● Small Company Stocks	12.7%
● Large Company Stocks	11.0%
● Long-Term Government Bonds	5.2%
● Treasury Bills	3.8%
● Inflation	3.1%

As you can see, only during the 1930s did large company stocks actually lose any money.

Large-cap refers to a company with a market capitalization, or worth, or over $5 billion.

Small-cap: Refers to a company with a market capitalization of $300 million to $1 billion dollars.

Mid-cap: Refers to companies with market capitalizations of $1 billion to $5 billion.

---

asset class on the Pig Pyramid. We want to invest in the stock market simply because we expect it to continue to do what it's always done: move higher and make us money.

As you can see from the chart, over the last 72 years, more wealth has been created in the stock market than anywhere else. One measly dollar invested in 1925 in large company stocks, or **large-cap** stocks, gained an average annual return of 11 percent, turning your $1 into a beefy $1,828.33 by 1997. Add some more zeros and things really get exciting. Eleven percent means that 500 bucks back in 1925 would have grown to almost $916,000 by 1997.

Even more explosive have been **small-cap** stocks, the stocks of smaller companies. One dollar invested in small company stocks back in 1925 turned into an astronomical $5,519.97, representing an compound annual growth rate of 12.7 percent. As you can see, small stocks have historically done better then even larger stocks. At the end of this chapter, we'll talk more about how to know what kind of stock investments are right for you.

Exactly how much is a stock "worth?" I'm always floored by the legions of well-clad Wall Street wunderkinder who regularly come on "CP" asserting that a particular stock is "undervalued" or "cheap" and should therefore be bought. While the price of a stock is based on a few concrete factors, like the company's earnings and future prospects, stocks are essentially traded like baseball cards. And just because you think your 1992 Michael Jordan basketball card is worth $350 doesn't mean someone will buy it from you. Just like any investment, stocks are worth only what someone else is willing to pay. It is commonly accepted, however, that a company's fiscal earnings, or it's profitability, are the most reliable indicator of its health, its prospects, and ultimately, its stock price.

STOCK OWNERSHIP: SOME SPECIFICS

Stocks don't "mature" like bonds or "expire" like the limited time-only deals at Dairy Queen. A stock represents ownership, remember, so as long as the company continues to be worth something, so will the stock. That's all a stock is—a valuation of a particular company's worth. How much is a company actually worth? That figure, called **market capitalization**, is the total number of shares of the company multiplied by the price of the share.

Shares of Stock Outstanding
× Price Per Share
= **Market Capitalization**

A company with a million shares of stock valued at ten bucks each would therefore have a market capitalization of $10 million. Fluctuations in stock prices are fluctuations in the perceived worth of the company. When investors think the company is worth more—they buy the stock. The stock price goes up and therefore, the company is worth more. MMmmkay? As a stockholder, you are protected by limited liability, which means you're not really responsible for much of anything. It's not like the company will come banging on your door, asking for cash if things get ugly. You are allowed to share in the profits, but (thankfully) not responsible for lapping up the losses. You'll be notified as to the company's operations by an annual report that will be sent to you for as long as you hold your shares. (More on that a little later in the chapter.)

Stock prices overall have risen and fallen with the general health of the economy. The market is thought to be "forward looking," which means it reflects investor's anticipation of the future. So when the market is up, investors are essentially betting the economy will be doing well. That's why, during a recession, an upward movement in stocks is the usually the first indication that things are beginning to get better. Investors who anticipate a turnaround in the economy start once again to buy stocks.

WHERE STOCKS LIVE

Okay, now we know *what* stock is (ownership in a company) and we know *why* stock exists (for a company to raise money). If I may slip into Ebonics for a moment, let us now discuss *where* stocks is.

Despite the presence of a physical "floor," a large percentage of the trading on the New York Stock Exchange is done electronically, with a minimum of human intervention.

NEW YORK STOCK EXCHANGE (NYSE). Surely you've seen pictures of the New York Stock Exchange, the Battlestar Galactica–style cavern located in Lower Manhattan. It's the world's most important stock exchange, and each day over 700 million shares change hands. Because the NYSE is the biggest and oldest of the exchanges, it's often referred to as the "big board." But other exchanges, including several regional stock exchanges located around the country, also trade stocks which are "listed" on the NYSE. To you as an investor, most of this stuff doesn't really matter. It's not like you have to specify which exchange you'd like to buy or sell your stock on.

Useless trivia: NASDAQ stands for National Association of Securities Dealer Automated Quotations.

NASDAQ. The other major U.S. exchange is called the NASDAQ (NAZ-dak) Unlike the NYSE, the NASDAQ doesn't actually "exist" anywhere. It's simply a network of computers that links 500 major brokerage houses around the world. After brokers get orders from their customers (you and me) they "post" them to NASDAQ to be traded at the best available price. NASDAQ, which is also called the **over-the-counter**, or OTC, market, has the reputation for listing more computer and technology-related stocks then the big board, as well as the stock of smaller, less well known companies. Microsoft (MSFT) and Intel (INTL) are just two of the big tech stocks that trade electronically on the NASDAQ. A stock can be traded on the NASDAQ *or* the NYSE, but not on both. In 1998, NASDAQ announced plans to merge with the smaller American Stock Exchange, which is located in New York City.

WHO SELLS STOCK

Here's an easy one: When you buy a stock, whom do you buy it from? Does the company sell you the stock? Do you buy it from the exchange? From a stockbroker? From TV's **Dustin Diamond**, better known as Screech from *Saved by the Bell*?

No! You buy stock from another investor. When you buy, another investor sells. That's the idea of a stock exchange; it's a centralized exchange where buyers and sellers can "meet" to exchange stock and money at mutually agreeable prices. The nuances of each exchange are slightly different, but the goal of everyone involved remains the same: Buy low and sell high. Nobody sells stock that they think is going up, and nobody buys a stock that they believe is heading toward the **securities** shit house.

It might seem elementary that stocks are traded between investors, but I regularly meet well-heeled listeners of "CP" who, when explaining why they didn't buy a particular company, tell me that they "don't want to support Philip Morris" (who makes Marlboro cigarettes). The logic, as you might now understand, just doesn't follow.

When you buy a share of Philip Morris, *the company receives absolutely nothing from you.* The money you put up to buy stock goes directly to the investor who sold it to you. It could be another individual, or an institution like a brokerage house or mutual fund. Philip Morris has *nada* to do with that transaction. When you buy stock in a company, you become an owner of it—not a fiscal supporter of it.

Securities is a general term given to any number of financial instruments, including stocks, bonds, mutual funds, options, or commodities.

The NYSE is a "specialist market," meaning that stocks are traded at a post by a single dealer who makes a continuous market. The NASDAQ is a "dealer market," meaning that several market makers post bids and offers in a particular stock.

The term **"over-the-counter"** (OTC) was coined over 100 years ago, when stocks and securities were actually sold "over the counter" of banks and other stores.

What makes that "I don't want to support that company by buying its stock" vibe so ludicrous is that *the most effective way to change the business practices of a company is to become an owner of one.* As a stockholder, even of one share, you are entitled to cast a vote in the company's major affairs, attend annual stockholders' meetings, and voice your opinion about the company's business practices.

Here's you: "Yeah right, like the head of some Fortune 500 company is really going to care." Here's me: "Didn't you see *Roger and Me?*" Activist shareholders are regularly able to raise enough ruckus to get their agenda heard. For example, part of Nike's decision to crack down on their sweatshop labor practices stemmed from a group of small but vocal shareholders. So if you are fed up with big business, don't be a complainer: Be an owner. Putting your money where your mouth is sends a big message that you mean business.

MARKET INDEXES

The stock market is literally a market of stocks. Thousands, in fact. Shares of over 9,000 companies are publicly traded in the United States, including not only shares of companies headquartered here, referred to as "domestic" stocks, but also the shares of foreign companies that trade on the major exchanges within the United States. This is made possible by means of proxies called American depository receipts (ADRs), which allow American investors to buy stock in foreign companies with U.S. funds on U.S.-regulated exchanges.

When you hear someone talk about what "the market" is doing—or has done, for that matter—they are most likely referring to one of the major stock indexes we use to track the overall direction of the market. Here is an overview:

Blue chips are companies that are the most stable, profitable, and have a long history of consistent revenue.

THE DOW JONES INDUSTRIAL AVERAGE. The most well-known index is the Dow Jones Industrial Average, which is an index of 30 **blue-chip** stocks that all trade on the New York Stock Exchange. Although this index is the most widely quoted, it's actually a weak barometer of the overall market. The 30 are all among the biggest companies in the world, which means that many small- and mid-cap companies are not factored into the Dow's dizzying dance. Another reason why the Dow is a lame index is because it is weighted, meaning that stocks with higher prices influence the overall index more. These little tasty factoids are more trivia than anything else; the important thing to know is that the Dow is the most commonly quoted and prominent of all the stock indexes. It's a useful quick glance at what the market is up to.

STANDARD & POOR'S 500 (S&P 500). A better measure of the overall market is Standard & Poor's 500, often abbreviated as simply the S&P 500.

The S&P 500 tracks stock of 500 of the largest companies in America. It's the index you should get to know best because it's the index most professionals use as their performance benchmark. When the pros talk about beating the market, they are talking about the S&P. Moreover, unlike the Dow, which is price-weighted, the S&P 500 is weighted by market capitalization, meaning that the largest companies have the correspondingly biggest impact on the index itself.

OTHER INDEXES. The Russell 2000 tracks 2,000 of the smallest publicly traded companies, those whose median market capitalization is approximately $500 million. This index is the benchmark index of small-cap stocks and is used as a proxy for the entire "small cap" market.

CP recommends that you become familiar with the broadest of the stock indexes, the Russell 3000. This highly diversified index measures the performance of the 3,000 largest U.S. companies, representing approximately 98 percent of the shares that are traded on U.S. exchanges. This index tracks almost every publicly traded company and is the broadest indicator of the direction of the market.

Each of the major exchanges has its own stock index, so toss the NASDAQ market index in there along with the AMEX market index for good measure.

As of late 1998, the 30 companies whose stocks are tracked by the Dow were AT&T, Allied Signal, Alcoa, American Express, Boeing, Caterpillar, Chevron, Citigroup, Coca-Cola, Disney, DuPont, Eastman Kodak, General Electric, General Motors, Goodyear, Hewlett Packard, IBM, International Paper, Johnson and Johnson, McDonald's, Merck, 3M, J. P. Morgan, Philip Morris, Proctor and Gamble, Sears, Union Carbide, United Technologies, Wal-Mart.

Dow Jones maintains several other popular indexes, including the Dow Jones Utilities Average (an index of interest rate–sensitive utilities companies) and the Dow Jones Transportation average (an index of companies involved in various areas of transportation).

Some of the more obscure stock indexes include the PLN (Airline stocks), the XAU (Gold/Silver stocks), DRG (Pharmaceutical stocks), or TOB (Tobacco stocks).

Indexes are very cool. They can tell us not only whether the market is up or down, but which particular areas of the market are shooting up (or getting shot down). For example, if the Russell 2000 is trading stronger (higher) than the S&P 500, it's an indication that smaller stocks are outperforming their large-cap brethren. Indexes are also important to understand because they serve as the benchmark by which we'll compare the performance of our own investments, namely, in stock mutual funds.

When making comparisons using an index, it's important to use the right index. For example, to judge the comparative performance of your small-cap mutual fund, you want to compare it to the Russell 2000 (the index of small companies) and not the S&P 500, which tracks mainly larger companies. Most mutual funds put return comparisons in their quarterly reports and generally seem to use the appropriate benchmark.

In CP land, asking someone their astrological sign is old skool—it's been replaced by the more contemporary (and arguably more relevant) interrogative de jour: *What's your favorite index?*

It's true: You can tell a lot about people by the stock indexes they choose to follow. Those who track the Dow are obvious laymen. Opting for the broader S&P 500 displays considerably more market panache, although it still reeks of populist homogeniety. Personally, when looking to impress the ladies, I opt to follow the SOX (Philadelphia Semiconductor Index). Highly volatile and unpredictable, the SOX is like me: *Dangerous, baby!*

THE MONEY (MARKET)

The stock market is the primary investment most investors use to reach their financial goals. This is simply because the shares of common stocks have historically beaten inflation and provided the highest long-term return. They've made a lot of people a lot of money. *You will be one of them.*

Reminder: **$3,000** invested now + $100 a month at 11 percent for 20 years becomes $113,386. In 40 years it becomes $1,099,516.22.

Data check: Once again, according to the brainiacs over at Ibbotson and Associates, large stocks have returned an annual average of 11 percent over the last 72 years, handily beating the return on bonds, precious metals, cash, even Beanie Babies. Need another "what if" scenario to get your blood pumping? Say you invest **$3,000** now into a stock mutual fund and set up an automatic investment program that will deduct $100 per month from your paycheck. Then you forget about it for the next 20 years. After only 20 years, you'll have well over $100,000. After 40 years—probably about the time you are ready to retire—you'll have over a million. For chrissake . . . somebody stop the madness!

The most striking thing about these generous returns is how easily they were achieved. Think about it: *These were the average annual returns.* It's not like they are returns were based on supercomplex arbitrage strategies, or savvy market timing. They came from investing. And waiting. And waiting. And watching the money continue to grow. *This is what investing is all about.* It's having the patience to ride out the financial typhoons that will inevitably touch down over the years. And if you know anything about the stock market, you probably know there has been some serious carnage throughout the years.

CRASH AND BURN

Crashes get the headlines, and deservedly so. The worst stock market crash occurred in 1929, right after Herbert Hoover was elected the nation's thirty-first president. How bad was it? In one day $4 billion of wealth was wiped out completely. Not to say it couldn't conceivably happen again, but I must note in fairness that the stock market at that time was highly speculative, with many investors borrowing money to get in on the action. For example, in 1929, investors only had to put down a small percentage of their investment dollars in cash. The rest could be borrowed. This led to rampant speculation with borrowed money, in other words, a recipe for a window jump. Today's market environ-

Compound Annual Rates of Return by Decade

	1920s	1930s	1940s	1950s	1960s	1970s	1980s	1990s	1988–97
Large Company Stocks	19.2%	-0.1%	9.2%	19.4%	7.8%	5.9%	17.5%	16.6%	18.0%
Small Company Stocks	-4.5	1.4	20.7	16.9	15.5	11.5	15.8	16.5	16.5
Long-Term Corp Bonds	5.2	6.9	2.7	1.0	1.7	6.2	13.0	10.2	10.8
Long-Term Govt Bonds	5.0	4.9	3.2	-0.1	1.4	5.5	12.6	10.7	11.3
Inter-term Govt Bonds	4.2	4.6	1.8	1.3	3.5	7.0	11.9	8.0	8.3
Treasury Bills	3.7	0.6	0.4	1.9	3.9	6.3	8.9	5.0	5.4
Inflation	-1.1	-2.0	5.4	2.2	2.5	7.4	5.1	3.1	3.4

ment, while equally speculative, is much more regulated: The amount investors need to put down in cash is a much more stable 50 percent, so direct comparisons are a bit far-fetched. Nevertheless, the crash ushered in the Great Depression, a pre-Prozac economic crisis that gripped the country's fiscal *cajones* until the beginning of World War II.

More recently, most of us remember "Black Monday." No, I'm not talking about UPN's hit night of urban family–oriented comedy, but the stock market crash of 1987, in which stocks went into a one-day free fall of over 22.8 percent. In the shakeout following 1987, most investment professionals believed that **portfolio insurance**, a smarmy scheme used by large institutional investors, helped exacerbate the panic. This prompted so-called "circuit breakers"—exchange rules on certain types of program trading—to be implemented from that time on. While they won't prevent a crash from occurring, circuit breakers will supposedly slow it down, kind of a market crash on Quaaludes.

Unlike the 1929 crash, which brought on the Depression and turned our entire country into an extended showing of *The Grapes of Wrath*, the 1987 crash was merely a blip on the radar screen of bullish returns. It was more of a symbolic event then anything else, marking the end of the "go-go" 1980s. Then the go-go 1990s rolled around.

Looking at a graph that includes both the 1929 and 1987 crashes, they are almost unrecognizable in the long-term trend, which is, as you can see, decidedly upward. There is no doubt in my mind that—unlike martini culture, bell bottoms, and high-protein diets—the rocky but vertical upward trend will continue.

STOCKS: THE BULLS VS. THE BEARS

Why am I so **bullish** on stocks for the long term? Investing in the stock market is having the simple and very reasonable expectation that our country's prosperity, quality of life, and tendency to innovate will continue. The only "bet" involved is the bet that some outrageous anomaly like, say, the Antichrist or Armageddon, won't come during our life-times. Even if it does come a few years down the road (and the Teletubbies are a shock-ing development toward that end), you still have some time to cash in and compound before the world comes a-tumblin' down.

The stock market will continue to rise, but it's not a rocket ship to *Runaways with the Rich and Famous*. There will be days, months, years—maybe even (gasp) decades—when the market returns a negative percentage, let alone the +11 percent we've come to expect as average. These periods of time, called **bear markets**, are more cantankerous than your common crash. Unlike a crash, where the market snaps back as it's hooked

> A **bear market** is a protracted period of declining stock prices.

up to a "buy on the dips" version of the Clapper, a bear market is a slow, undulating decline in prices. I've never lived through a severe bear market, but you don't have to pull a Marty McFly to know that few things suck more than sinking stock prices.

In his appropriately titled *Bear Book*, longtime grizzlymeister John Rothschild points out some examples of the market's slothful spells. For example, in 1937 the Dow reached 194. Twelve years later, it still stood below that point. Shocked? In 1961, the Dow hit 734, not breaking that barrier again until New Wave reigned in the early 1980s, 19 years later.

In 1973, stocks tumbled to the tune of −45 percent over a 20-month period. Even as recently as the early 1990s, stocks lost almost 20 percent of their value. It happened then and will undoubtedly happen again.

No one can predict when the next bear market is coming, or what series of events would prompt Ol' Smokey out of hibernation. We might even be in one right now, for all I know. One theory holds that as soon as our best friends (you know, the baby boomers) start to retire, they'll pull their money from the market, sending it spiraling downward. *I don't buy it.* For one thing, most of their wealth will not evaporate, but will be passed on to their heirs in trust (isn't that right, Mom?). Furthermore, life expectancy has increased dramatically in recent years, prompting even old fogies to keep a large stash in stocks up until the very end.

So what's this bear market bullshit mean to you? Should the stock market's unavoidable downswings deter you from stuffing your money into stock? *Absolutely not.* I'll ask you the same ques-tion **Gordon Gekko** asked Bud in *Wall Street*. It's simple question. Straightforward. And to the point: *Are you with me?*

Think about it. When it comes to investing in the market, *you're either in or out.* Don't expect to bail from stocks whenever your leg begins to twitch, or if a black crow lands on your windowsill, or you get some secret sign of the impending market maelstrom. There's no predicting what the market will do over the short term.

THE LONG HAUL

> **"Life moves pretty fast. If you blink, you might miss it."**
>
> —Ferris Bueller's Day Off

Don't miss it! According to a recent study at the University of Michigan, missing even a few of the "up" days in the stock market—which you're likely to do if you're jumping in and out—can seriously hamper your return. For example, if you missed just the top ten days of the 1982–87 bull market, your return would have dropped from 26 percent a year to 18 percent. If you missed the top 40 days, your return would have completely wilted to a paltry 4 percent. Unless your Bat-Belt contains a crystal ball with a hell of a lot of Windex, timing the market so you hit only the peak days is just not an option. *It simply can't be done.*

The other reason that long term is the only way to invest is that by holding stocks through all market conditions you avoid paying taxes every time you sell and commissions every time you buy or sell. Taxes are tough. As you now know, the government gets a piece of the action whenever we make money, and stocks are no exception. Money made from stocks held less than one year are taxed at your normal income tax rate, while longer-term holders still get whacked with a slightly more palatable tax bite of 20 percent. Buy buying and holding . . . and holding . . . and holding . . . you defer these taxes until you want to pay them, most likely closer to retirement. If you choose to invest in mutual funds, you will pay capital gains tax each year, but funds with low turnover (more of a buy and hold strategy) will drain your coffers by a much smaller amount.

So you can't predict the market. If you're in . . . stay in. If you're out, return this book for something by Robert Foster Wallace and forget about ever reaching your financial goals. If you want to get in the game . . . you've got to stay in the game . . . period.

But there is risk. Knowing the volatility, danger, and risk inherent in the stock market, you do make a bit of a leap of faith when you invest. The leap you're making, however, is not a reckless one. You are assuming that the world will continue to spin, that people will continue to need products and services, and that companies will be able to make a profit delivering those goods and services. Not exactly hoping for anything too crazy (like say, the Cubs winning the World Series or anything). When you think about it in those antifinance terms, it's not that much of a stretch to believe that the stock market will continue to rise over time . . . which *it will.*

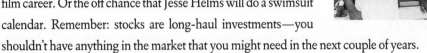

If you are frightened of investing and worried that a crash or prolonged bear market will turn your life into an episode of *Good Times . . .* you must chill! There are plenty of more important things to worry about, like the distinct possibility that those hilarious pranksters from **Good Burger** will have a legitimate film career. Or the off chance that Jesse Helms will do a swimsuit calendar. Remember: stocks are long-haul investments—you shouldn't have anything in the market that you might need in the next couple of years.

The CP consensus: Don't waste the Zoloft worrying about the market. Keep focused on your goals and the stats. To quote Hans (and/or Franz), "Listen to me now and believe me later." Over a long period of time, *stocks go up.* Over a 20-year time horizon, the market's *worst* performance has been about 2 percent.

I know . . . I know . . . money is tight. You "can't afford to invest" right now. Without sounding too much like an after-school special, the reality is you can't afford not to. With inflation humming along, common stock is the only asset class that will consistently keep you ahead. Besides, don't you see how painless a process this is? We're not talking about giving up everything and living in squalor. Use some of the strategies from Chapter 3 while aggressively stuffing money into a variety of investments, including stocks. Investing doesn't take much involvement—it just takes time.

Does history repeat itself? Perhaps. You'll undoubtedly hear the pundits—guys who love to argue that market statistics are historically based—warn that "past performance is not an indicator of future results." So how do we really know stocks will continue to do well in the future? Stocks are not insured. There's no guarantee the entire market won't collapse *forever.* But know that in the unlikely event this occurs, you'll have millions of new best friends to complain about it with. Public participation in the stock market has recently reached an all-time high, with over 40 percent of households holding some form of equity investment. With this many individuals "banking" on the market, I'm confident that over the long term, it has no place to go but up.

But have some *realistic expectations!* Lest you've been sucking on a crack pipe, you probably know that 1995, 1996, 1997, and 1998 were outrageously profitable for the stock market. Miss out on the gains? *No big whoop.* "Home Runs" look great on the cover of *Money* magazine, but real wealth is born over time. Remember compound interest from Chapter 4, the titillating phenomenon of earning interest on interest. That's how we make money in the market. If the 11 percent a year average sounds ambitious and you want to play it safe when calculating your anticipated wealth, use 7 percent instead. Even at this historically low rate of return, saving 100 bucks a month for 30 years will compound into over $121,000.

Hey now! This "get-rich-slowly" scheme won't get your picture in *Barron's*, but it will provide for an adequate retirement, if that happens to be one of your goals. After all, $100,000 will buy hell of a lot of Geritol once you get to Florida.

INVESTING AND TRADING: SOME DRASTIC DIFFERENCES

Few things make me more annoyed than when people call my show espousing the "investment" vibe while in the same breath asking for a "hot tip" on a particular stock. If you are buying and selling stocks, you are not investing. You are trading. The idiotic investment community, in a rush for your investable assets, has encouraged this mayhem by focusing on cheap commissions and the ability to trade from almost anywhere via phone or the net.

Don't get me wrong. *I love to trade.* I actively trade stocks, options, and even futures with my own cash. But trading is not investing, it's speculating. Speculating involves taking profits and losses. It's a game. It's action. It's fun. But it's not investing.

If you hold stocks for one year only, you have about an 18 percent chance of losing money. Hold on for five years, and your risks fades to a mere 7 percent. After ten years, stock risk fades to just under 5 percent—quite a contrast. This is why investing is decidedly less risky then speculating. Over the short term, price movements are the fiscal equivalent of Jenny, my old girlfriend: They're erratic, unpredictable, and irrational. That's why it's so hard to predict where stocks are headed. Just because I broke up with Jenny doesn't mean you should sever your relationship with stocks.

Now I'm no **B. F. Skinner**, but I do harbor a few notions about human behavior. I honestly believe that most of us are wired to enjoy basically similar activities. The three that pop immediately to mind are eating, screwing . . . and gambling. Reserving comment on the first two, let me tell you that gambling is alive and well in America: on riverboats, on Indian reservations, *and in the stock market*. The Net has made trading so cheap, effortless, and gosh-darn FUN, that it's hard not to want to take a flier on a stock or two. A few on-line brokerages add fuel to the fire by tracking your portfolio tick by tick, with every dollar and decision always accounted for.

We'll talk about speculating in depth in the next part, but let me just remind you why we invest. We want to make money. Looking for thrills and spills? *Get on a roller coaster.* Want some action? Hit the Strip. More money is made in the market by *not* trading than trading. In fact, the best trade anyone could have made during our lifetime was to have gone "long" in the market after the '87 crash, and then gone out for pizza. For the next 13 years.

As an investor, you won't have to even look at the stock tables. Maybe once every couple of months you'll check out your funds, but more out of curiosity than the need to make any serious adjustments. *Need to play with something? Play with kids, your car, yourself* . . . anything but your investments. In CP land, our investments are loved, cared for, but *never* touched.

But the market is going **meshugge**! Yes, yes, I know that volatility is frightening, but it can't shake your long-term strategy. So even when CNBC's Ron Insana, always quick to jump on the "Is this the big one?" bandwagon, starts yapping, you've got to tune out

the noise and nonsense. Lots of factors create short-term volatility in the markets, everything from changes in monetary policy by our government to weakness in markets you've never even heard of. Treat this stuff like Steely Dan in the proverbial compact disk of your consciousness. It's background music that, after a few years, all starts to sound the same anyway.

CAPITAL GAINS AND DIVIDENDS

Mo' Money: Two Ways to Get Paid

CAPITAL GAINS. There are two major ways we make money in the stock market. One is through capital gains, which is the difference between the price at which you bought and the price at which you sold. So if you bought a stock at $10 a share and sold it later for $15, you would have made $5 in capital gains. Most likely, though, you wouldn't just buy one share, but a **round lot** of 100 shares. Now you've made $500. *Chump change in the world of Wall Street.*

A **round lot** generally refers to 100 shares.

Unavoidable buzzkills include the fact that you have to pay taxes on all capital gains, somewhere in the neighborhood of 28 percent. That's right. Up to 28 percent of your return is immediately lost to the federal government—but only when you sell. Before you actually sell and "take a profit," the gain on your stock holdings is referred to as a "paper gain" and is not taxed. But when you sell, *you pay.* That's the price of freedom, I guess.

You'll also have to pay a commission to a stockbroker to execute the trade. Up until 1975, commissions were fixed, not a Bob "Neuter Your Pets" Barker type of fixed, but standardized and set by the various regulatory bodies in the securities industry. Deregulation, which is often referred to as the "big bang" in the brokerage business, brought increased competition and lower commissions. Commissions used to run into the hundreds of dollars per transaction, but these days, especially on-line, you can trade for as low as $5 a pop.

Even that can add up, however, especially for frequent traders.

DIVIDENDS. The other way we make money in stocks is through a **dividend,** a quarterly cash payout that comes from a company's earnings. Most of the companies that pay dividends are larger, blue-chip companies that decide to distribute their earnings back to the shareholders, rather than reinvest the money back into the company's operations. Companies that have historically paid dividends include those that are past their main growth cycles, utility companies, or companies that generate a lot of excess cash.

Dividends are earnings that are paid directly to shareholders.

Dividends are expressed as a numerical cash value per share of stock. Boeing, the aircraft maker, for example, pays 56 cents in dividends per share. This number is extrapolated into a **dividend yield**, which is the annual number of dollars, or yield, you can expect to receive from holding a particular stock. With Boeing's stock trading at $36, a $.56 dividend represents at 1.5 percent yield.

The **dividend yield** is determined by dividing the dividend payment by the current stock price.

Aww, what's a lousy 1.5 percent? Dividends do matter! One and half percent seems like a pitiful return, but remember that you are receiving the dividend while also being able to snag any capital gains (increase in price) of the stock. It's almost as if you are being paid 1.5 percent a year to hold the stock, just waiting for it to rise. The return from capital gains combined with the dividend is known as the total return.

To give you an idea of how much dividends do count, check out the following graph of large company stocks from 1925 to 1997.

One dollar invested in these suckers returned 11.0 percent, but only when the dividends were reinvested. Without dividend income, the return shrinks to a lethargic 6.2 percent, and the $1 you invested in 1925 becomes only a meager 76 bucks.

Large Company Stocks

(with and without dividends)

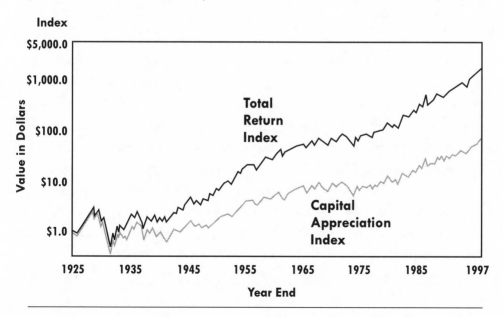

One good place to find out more information about companies that do **DRIPS** is through a newsletter called "the Moneypaper," which can be found on the net at www.moneypaper.com.

While the prospect of getting a quarterly check for a few bucks can seem mighty appealing, you'll definitely want to have the dividends reinvested back into buying more stock. Some companies offer their shareholders automatic dividend reinvestment plans, also called **DRIPS**, which make the process a bit easier. Instead of sending you the check, they company will automatically reinvest your dividends into more shares. This process, which is especially popular with a lot of the larger, more established blue chips, is a great idea for long-term holdings.

When you invest in stocks through mutual funds, the process of reinvesting dividends is even easier—all you will do is check a box on the fund application.

Not all companies pay dividends, and even those that *do* are not obligated to keep paying them in the future. Nothing says that a company can't change or suspend its dividend at any time. For example, sometimes when a company gets into a financial fiasco, it might have to *cut its dividend*, holding back the cash to finance internal operations. More likely, especially with the larger companies that have long histories of paying steady dividends, it will regularly get *increased*.

GOING BACK TO GOALS

Glitz, glamour, and glory aside, make sure you remember why we are investing to begin with. To quote that crazy soccer announcer on the Spanish station, it's all about "GOAL!!!" Or goals, I should say. It's *One Life to Live, mis amigos,* and part of growing up means taking the steps necessary to ensure that your goals become a reality. It's up to us as individuals. Unless you've got some horribly debilitating malady, the Make-A-Wish foundation isn't going to show up at you doorstep with a sack full of money. Reaching your financial goals involves you . . . that's all. Don't make a *wish* but a *plan*. When you take the steps to make it happen . . . when you commit yourself to a realistic plan for success . . . it will happen. You will succeed.

Stocks and equity investments are the best way to increase your net worth over time . . . but there are risks. As you can see from the Pig Pyramid, stocks fall decidedly near the top, meaning that what we get in return we give up in safety of principal. The stock market goes up, but not in anything even remotely resembling a straight line. We've talked about the sexy stuff—the crashes, panics, and even bear markets—with a decidedly relaxed sense of "yeah right." Not to sound alarmist, but don't take the market's fluctuating nature lightly.

When the market is bullish, it's easy to be bullish. But if you want to invest, you've got to mentally and psychologically prepare yourself for periods of time, perhaps long periods of time, *when nobody wants to own stocks.* For the past few years, the stock market has been as hot as the Tommy Lee video, and it's exceedingly easy to get wrapped up in the euphoria of the quick buck. Watch **CNBC** for a while—it feels like the financial equivalent of *NFL Gameday* or any other sports show. Baseball? Baloney. The stock market has become the national pastime.

I too get wrapped up in the titillating excitement of seeing huge swings in the major indexes, but it is vital to keep in mind that investing is not a game. Long term means long term. When popular consensus says stay out of stocks, pull out the history books, check out the charts, and chill. Your goals deserve nothing less.

The coverage by **CNBC** of the market and of major league sports are decidedly similar. CNBC goes as far as to broadcast a "halftime report" of midday market action.

8 BEHOLD: STOCK MARKET MUTUAL FUNDS

Still scared of stocks? *Stop.* Because after all of the worrying, the crisis, the crashes, the economic contusions and conundrums . . . we've got to face the facts—and they're fantastic!

Check out the chart on page 129.

For the past 70 or so years, there has never been a 10-year period when you would have lost money investing in the stock market. Not in large stocks, small stocks or any size in between. This is why if your investment goals are more than 10 years out—stocks are a mighty safe place to store your stash.

The ironic thing, however, is that you could very easily invest in the stock market without ever buying a single share of stock.

Whatchu talkin' 'bout, Willis?

The way you'll accomplish this feat of investing in the stock market without buying stocks, is of course, through the use of mutual funds.

Ohhh, my mutual funds! How do I love thee! Let me count the ways! For most investors, especially those without the Boesky billions, stock mutual funds are the easiest, most efficient, and most effective way to get into the stock market. The low initial minimum requirements, professional management, and painless bookkeeping make funds a solid choice for investors of any age, let alone young investors or those without a ton of money. In Chapter 6 I outlined the basics of mutual funds with regard to bonds. While stock mutual funds aren't terribly different, there are some notable differences, which I'll cover later in this chapter. Below, a quick recap of some of the salient facts on funds.

The idea behind the mutual fund is simple. Many people pool their money, which is then collectively invested in one fund, which in turn invests in various types of securities, in this case, stocks. Each investor shares in the gains and/or losses the of the fund's investments. Using mutual funds to invest in the stock market offers many of the same advantages of using them to invest in the bond market, namely, the professional management, automatic diversification, and low initial minimum cash requirements.

Don't dis diversification! The farther we move up the risk pyramid, the more important it is to remember to diversify our investments. Stocks are volatile. Some go up. Some go down. Some stay down.

Owning just one stock, even the bluest of blue chips, is way too risky, so don't bet the farm on just one animal. When stocks move, they *really* move, especially to the downside. Look in the business section any day of the week and you will see a listing of the top percentage gainers . . . and losers. Nothing, not even an evening of *Babe Winkleman's Good Fishin'* reruns, will make you as sick as will seeing your entire net worth slashed by 20, 30, 40 or even 50 percent. Don't be dumb: Diversify.

Owning a diversified portfolio of stocks means that you'll own lots of stocks from different industries. You'll own stocks of different sizes. You'll own stocks that move in different directions. And mutual funds are the ideal way to do it. Most funds hold between 100 and 150 stocks. If one stock makes up, say, 2 percent of an overall portfolio, even if it tanks it won't destroy an otherwise profitable assortment of companies.

Without mutual funds, you could probably never achieve this level of diversification. To assemble a portfolio of 100 different stocks, even if you bought small amounts of each, you would need literally hundreds of thousands of dollars. Sure, you'd be able to pick up one share here and there, but it would take you literally eons to get 'nuff diversity. Buying a mutual fund, however, you are able to buy just a small piece of a lot of different companies. You get all the diversity without all the dollars. Most mutual funds, as you remember from Chapter 6, will allow you to open an account with as little as $1,000. Some have minimums that are even lower.

The Danger of Non-Diversification

Einstein's Bagels

Bagels, or the traditional Jewish bread, feature a soft texture with a hole in the middle. Investors in Einstein's bagels, however, we're more likely to want to put a hole in their head after its dismal performance throughout most of the 1990s.

Small minimums are a big deal. Take Microsoft, for example. Let's say you had $1,000 to invest. With Microsoft trading at 85 bucks a share, there is no way in hell you could buy Microsoft and still have enough money left over to diversify into other companies, let alone other industries. Let's say you buy ten shares at 85 bucks a share. You've spent 850 bucks (before commissions) and put 85 percent of your portfolio into one company, making your portfolio about as diversified as a potluck dinner at David Duke's house.

But be wary! Mutual funds are like condoms: one size *does not* fit all. They come in a variety of shapes, sizes, colors, and, umm . . . flavors. With thousands of them in existence, there are funds for almost every particular investment style. Some get really specific. Interested in small-cap growth and value biotechnology firms in unincorporated areas of lower Jakarta? How about companies that specialize in **sin**.

Some funds that will allow you to invest small amounts of cash:

The Muhlenkamp Fund ($200):
800-860-3863

Nicholas Fund ($500):
800-227-5987

There are funds that focus on the most arcane and specific segments of the market. Often called sector funds, these investments might hold a lot of companies, but all from a similar industry, allowing you to make a "sector" bet. *This is not diversity!* You want to own mutual funds that invest in a variety of different areas of industry—not just lots of companies within a particular industry. Sector funds could be one part of your portfolio, but not the whole part.

So will your portfolio look like? Depending on your asset allocation, it could take any number of guises. Besides your cash reserve, kept in a money market, CD, or similarly safe instrument, you might choose a balanced fund—the kind that holds both stocks and bonds—and be done with it. You might opt for a few different funds, for example, a large-cap index fund along with an actively managed small-cap fund. I'll suggest some asset allocations toward the end of this chapter.

> One mutual fund, Morgan Funshares, invests its assets in companies that derive their revenue from "**sin**"-related businesses such as liquor and tobacco manufacturers and the like.

CHOOSING MUTUAL FUNDS

In choosing a mutual fund, especially a stock fund, we're looking to make a long-term commitment. It's kinda like marriage. I mean, you are trusting this *thing . . .* this mutual fund, to provide for your future. As Dan Quayle would say, that's no small "potatoe."

Trust. It's a big concept. I mean, this is money we're talking about. *So who do you trust?* There are a lot of good funds out there. You can put your resources here or there or there. The choice is up you and it all comes down to trust.

From clear beer to credit cards, the Neutron Dance to the Noid, we're no strangers to marketing. Most of us have grown up in an environment of jingles, slogans, logos, and catchphrases—each the product of a marketing campaign determined to sell us a product we may or may not want. The products called financial services—where you put your money and who you put it with—are no different.

Marketing is *everything* in the mutual fund business. Surprised? Remember, mutual fund companies are, first, in the business of selling us shares in mutual funds. The more they can get us to invest, the more they'll make in loads, commissions, and management fees. Now, it doesn't mean we shouldn't buy what they're selling; it simply means we need to be we aware of their very vested interest in selling us their products.

You've probably already seen a couple of the marketing approaches in television commercials, print advertising, or fund literature.

Some of the fund companies, especially the ones with the older, well-known brand names, stress their conservative values, as in Smith Barney's infamous "We make money the old-fashioned way, we earn it" slogan. Other funds advertise their extraordinary performance, putting 30 or 40 percent return stats in the middle of CNBC's *Market Wrap*. Others trumpet their "star" manager or particularly quantitative approach. As in selling soft drinks, sneakers, or any other product, there are any number of tacks the firms take.

But what are they selling? Past performance, as you know, is NO indicator of future performance, so just because a fund did well last year doesn't mean it will do well next year. In fact . . . most don't.

How about that star mutual fund manager, the guy or gal with the magic touch? Michael Price is a good example. As head of the Mutual Series family of mutual funds, he posted several years of excellent performance, racking up returns of 29 percent in 1994, 20 percent in 1995, and 26 percent in 1996. He became the guru du jour, and the mere whisper that he was interested in buying a company's stock sent its price soaring. His star status attracted million of dollars of new money to his funds—thousands of investors willing to pay the outlandishly high 1.75 percent expense ratio to have their money managed by the "prince" called Price. Price is no fool: He promptly sold his fund company to the Franklin Templeton Group for a fat $800 million. In recent years, the fund's performance has faltered, and Price, obviously better at managing his own career than his once-hot mutual funds, has promptly bailed out of the day-to-day duties of stock picking, content to count his bonus bonanza while his fund's shareholders continue to suffer . . . which they do to this day. So much for chasing the star manager.

The marketing, by and large, is bullshit. It's put together by the same advertising agencies that sell us every other product. Remember: Mutual funds make no guarantees. They get paid (through their loads and expense ratios), whatever happens. So while an advertisement might perk your interest in a fund, you've got to dig deeper than the pages of *Smart Money* before you decide whom to trust.

No matter how savvy the marketing, I will not have you "picking" mutual funds like you pick items off the menu at Steak 'n' Shake. Don't just page through the ads in *Money* magazine, saying, "I'll have one of these and one of those." We're going to be making long-term commitments to our investments, and the investments we choose should fit our own particular goals.

How Not to Pick a Fund

Every year *Money, Smart Money,* and all their ilk publish their "Top 10 Mutual Funds You Need Right This Moment" issue, profiling the highest-performing funds in recent months. It's a securities **shanda**. It's the financial equivalent of *People*'s 50 sexiest people. Everyone races to see who's in . . . and who's not. Strangely—picking the previous year's best-performing funds is a strategy that tends to underperform the market, meaning it does worse than the market average. Besides,

picking the hot fund du jour is no way to reach your financial goals. Actively trading mutual funds—buying one fund today and selling it next week—is even more idiotic. Mutual funds are long-term investment vehicles. Like, 20-plus years long. Okay? Besides, it's one of the ironies of mutual fund investment that a fund that makes the list one year tends to underperform the following year. I'll give some more examples later in the chapter.

I want you to get in the habit of seeing mutual funds as *products.* That's the way the fund companies treat them, and that's the way we should treat them. You see, the marketing often puts a little bit of a "switch-a-roo" into our heads. Because mutual funds are used to achieve our goals, stuff we want to do and own, much of the marketing goes as far as to equate them as being identical. Here's what I mean: A secure retirement is a goal for most of us. So mutual funds will often run ads that say something like "Fund X, here today to provide you with a secure tomorrow." See the switch-a-roo? They've taken a fund, which is a product, and turned it into a goal in one shady maneuver.

SHOPPING FOR MUTUAL FUNDS

Mutual funds are products. They're like cars . . . or camcorders. We need to "shop" for a mutual fund the same way we shop for a stereo, or anything else we might buy. This means evaluating the costs, the features, the benefits, and the risks. It also means making sure that the product, or fund, we choose fits our own needs.

Active vs. Passive Funds

Before you decide anything else about mutual funds, I believe you've got to find your mutual fund 'hood, that is: Are you into active management or passive? Do you want your money managed by an actual person choosing stocks, or would you rather have an unmanaged portfolio of stocks that merely tracks a particular index?

ACTIVELY MANAGED FUNDS. There is something profoundly reassuring about putting one's faith in the ability of another person. If a mutual fund manager holds enough of your money, he becomes your spiritual Buddha of bounty! Portfolio managers, especially the most successful ones, indeed take on a cult or celebrity status, the best example being that of Peter Lynch who during the eighties rose to fame with Fidelity's Magellan Fund. When your fund has an active manager, there's someone human to put your trust in. Somehow, their credentials, age, and experience seem to represent a comforting level of reassurance, especially when compared to the *Tron*-like and computer-vibed impersonality of an index fund, which just tracks the index.

I mean . . . the fund manager's picture is plastered right there in the reports. It's a real, usually very sensibly dressed person. And we (the shareholders) are thinking to ourselves, "This person looks okay. He's not going to go crazy, I think I can trust him." You may not want to admit it, but there's a little voice inside your head that's seeking some modicum of safety and predictability in that person's face. I do it, too. There's something very comforting about knowing that there's someone watching the markets when we're not and someone to *blame* should things go wrong. With an index fund, you can only blame the market. The market doesn't return your phone calls.

Look at the fund literature from the average actively managed fund—I mean, they seem so active! Almost every actively managed fund touts its extensive research capabilities, how its managers diligently visit the companies in which they invest, their superior trading technology, *blah blah blah.* One particularly memorable ad campaign for Franklin Tempelton shows the portfolio guru and Marshall Applewhite–lookalike Mark Mobius careening his way through some Third World barrio, something like the Wall Street Indiana Jones, I guess. Who pays for Mr. Mobius's malaria shots? Who pays for that airfare to Bangladesh? Who pays for the huge staffs of researchers that active managers employ?

We do.

That's right, you, me, and the shareholders are who pay for the heavy infrastructure of active management. It shows up in plain black and white on page 2 of every mutual fund's prospectus, in the fee tables. Actively managed funds **cost** more to own then passively managed funds, that is, they charge a higher annual fee,

And the **cost** is going up. According to Morningstar, the average expense ratio of a U.S. diversified stock fund in 1981 was 1.09 percent vs. 1.41 percent in 1998.

which you pay every year, regardless of whether the fund does well or not.

None of this benevolent "we-make-money-when-you-make-money" crap on Wall Street. It's more like, the mutual fund makes money, or they make *more* money. Imagine if you had to pay for cable TV, even if it never worked. That's what the realities of paying **management fees** are like. We pay a percentage of our money every year to the managers, even if they totally suck and make us nothing. Of course, as shareholders, we always have the right to sell out of a fund (or not buy one in the first place), but remember that whatever happens in the market, the fund gets paid.

It's weird. All things being equal, the *fees, commissions, and costs of a fund are its only certainties.*

Here are some facts about a fund's costs and the ongoing debate concerning active vs. passive management. According to Morningstar, the average expense ratio of the average equity mutual funds is 1.41 percent, compared with the .20 percent annual expense ratio of the average passive stock index funds. During the ten years that ended December 31, 1997, the S&P 500 index, the most popular index fund to own, outperformed 81 percent of all actively managed funds. The lower cost of owning an index fund was a big factor in this superior performance.

Funds that are managed by gurus charge even more, like Franklin Tempelton, which charges the ridiculously high 2.76 percent for the services of **Mark Mobius**.

While many of these active managers are talented stock pickers, I seriously doubt anyone's ability to consistently beat the market over the time period for which most of us will be investing. In fact, from over a five to ten year period, only a small handful of actively managed funds have beaten passively managed funds in total return.

Here's what usually seems to happen. A hot manager (meaning "hot" in the most economic of senses) might turn up some good numbers for a few months. People see this. "Gee . . . Fund Manager Fonzie is on the cover of *Money* magazine!" Investing in the fund becomes the subject of a kind of locker-room stock talk: *"Yeah, I've been in Fonzie's fund . . . made a ton of bucks!"* Word goes around that Fonzie's got the magic touch on both the pay phone *and* the portfolio. Fonzie's fund gets flooded with new cash—to the tune of millions

That's one of the things I find most troubling about actively managed funds. They are overwhelmingly, for lack of a better term, *a ripoff.* An actively managed fund might charge 1.5 percent of its entire portfolio every year for its services. Considering the market only does about 11 percent a year, that represents quite some ego premium.

As of late 1998, **Mobius's** Developing Market's Trust was down some -34 percent.

and millions of dollars a day. Fonzie, desperate to put the new cash to work, deviates from the style that has made him great. The fund's performance suffers. It happens all the time.

Here's one example. Foster Friess was the superstar manager of the Brandywine family of funds. They returned more than 30 percent annualized from 1994 to 1997. The press loved him. Investors thought they had found the Messiah of the mutual fund . . . and money poured in. In 1990 Friess managed $1 billion; by the end of 1997, that number had skyrocketed to $12 billion. But Friess lost his touch. "Sometimes you make a decision on instinct," he told the *Wall Street Journal*. That "instinct" told him to sell over 40 percent of the stocks he owned over a ten-day period in 1998. Needless to say, he made the wrong call. As of late October 1998, returns on his funds have been clobbered. Down 25 percent since January of 1998, underperforming 87 percent of similarly managed funds. So much for star power. Oh, and did I mention Mr. Friess's expense ratio—*1.04* percent?

Another ubiquitous disclaimer: Mutual funds are not FDIC-insured, and fund companies also include a declaration of this fact in their literature.

As you can probably tell, star fund managers annoy me. They boast about performance, then hide behind the fact that "past performance is no indicator of future result" when they do poorly.

It's almost as if you said to a prospective employer, "Hey, don't mind the fact that I'm an uneducated crack addict, I mean, my past performance is no indicator of what I'll do in the future!" *C'mon!*

Mutual funds take a yearly percentage of the entire assets under management. So the more money they have under management, the more money they make. A mutual fund company might have $10 billion . . . that's right, $10 billion under management. So even 1 percent makes them a quick 100 mil every year—like clockwork. But fees have been going up even as the amount of money coming into stock funds has been skyrocketing. Over the last 12 years, mutual fund ownership has quadrupled. They're charging more, even as the economics of scale point toward charging less.

Another concern is that actively managed funds almost always buy and sell more stocks throughout the year than index funds, which make very few changes to their portfolios. The actively managed portfolio's trading, or turnover, generates a higher tax bill for its investors at the end of the year. As shareholders, we get hit with a bigger tax bill. If the manager is outperforming, that's one thing—but according to the stats, over the long run it just doesn't happen. These funds are simply more expensive to own.

So I'm not going to pay a lot for this muffler . . . or this mutual fund. I strongly believe that when you're choosing a mutual fund, the fund's fees are probably the most important criterion to consider. When you're leafing through the glossy pages of *Smart Money* magazine, replete with brazen managers in a variety of inspiring poses, don't forget to *consider the cost.*

INDEX FUNDS. Enter the index funds! Talk about cheap! Once again, stock index funds cost as little as .20 percent per year to own—a much lower percentage than the 1 to 2 percent actively managed funds routinely charge. You get diversification at low cost. And taking a look at the returns of the average actively managed fund vs. the unmanaged S&P 500 over the last 20 years, you also get superior returns to boot.

Why can't managers beat the index? Experts call it the "efficient markets hypothesis." You see, the SEC requires that all companies' financial information, their "books," so to speak, be publicly available to everyone. So if there is a piece of financial information that would affect the price of a stock, like high earnings or increased profits, it has to be available to the entire investment community, not just whoever the company wants to tell. Thus, is it said, the stock market is an "efficient market," because all available information is freely available to all players. All the market participants know everything there is to know, so the current stock price of a particular company should have all relevant information already factored in. So it's not like one fund manager can secretly know that Intel is going to have higher sales, and buy stock before everyone else does. That's why once information is released, usually through a press release or "conference call" with analysts, stocks often make huge swings upward or downward. The market reacts immediately to any new and relevant information, and is thus said to be "efficient."

OTHER CHOICES WHEN FINDING FUNDS

So you've got the two major styles of mutual funds, passive and active. Active funds are managed by an individual or team, while passive index funds seek to replicate a preestablished index. Whichever 'hood you're from, you'll have innumerable choices when it comes to styles of investing. There are both actively and passively managed stock mutual funds for almost every conceivable investment objective, from the most conservative to the most aggressive.

GROWTH VS. VALUE

Let's talk style. There are two major categories of investment style: growth and value. While some managers opt to employ elements of both strategies, you should know what each of them means and the difference between them.

Growth Investing

Understand: You want growth, not "a growth." With few exceptions, you buy a "growth fund" and you get "growth stocks." Growth fund managers are interested in rapid earnings growth, so they will buy the stocks of companies whose earnings are growing faster than the overall market, even if the stocks seem "expensive" at the time. Growth managers aren't looking for bargains in the market; they're willing to pay high stock prices for companies that are growing their earnings quickly, as they are confident the stocks will continue to follow earnings upward. This is why many of these companies have market capitalizations that dwarf their earnings, meaning that the market values of some companies that have never made a dime are "worth" hundreds of millions of dollars. Growth companies, or, more specifically, growth stocks, can be found in several

Growth Investing

Globe.com is one example. In the fall of 1998, Internet community globe.com went public at $9.00 per share. Euphoria was so high, the stock opened north of $60/share ... quickly pushed up to $90/share. Immediately, investors were giving a company with no earnings or profits whatsoever a market value north of 1 billion dollars. Investors were willing to bet that because of globe.com's huge potential, it was a solid investment even without a dime of profit.

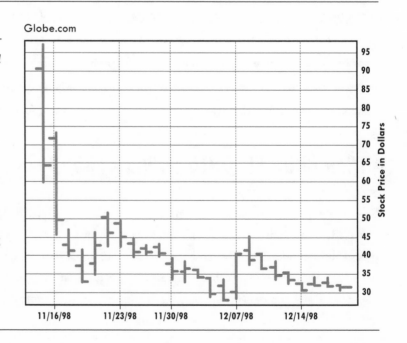

Globe.com

industries, most notably technology. Growth funds invest in companies with big potential, but just as much risk. This means companies that are growing and expanding rapidly, or companies that are currently highly valued in the market.

A Few Types of Growth Funds

AGGRESSIVE GROWTH FUNDS. These mutual funds invest in growth stocks, or stocks of companies with rapidly increasing earnings, profits, or momentum that carry big potential for long-term capital gains. Besides sector funds, aggressive growth funds are among the most volatile of any type of stock mutual fund. The companies in which the funds invest are often unproved or are new companies in rapidly changing industries, like technology. These stocks rarely pay dividends, so don't expect much in the way of dividend income. Most of your gains in aggressive growth funds come from capital gains, so when the market is strong, aggressive growth funds usually lead the way. Consequently, during bear markets, when investors flock to companies with more established histories of solid returns, aggressive growth funds can get whacked. So the risk is highest, but so is the potential return. Aggressive growth funds have returned an average of 16.10 percent a year over the last 20 years, according to Lipper Analytical Services, meaning that $1,000 dollars invested in the average aggressive growth fund turned into $19,799 over a 20-year period. Aggressive growth funds are perfect for long-term investments, and their volatility makes dollar-cost averaging (see page 150) a solid choice as well.

GROWTH FUNDS. Somewhat less risky are growth funds, which are slightly tamer versions of their more aggressive counterparts. Same basic idea as aggressive growth funds, although growth fund managers typically buy more predictable, less volatile stocks that have somewhat better track records of consistent earnings. So some of the more rapidly growing blue-chip companies might reside within the portfolio of a growth mutual fund, as might the stocks of some smaller, more speculative firms. Growth funds don't seek to buy stocks that pay dividends, so there won't be much investment income. They concentrate on capital gains, and thus also are appropriate for long-term investments.

GROWTH AND INCOME FUNDS. Growth and income funds are designed to provide both growth and income. Some *growth,* meaning that the fund will invest some of its assets in the stocks of growth companies for capital gains, and some *income,* meaning that the fund will hold some stocks and/or bonds that pay dividends and/or interest. The stocks in growth and income funds tend to be more stable and less risky than stocks found

A close cousin of the growth and income fund is the "equity income fund," although managers of equity income funds tend to avoid growth stocks and focus on stocks that pay high dividends.

in more aggressive funds, but the income is the kicker: The fund will also invest in securities that pay either dividends, like dividend-paying stocks, or interest, like a bond. The idea is that a mixed portfolio of stocks and bonds will give you potential capital appreciation (with the stocks) combined with the income interest on bonds or dividend-paying stocks. What does this mean? Less return on the upside than a fund composed solely of stocks, but more stability from the income side of the equation.

Of course, unless you're living in a retirement home or need the cash, the income your fund provides should be reinvested in your fund as shares, not sent to you in the form of a check. That choice is easily accomplished by checking a simple box on the mutual fund application form, or calling your mutual fund company's 800 number to make the switch.

We've talked about growth, one of the major styles of stock investing. The other is value.

Value Investing

If you've ever clipped a coupon, waited for something to go on sale, or spent an afternoon at the PriceClub, then value investing will be of special interest to you. What is it? Value investors focus on stocks they believe to be temporarily undervalued or unfairly "beaten down" in price. Unlike growth investors, who buy the stocks of companies with rapidly growing earnings—at any price—a value investor is looking to get a good deal or to buy stocks that are for some reason being undervalued by the market. Hence, we say that value investors buy "value stocks."

Value stocks appear to be inexpensive relative to their current earnings and profits—and what the Wall Streeters call fundamentals. So value investors go looking for companies whose underlying businesses are being undervalued, essentially hoping that people will realize how cheap the stock is and bid it up to a higher price. Value investors spend a lot of time crunching numbers—adding up a company's assets, including inventories and real estate—trying to get a handle on what they think it's actually worth. These figures are then extrapolated into a stock price. Value investors believe that if their calculations are correct, the stock should eventually return to its rightful valuation.

This usually leads them to stocks with low **price/earnings [P/E] ratios** or stocks that supposedly are "cheaper" than they should be. While a high-flying growth stock like Yahoo! might trade at 100 "times earnings," a value stock like Philip Morris, which makes cigarettes, might trade at only 15× ("times earnings"). From an investment perspective, Philip Morris is much cheaper. Value mutual funds tend to be slightly less volatile than their more expensive growth counterparts.

Get the value thing? Here's a cinematic example: *John Travolta*. Sucked in the eighties. Unpopular. Made shitty movies—*Look Who's Talking* springs to mind. Now he is racking up over $20 mil a flick. The movie market has "rediscovered" Travolta. He was essentially a "value" investment for all of the eighties, up until he was "discovered" by the market when Quentin Tarrantino made *Pulp Fiction*. Don't you wish you could have bought some "**Travolta**" some time after *Perfect* and sold out after *Phenomenon*?

There's a difference, however, between companies undervalued by the market and crappy companies. How can fund managers tell the difference? They do their homework, finding out the numbers behind a company's earnings and profits, attempting to find the true value of a company's assets and stock price.

No matter which style of investing you choose, don't invest in "fads"—especially "fad funds." In recent years, more and more funds have popped up that are more deserving of a place in the loony bin than in your portfolio. One of the more bizarre offerings was the "Tombstone Fund," a fund that invests only in the stocks of companies associated with the death industry, or the Sports Fund, a mutual fund that can buy only the stocks of companies involved in sports-related activities. Not only are these funds totally nondiversified, but many of them charge above-average fees—in the case of the Tombstone Fund, a whopping 4.1 percent.

The **price/earnings ratio** is found by dividing a stock's price by the company's current or estimated future earnings per share. For example, if a stock is selling at $86 and its earnings per share is $4.05, it trades at a P/E of about 21. The P/E ratio helps you determine if a stock is over- or undervalued.

This type of trading actually exists, on the Web's niftiest little site: the Hollywood Stock Exchange (www.hsx.com).

GLOBAL AND INTERNATIONAL FUNDS

In the final moments of *The Wizard of Oz*, we hear the now-famous sentiment: "If I ever go looking for my heart's desire again, I won't go looking any further than my own backyard."

Dorothy might have been one hell of a piece of Kansas-ass, but I wouldn't want her managing *my* portfolio. With that attitude, she misses the point of going global.

Global or international funds are mutual funds that will invest your money in the stocks of foreign companies or companies that do most of their business outside the United States. International funds invest solely outside the United States, while global funds may generally buy stocks of U.S. companies, depending on the manager's investment outlook.

If investing overseas conjures up images of flea-bitten Ethiopians sipping gruel from a Red Cross truck, you've got a lot to learn. There is serious investment opportunity across the globe.

In 1970, foreign markets accounted for only 34 percent of the world's investments. According to Morgan Stanley, by 1997 that number had increased to 57 percent.

In May 1998, the **German** automaker Daimler-Benz and the American automotive giant Chrysler announced that they would merge to create one corporation called Daimler-Chrysler.

Why do we do it? Investing overseas, especially through a mutual fund, can add some juice to your portfolio in a well-diversified fashion. Notwithstanding the egocentrism of us obnoxious Americans (guilty as charged), there are investment opportunities all over the world, from Johannesburg to Jakarta and more. For example, Belgium's stock market rose 27 percent in 1997, and posted beefy gains in 1998. And Poland's market capitalization, or the value of all the stocks traded in Poland, jumped from $2.7 billion in 1993 to $12.1 billion in 1997. As more business is being done across borders, the line separating one country's companies from another's is truly starting to fade.

Diversification is another argument for goin' global. Historically, stock markets from different countries moved in different directions. So if the Dow took a tumble, perhaps the Dax, made up of 30 **German** blue-chip stocks and considered the most popular index of German stocks, would fare better. Stock markets overseas, while volatile, regularly rank up returns that put those of the United States to shame.

Goin' Global

As you know, there are several stock exchanges here in the United States, the most famous and largest being the New York Stock Exchange. There are, however, stock exchanges all over the world: London, Frankfurt, and Tokyo are three of the most developed and active, while less developed countries like Malaysia, Singapore, and Argentina are increasingly attracting investors' capital to their markets. While the investment returns can be quite volatile, they can also be quite tasty.

But buying individual stocks on foreign exchanges is a tedious task best left to institutions, making mutual funds again a good choice for getting some cross-border exposure. You'll get the advantage of being able to invest in U.S. dollars, meaning that you won't have to exchange your bucks for **Baht** anytime soon. You'll also enjoy the other major advantages of investing through funds, including low initial minimums, simplified bookkeeping, and, depending of the fund, diversification. I make that small disclaimer because some international funds focus on one particular country or region, making them more volatile and risky than funds that invest in countries all around the globe.

A sidenote: As information spreads ever more quickly around the world, there is actually a trend for many of the world's stock markets to show positive correlation, or to move more in sync with each other—which would cut down on diversification. A good example of this was in October of 1997, when a currency crisis sent the entire world's stock markets reeling, not just the Asian countries where it originally started. Even apart from major economic crises, day-to-day price movements of the world's markets are more apt to show positive correlation than they were in the past. If Wall Street closes strong, it's likely that the Asian markets will start strong the next day. If the European markets are weak, it will usually mean a weaker opening on Wall Street. Long-term stats still argue for diversifying overseas, but things could change. In the next few years, we'll just have to wait and see whether seeking shelter from U.S. markets overseas still works as it has in the past.

Baht: The national currency of Thailand.

AVERAGE ANNUAL TOTAL RETURN OF GLOBAL MARKETS, SEPTEMBER 30, 1987, TO SEPTEMBER 30, 1997

Hong Kong: 17.10 percent

Netherlands: 17.83 percent

Sweden: 16.73 percent

Denmark: 17.93 percent

United States: 15.00 percent

Germany: 11.22 percent

(Source: Morgan Stanley)

(Non)domestic Disturbance

But let's talk risk. Investing overseas, even through a U.S.-based mutual fund, still carries serious risk. For one thing, foreign markets tend to be more volatile than the more established U.S. stock market. Add to that the serious currency risks, meaning that the dollar value of your shares in overseas companies might go up or down, depending on the price of the local currency. Let's say you owned a international fund that invested in Japan. If Japanese stocks rose but the value of the yen fell, the value of your fund could quite possibly fall as well.

Lots can happen overseas: Exchange rates fluctuate, leaders get assassinated, and countries go belly-up. Remember: *Foreigners are the people who made David Hasselhoff, Mr. Bean, and the Spice Girls famous. Anything can happen!* So while international investing should remain an option to consider, I'd be queasy about putting too much of my portfolio overseas, certainly no more than 30 percent. Most financial professionals would agree that 5 to 15 percent in overseas funds would be a relatively conservative allocation for a young person.

International funds are available in all types of styles; active, passive, growth and value are all represented—and be sure to keep an eye on the fees.

> **Because of the additional research, expertise, and cost of doing business overseas, the expense ratios on international funds tend to be higher then domestic or U.S.-based funds.**

NUTS AND BOLTS

When you've decided which categories of funds are best for your investment goals, you'll need to research several individual funds in those categories. Most of the major mutual fund companies offer dozens of individual funds. Fidelity, for example, the largest mutual funds "family," offers over 70 stock funds, 19 bond funds, and 29 international funds.

First things first: Look for low fees! This includes any loads (front-end loads are changed when you buy into a fund, back-end loads are charged when you cash out), the management fee, **12b–1 fees**, and any other shenanigans the company is trying to pull. The best place to find this information is in the fund's prospectus. Each of the fees

> **12b–1 fee:** A yearly fee that pays for the fund's advertising and marketing costs. It is named for the regulation that created it.

will be outlined, itemized, and totaled under the heading "total fund operating expenses." The prospectus will even give a few hypothetical examples of what fees you'll be paying over a 1-, 3-, 5-, and 10-year time period. Unless Alan Greenspan, Jesus Christ, or David Byrne was managing the fund, I'd be hard- pressed to pay more then .50 percent in operating expenses—period.

What's a puny point? Over a 40-year time horizon, the difference between making 10 percent and 11 percent on a $1,000 investment is monster: $45,259 as compared to $65,001. Remember, if you're opting for a low-cost index fund, the performance will always simply match the index. If you decide to go with an actively managed fund, I strongly urge you not to pick the top-performing funds. Why? Chances are that they just won't continue to be that strong.

Leah Modigliani, a strategist at Morgan Stanley, ranked 660 mutual funds over a ten-year period. She looked at all types of stock funds, from growth to value, biotech to large-cap. What she found was that the funds whose return was in the top 25 percent in the first five years had only a 28 percent chance of being in the top 25 in the next five years. In fact, top-performing funds had only about a 50 percent chance of being in the top *half* of the funds in those next five years. The *Wall Street Journal* columnist Robert McGough summed it up quite well when he wrote: "In essence, it was a toss of a coin whether a top performing fund at the end of 1992 was also a top performing fund at the end of 1997."

So don't chase returns. If you pick an active manager, find out how long he/she has been managing the fund. What is his/her track record like? Morningstar (www.morningstar.net) has lots of this information, as do most of the brochures available from the fund companies themselves.

Another factor: The fund family itself. They have an 800 number . . . give them a call. How accessible are they? How well do they answer your questions? What's their minimum initial investment? Can you buy shares in small denominations? Do they have any giddy restrictions about when you can *withdraw money* from the fund. Do they have reports that you can understand and . . . (gasp) enjoy?

Yet another factor: The fund's strategy. What is its game plan? Does your fund keep any holdings in cash? Does it invest overseas? Understand the risks of the particular fund. Does it invest in any particularly risky areas of the market? If so, are you prepared to take those types of risks?

As a mutual fund shareholder, you should be able to withdraw money from your account on any business day. Funds will send you a check immediately, or many will allow you to have the money electronically wired to a bank. Keep an eye out for redemption fees. Several fund families, including Fidelity and Vanguard, charge a fee for redemptions on shares of the fund not held for a specified amount of time—usually a year.

You'll find that most of the larger mutual fund companies offer a similar menu of funds, from highly volatile stock sector funds to the more conservative equity income funds. But here's a warning: Don't buy into a fund on the basis of its name alone. Mutual fund companies can essentially call 'em as they see 'em, meaning that they can call a fund whatever they want. Some of the more common adjectives tossed around include "growth," "opportunity," and "high return." Again, this is merely marketing. Fact is, the name of the fund isn't nearly as important as its objective, which is printed clearly in the prospectus. You need to know the name of the fund, but also its stated objective, because sometimes the two just don't jive. You'll also want to find out some of the fund's top holdings, meaning that you'll want to look in the prospectus or ask the 800 number person what some of the largest positions in the fund currently are. That way you can be sure your actively managed fund is actually buying what it's supposed to. Passively managed funds, or index funds, obviously never have this problem.

One example of a fund buying stocks unrelated to its name came in 1996, when mutual fund giant Fidelity Investments revealed that their "blue chip" fund actually held very few blue chips. Looking to boost returns, the actively managed fund had gone dipping into mid-cap companies—not exactly the stocks a fund called "blue chip" should be investing in. So know that a fund's name is just a starting place for a general investment style.

RESIST THE PENCHANT TO PANIC

Here's a "what if?" scenario you *don't want to hear*. You spend a few hours in the library or on the Net with Morningstar, looking through its listings of highly rated but low-cost funds. You choose a fund, mail off your check, and pat yourself on the back for being responsible. A few days later, as normal, the fund sends you back a confirmation of your purchase, welcoming you to the world of Wall Street. Then, feeling like a Boesky-to-be, you pick up a copy of an investment magazine that labels your fund as a long-term . . . loser.

If your fund does come up on a ratings loser list, don't panic. Find out *why* the fund has underperformed. Analyze the criteria that put your fund on a loser list. Don't just jump ship! Did the entire market underperform, or did your active manager just screw things up? Again, one of the beauteous things about index funds is that, no matter what, you'll always get the market return. You'll never have to worry about underperforming the market, because whatever the market returns—so will you.

When index funds were first introduced, they were decried as being "unpatriotic." CP says: Unpatriotic? Low expenses, high returns . . . *index funds couldn't be more American!*

But to return to your "loser" fund. First, most "buy/sell/hold" recommendations for mutual funds are based on that fund manager's past performance and we *know* how reliable an indicator that is. Secondly, take a moment to remember why you got into the fund in the first place. If small stocks, which have historically outperformed larger stocks, are getting creamed, how well can you realistically expect your small stock fund to be doing? When sectors are out of favor, it's easy to pick on a particular fund or group of funds. Stick to low-cost funds that suit your investment objectives. Think long term. Make rational decisions, not impulsive gambles.

PUTTING IT ALL TOGETHER

By now you're aware of the different types of securities we call investments (stock mutual funds, bond mutual funds, cash). The question now becomes that of *asset allocation*, or how much money you'll invest in which instruments.

How do you decide? Three main factors determine how to structure your asset allocation. First, and more than anything else, the main determinant of where you put what should be your own goals. You are investing for a purpose, for a *reason*, on a certain time horizon, and how you structure your portfolio should be in line with your own objectives and goals for the future. Go back to some of the goals you considered in Chapter 2. Prioritize them. Now that you know how each of the investment products have historically performed and how much risk each entails, you can match up your goals with the investments that will get you there. The bigger the goals you have, the bigger a commitment you will have to make to investing in order to reach them.

I have mentioned retirement a few times. Even if we're not planning to load up the Winnebago and head for Florida when we're 65, most of us will at some point want to

It is estimated that when you **retire**, you'll need 60 to 80 percent of your preretirement income. CP says: I'll need more. According to a report issued by the National Bureau of Economic Research, many of today's retirees have unexpectedly been forced to cut their spending sharply when they left the workforce, simply because they underestimated the amount of money they'd need to retire on. "On average," the researchers report, "individuals who arrive at retirement with few resources experience a surprise—they discover that their resources are insufficient to maintain their accustomed standards of living."

stop working as hard as we do now. Retiring from work takes a lot of money. This is why I think **retirement** can serve as a good proxy for most of the long-term goals we might harbor for ourselves. Your investments will provide that financial support.

Earlier in this book I made the distinction between active and passive wealth creation. Active wealth creation is our jobs; passive wealth creation is our investments. I've made a big deal about compound interest because your money can't compound, or grow exponentially larger, if you're dipping into it to buy one of our favorite Nine Inch Nails albums on minidisc.

STOCK MUTUAL FUND DATA BANK

Where: Mutual fund companies.

Investment return: While volatile, the long-term investment return on stocks averages 10 to 13 percent.

Safety of principal: Low. Over short periods of time, it's possible to lose a large portion of your initial investment.

Purpose: To achieve highest long-term returns. Stock funds are ideal for goals 10 to 40 or more years into the future.

Tip: Chasing a fund on the basis of last year's performance record is a statistically losing strategy. Better to concentrate on finding funds with low expenses, low turnover, and a long-term history of success.

Because we want our money to compound at the highest rate possible, we are better off choosing financial instruments that have consistently offered the highest returns. Simply put, this means investing in stocks. Using retirement as our "goal" proxy, I can confidently say, that providing all your consumer debt is paid off, you should have a large portion of your long-term portfolio in stocks of some sort, be it a single diversified mutual fund or several mutual funds that concentrate on different sectors.

Before you start counting your millions, keep in mind that this is a *long-term* portfolio. The 11 percent annual average return that large-stocks have provided is an average, not a "floor." There will be tough years, years when your portfolio will actually lose significant amounts of money. But stay in stocks! Because for most of us, retirement is far enough away so that we'll be able to ride out the inevitable ups and downs of the market. This brings us to the second factor in determining your asset allocation: time horizon.

Time horizon is when you expect to need your investment dollars back. Although we'd all like to buy shares in the fictitious "get rich quick fund," the reality is that if the time horizon for your investments is anything less than ten years, you'll need to steer most of your portfolio away from stocks toward bonds and cash investments. According to Ibbotson and Associates, over a five-year period large-cap stocks returned anywhere from 23.92 percent compound annualized rate of return (1950–1954) to -12.47 percent (1928–1932). Moving out just five additional years, however, reduces the "worst case" from -12.47 percent to a measly -.89 percent, meaning that historically, stocks have almost never lost money over the average ten-year period. While there is a great deal of pressure for young people to be as "aggressive" as possible with their investments, if you're planning on using the cash anytime soon, a portfolio entirely invested in stocks is just too risky. So if putting a down payment on a house is in your not-too-distant future, the time horizon dictates a less aggressive approach. Better to choose a more conservative blend of stocks, some bonds, and even some cash equivalents.

A FEW SUGGESTED PORTFOLIOS

PORTFOLIO #1: FAR-OUT FUTURE— 40 YEARS OR MORE

Cash: 5 percent

Bonds: 5 percent

Stocks: 90 percent

SOMEWHERE OUT THERE: 20–40 YEARS

Cash: 5 percent

Bonds: 15 percent

Stocks: 80 percent

SOONER THAN LATER: 10–20 YEARS

Cash: 5 percent

Bonds: 20 percent

Stocks: 75 percent

A FEW YEARS DOWN THE LINE: 5–10 YEARS

Cash: 10 percent

Bonds: 30 percent

Stocks: 60 percent

THE NOT-AT-ALL SO DISTANT FUTURE: 0–5 YEARS

Cash: 50 percent

Bonds: 30 percent

Stocks: 20 percent

I've concocted a few very general suggested asset allocations, based on your particular time horizon. Use these models as a starting point for thinking about how to structure you own portfolio, taking into account the other factors we've discussed, most notably your goals and tolerance for risk.

Finally, there's your risk tolerance. While there is certainly a risk in investing, especially investing in the stock market, I hope you now understand that it's a reasonable risk, and, for most of us with big dreams and little money, a necessary one. Nevertheless, if you can't afford to lose a penny, you can't afford to risk a penny. Therefore, the most risk-adverse portfolio—primarily cash and cash equivalents—would be most appropriate for you, at least until you've saved enough to party with the big boys.

Also, if every swing of the market makes you break out in hives, you've probably taken on too much risk. Pick an asset allocation that you can sleep with, but remember that it's not set in stone . . . perhaps you'll start slowly and then move up as you become more comfortable with the market's movements. You might want to reread about the market's historical performance and how a long-term focus can quell short-term fear.

PART 3:
SPECULATING

9 INTRODUCTION TO SPECULATING

Not a window in my entire apartment building is illuminated, save one—mine. The usually busy streets are dormant and dark; rush hour is still hours away now, according to the glowing purple collegiate clock tower that stands watch over the sleeping Chicago suburb I call home. Yes, at five-fifteen A.M., the world is still sleeping. I, however, am not.

They say that money never sleeps. And when you love money as much as I do, you find little or no time for slumber yourself. In the precious few hours between *Snyder* and *Squawk Box*, millions of dollars change hands. The **Hang-Sang** hits a high. The **Footsie** has faltered. Money is moving. Moderately mortal, I must catch a few winks here and there, and it's annoying, to say the least. The markets never sleep, so why must I?

Alan Greenspan made a comment on job growth last night, prompting overseas currency markets into total turmoil. The All Ordinaries, an index of Australian stocks, got hit, as did the price of the Japanese currency, the yen. There's been a "flight to quality" in the U.S. bond market, which continues to trade overnight despite the fact that most of the United States has long gone to bed. The U.S. Treasury bond is up a full point, or 32 "ticks," bringing the yield on the bond way down in frantic trade. The "spoos," or electronically traded S&P 500 futures contract, is **limit down**, and I'm splashing cold water on my face and looking for khakis, corduroys, or anything that's actually been cleaned within the past few weeks.

Hang-Sang is the nickname of a popular index of Hong Kong stocks; **Footsie** refers to the FTSE 100, a major stock index of the United Kingdom.

Limit down is the term used to refer to a futures contract that has moved down the maximum daily amount set by the exchange.

Ten minutes later, I'm on the "el," the elevated train that cuts its way through the rising sunlight and toward the city of big shoulders, Chi-town. Lake Michigan is on my left, and as the train winds its way through the still nocturnal neighborhoods that make up the city's outer rings, I'm scanning freshly faxed brokerage reports, *Investor's Business Daily*, the *Financial Times*, and of course, the *Wall Street Journal*. A little light reading, or night reading, as the sun has yet to rise above the lake lapping the shore a few hundred yards east.

At the LaSalle/Van Buren stop, I scramble down the steel staircase and stride into the Chicago Board of Trade, where I spend most of my mornings trading futures contracts on the floor of the exchange's "Mid-Am" subsidiary. I snag a latte at the coffee shop, pull on my trading jacket, and get ready for battle.

Game time. On the floor there is a palpable sense of uncertainty in the air. The traders await the opening with feelings of anticipation, fear, hope, and excitement. News tickers update the latest quotes from exchanges all around the world, from Belfast to Borneo. A buzzer sounds, digital numbers flash, and the place goes crazy. It's 7:20. Like a great Greek chorus of capitalism, hundreds of traders explode into action. The U.S. Treasury bond futures market is open for business.

"Six for two!" "Six for two!" "Six for two!"

On the floors of futures exchanges, bids and offers to buy and sell are made through a system of "open outcry." The method is simple and efficient. Palms out: You're selling. Palms facing inward: You're buying. When you're buying, or bidding, the first of the numbers being shouted means the price, the second, the quantity to buy. Thus, "six for two" means I'm bidding a price of "six," or 120 26/32 (we only say the last number), for two contracts. 120 26/32 refers to the U.S. Bond Futures Contract, which trades in thirty-seconds. If I wanted to sell, the routine would be reversed to quantity then price, i.e., "two at six."

I'm bidding. "Six for two!!" I'm bidding because the yen is breaking, hitting new lows, which should push bonds higher, if only for a moment. I'm bidding because a notable **hedge fund** has gone belly up, and is supposedly short millions of dollars of bonds—and if they have to "cover," or buy back the bonds, it would force the price up even faster. I'm bidding because it looks like a sure thing. Harry, a rowdy trader who stands across the pit sells me a bond. "Sold!" he screams, and we quickly "card up" our trades. "Six for one more," I scream, still con-

A **hedge fund** is an unregulated and often speculative pooling of assets from institutions and high-net-worth individuals.

fident that we'll soon go "seven bid," meaning that the market will have moved up a tick, making me $15 in quick, hard cash. Harry "hits" me, or sells me my one-lot at six. And in my head, the money is already spent.

Seconds later the big broker across the pits offers 100 contracts at six. Then 100 at five. Then 100 at four. *What??? The price is going down???* I buy two more at four. "One hundred at three," screams another broker. It's a "small" two bid, as they say, I'm down over 200 bucks before eight o'clock. I'm also having the time of my life!

Screw the NBA: I love this game!

THE FERVOR, THE FEVER

I'm obsessed with speculation. Speculation is extraordinarily exciting and potentially profitable. It's dynamic. It's dangerous. And it's more fun than I've ever had in my entire life. And it is that art of speculating to which the entire third part of this book is devoted.

The *entire* third part? Absolutely. Here's why:

The fact is that *most of what constitutes investing is patience.* I mean, there's just not a lot to *do* when it comes to investing. You'll cut down on your consumption. You'll save. You'll start understanding the importance of valuing your biggest resources, namely time and money. You'll pick some bond and stock mutual funds that offer you diversification and low fees, start a regular investment program, and let compound interest get things funky. Then you'll wait around for the next 40 years and let the stock market do it's thing. *That's it.* Investing doesn't require a lot of fiddling, touching, or trading.

Speculating, on the other hand, is everything that investing is not. I'll use the word "speculating," instead of "trading," because even as investors we might very well make some trades. We'll have to: I mean, buying a mutual fund is a "trade" but not a speculation. Trading is the mechanics of buying and selling. Speculating is the business of making knowledgeable, concentrated, and short-term price predictions.

But don't get lost in the lexicon: Speculating isn't gambling, either. When I first joined the Chicago Board of Trade, many of my radio colleagues questioned the validity of making money on price fluctuations in the financial market. "Isn't it just gambling?" they'd ask. For most people, playing individual stocks or derivative instruments is indeed akin to gambling, in the sense that they just throw their money down, hoping some luck will come their way.

As speculators, we're not going to be gambling. We're not simply going to be "throwing darts at a board," as Gordon Gekko puts it, but using our skill, knowledge, and experience to make much more knowledgeable bets than any gambler would ever undertake. Pick a stock out of the paper, and there's arguably a fifty-fifty chance it will go up the next day. This is **gambling**. What good speculation is about, however, is learning how to narrow those odds so that we're not just tossing the dice and hoping to get craps. If that sort of mindlessness appeals to you, I urge you to jaunt on down to your local casino and help put some Native Americans' grandkids through college. What separates gambling from speculating is the knowledge and know-how that we, the "market participants," bring to the proverbial table.

GUESSING FOR MONEY

Is it going to rain tomorrow? Everyone has an opinion on this very simplistic question, although we trust the mighty meteorologists because of their superior skill, access to information, and experience. Although weathermen are not right all of the time, their predictions are by no means gambles. They've got a better than average chance of being right. As speculators, we don't want to just hope and pray it will be sunny (or that our speculations work out), but be so well informed that it's hard to imagine them not working out, and making us some money in the process.

Even so, some of them won't . . . and that's okay. Nobody wins every bet, and as a speculator, we're going to be looking to limit our losses and maximize our profits—so that the losses we do take hurt our hearts more then our wallets.

We'll talk about speculating in stocks, or individual stocks, but also about more esoteric stuff, like options and futures, which I happen to believe are even better than stocks. Why? The leverage. Highly leveraged products like futures and options allow you to make big bets with small antes. The point of speculating is not to win every bet, but to lose as little money as possible.

CP isn't interested in **gambling**. When you gamble, say, at a casino or in the lottery, the house has the edge, meaning that statistically you have a better chance of losing than winning.

We are socialized to speculate. From Baltic Avenue to Bingo, few things seem as common as playing with one's money. Most of us have been doing it for years with Monopoly, Parker Brothers' perennially popular board game that has sold over 90 million sets since 1935. Parker Brothers is a bigger printer of money then the U.S. government—there is more Monopoly money in circulation than U.S. currency.

WHAT'S IT FOR?

Let's go back to goals for moment. *Why do we invest?* To make money and reach our financial goals. That's clear. Investing over the long term is the best way to build wealth.

So why should we speculate? Two reasons: Because it's a hell of a lot of fun and because it can teach you a great deal about the markets. Unless you are truly a professional, with access to institutional trading desks or membership in an exchange, speculation should be viewed first and foremost as entertainment. It's true. If you just want to make money, investing (not speculating) is the only option for you. That's because, by and large, investors go to Boca—speculators go broke.

So while we're going to *try* and make some money speculating, it's far from a sure thing. Way far. Before you plunk a penny into a brokerage account, understand that what you can be certain of getting is excitement and education. Actually making money as a speculator? Think of it simply as icing on the capitalist cake, because if you speculate, you will undoubtedly lose money at some point. Everyone does. In the futures business, it's estimated that over 80 percent of all individual, or "retail," traders lose money. When it comes to trading stocks—the strategy you'll probably start with—the stats ain't that pretty, either. In a 1998 landmark study, two researchers at the University of California–Davis found that frequent traders—individuals who traded more than 48 times a year—made a third less on returns than investors who just sat tight with their investments. There's no doubt that you'll make more money with a consistent investment plan than you will by actively speculating.

But excitement? Speculation is *all that*. There is nothing like the feeling of researching a stock, tracking the charts, making the trade, and ending up a dollar-denominated winner. As Gekko says in *Wall Street*, "It's better than sex."

Losing money is just as big a part of the game, and in a strange way *even that's* kind of exciting. At the exchange, traders live and die by the morning statement that indicates what they've won or lost in the market the previous day. When you lose, it hurts. *It should.* Just like the pain we feel from being burned on a stove, the pain from being burned on a stock makes us sharper—as long as we learn from our mistakes.

And you will definitely learn about the markets if you begin to speculate. You'll start reading the financial pages, looking at annual reports, and becoming better educated about the *business* of *business*. After all, it's the knowledge that gives the speculator the edge that differentiates speculating from gambling. Besides, most people find that part of the *fun* of speculating is not just *being* right about a particular stock or financial instrument, but knowing *why* you were right. So if you want to play individual stocks (meaning that you'll buy and sell stocks for short-term profits—and losses), you have to commit yourself to being the most knowledgeable market participant possible. That might mean calling companies, crunching numbers, or culling the Web. When it's your account, it's your money and your decisions. The best speculators are the ones who make the most informed decisions.

What usually happens when people start speculating is that they start losing money . . . and consequently lose their taste for speculating. That's okay. You've *learned* something in the process, and it's not as if you need to play the markets to have a virtuous life. I'd rather you lose a few hundred bucks and understand a lot about the markets. It's cheaper than business school and ultimately, more useful.

The other scenario that usually occurs when people start speculating is that they start winning, and get cocky and lazy. They start laying down bets without doing the research, or without attempting to limit their losses. Upshot? They end up losing all their winnings . . . and then some.

This is why we're going to start slowly. The more you know about the process of speculation before you start, the more likely you will be able to avoid either one of these unpleasant scenarios.

You might be confused as to why stocks are classified as an investment in the previous chapter and a speculation in the next. The fact of the matter is, unless you've got enough money to assemble a diverse portfolio, *buying individual stocks is speculating*. For example, if you only have $2,000 to invest, putting the entire stash into one or even two stocks would be considered highly speculative, since your portfolio would be totally non-diversified. Affluent or high–net-worth individuals have large enough portfolios (like $100,000 or more) so that they can be diversified enough by picking individual stocks, essentially assembling their own mini-mutual funds. Surely you and I will reach that status at one point. But for the undoubtedly more intelligent albeit currently less affluent readership of this book, we'll consider buying individual stocks to be speculation.

HOW MUCH MONEY DO YOU NEED?

So how much do you need to get started? There are no hard and fast rules, but it is safe to say you need at least $7,000 to $10,000 in your total *investment* portfolio before you make any type of speculation. That's because we're going to be playing with only a small part of our overall portfolio, *certainly* no more then 10 percent—tops. Remember, at the end of the day, we're looking to make money to meet goals, and it's the long-term investments that are best suited to accomplish that task.

You need $7,000 to $10,000 to begin because it takes about $700 to $1,000 to begin to speculate with even the least expensive products, like buying call options or buying round lots of low-priced stocks. (Futures, as you'll read in Chapter 12, require even more capital.) If you don't have that kind of stash, read on anyway, and salivate as you think of the time when you will be playing the market like a store-bought Stradivarius.

If you are too low on cash to actually begin to speculate, you might consider paper trading, or just pretending to play the market. Research stocks, keep a log of your fictitious buys and sells, factor in a commission, and see how you do. It's a simple way to get the hang of it without actually putting any of your money at risk. Some of the largest, most successful traders I know still paper-trade their speculative ideas for a few months before actually making a trade. And these guys are worth millions.

I know, I know, it's not as exciting as actually putting your money on the line, but paper trading will definitely give you a sense of what it's like to follow a particular stock and do the requisite research. Do it as realistically as possible—actually "buy" or "sell" the stocks on particular days, factor in commissions, and see how you do. It will definitely give you a taste of what speculating is really like. Another option is to use one of the electronic "portfolio trackers" or investment **games** that are regularly being played on the Net. They'll track your trades for you, and tally up the numbers so you won't have to bother with the math.

Heed these words: Don't play individual stocks, options, or (god forbid) futures with anything other then *total risk capital*. This isn't money you need for the long term—or any "term" at all. Risk capital is a stash you're prepared to lose without the fear of eating out of garbage cans and stealing soap from the Hilton.

I really want to stress that speculating should come *only* after you've already got a tight, firm, and tasty investing plan well under way. That means that you must follow the investment pyramid from one level to the next. You can't skip grades like some Wall Street Doogie

Sites where you can play these **games** include both www.virtualstockexchange.com, www.finalbell. com, Standard & Poor's Personal Wealth (www.personalwealth.com), a site run by the *Wall Street Journal* (www.wsj.com), and the excellent (and free) Yahoo! (www.yahoo.com). These are a few ways for you to try your hand at speculating without losing your ass.

According to the February 1998 issue of *Smart Money* magazine, the average on-line commissions dropped over 45 percent between June and October 1998.

Howser. That means investing in stock mutual funds. That means investing in bond mutual funds. That means a checking account with some emergency cash in it. While you have no intention of losing your speculating money in toto, you've got make sure that in the event do you blow it, your long-term plans—and investments—won't be in the least bit compromised. Getting burned in the market is one thing. But getting burned and having to move in with your parents is just plain pathetic.

PULLING THE TRIGGER

If you have determined that you have enough money to potentially get into speculating, take some time to think about whether it really suits your style. Even an hour's worth of introspection will be enough for most of us to decide whether we want roll the dice. Many people, especially those who are already "speculating" in other areas of their lives (like paying for college or starting their own business), just decide that they can't afford to play. Others know they just don't have the time or desire to do all the market research good speculating requires. *And that's okay!* Those of you who can withstand the call of the wild will make more money with less hassle than any of us gunslingers.

Those of us who, to quote the **Mav-ster**, feel a "need for speed" find speculating in the financial markets to be a much more socially acceptable high than the stuff you inject. While I've never tried heroin, I can't imagine it's more exciting than riding a ten **lot** from its seven-tick **retracement** on up.

I do not believe in segregation, but separation. Church and state. Business and pleasure. Burt and Loni. *All of it!* When it comes to your speculating money, separation is vital—separation from your investment money. You will open an account just for your speculating money that is *totally* separate from everything else—that means your stock and bond mutual funds as well as your liquid reserves in CDs, money market accounts, and checking accounts. Even if you trade with a broker like Charles Schwab, who offers consolidated accounts—the type where you could easily hold both mutual funds (investments) and stocks or stock options (spec-

Lot: Trader slang for one individual futures contract.

Retracement: The tendency for a security that's on an upward or downward trend to experience a predictable temporary reversal before continuing on that trend.

ulations)—CP says you must *divide to conquer.* Open a separate account with your trading capital . . . you've got to physically separate your "spec fund" from everything else. You'll be handling it much differently than your slumbering mutual funds.

Speculating is a blast, but you've got to separate *that* cash from your investments in order to keep some sense of balance . . . and discipline. The main reason to separate your funds is that if you don't, it's just too easy to raid your investments to keep speculating.

A common scenario: "**Natalie**" wants to start speculating. She has $9,000 divided up between a few stock funds, bond funds, and certificates of deposit, and decides to take $900, or 10 percent of her portfolio, and open up a brokerage account with a **deep-discount broker**. She buys a few shares of a **penny stock** and a few **call options** on her favorite high-tech company. The stock suffers (and doesn't stop) and the call expires worthless—Natalie's "spec money" is gone. But her investments, her mutual funds, have done very well. In fact, she's made another $1,000 on her stock fund alone just from the time she started speculating. Natalie withdrawals another $900 from her investments, determined that "this time" she won't lose it. *Bad idea.*

Open a stock account and consider it "play money." *When it's gone . . . it's gone.* No way can you go back to withdraw money out of your investments to refinance a depleted speculative account. Give yourself a sense of "fiscal finality." When you initially deposit money into a trading account, it's all you've got to work with. People who can't develop the discipline to stop speculating shouldn't be speculating at all.

A **deep-discount broker** is a broker who will execute your orders to buy and sell securities for commission rates much lower than those of a full-service broker. Deep-discount brokers generally offer the lowest possible execution rates in the industry, but they do not provide guidance or recommendations.

Some define **penny stock** as stock that costs less than $1 per share; others say it can cost up to $5. The main things for you to know are (1) that penny stocks are cheap and (2) that they're cheap because they're issued by companies which are more speculative and marginal than the companies issuing higher-priced stock.

Call options give you the right to buy stock at a certain price and date in the future (see Chapter 11 for a discussion of options).

HOW TO BE A PLAYER

Though it's not necessary to wear black leather pants and wield a riding crop, if you want to be a speculator, you do need to learn how to give orders. Orders to your broker, that is.

The broker is the company where you'll have an account, to one of whose representatives you'll give specific instructions regarding what to buy and sell. *Full-service brokers* will offer you ideas about where to put your money, as well as access to research on any number of stocks. You'll pay a higher commission rate for this service.

A deep-discount broker, on the other hand, won't offer you trading ideas but will simply buy and sell stocks on your command. You'll give the same types of orders to both types of brokers.

Order placement is important. Order placement gets things done. Order placement can make or lose you money.

Placing an order to buy or sell is called an *execution*— and if you're not careful it can easily become one. Trading is easy. Sometimes too easy. You call your broker and tell him/her what you want to do. Not exactly difficult. Trust me, Forrest, if you can use the phone you can make a trade.

Many of the broker's research "tools" are available on the net to anyone. One good place to start is with Hoovers (www.hoovers.com), a service that offers detailed descriptions of thousands of different companies.

Placing a trade involves deciding what kind of order to use, and there are several, from the ubiquitous *market order*, an order to buy or sell immediately at the best available price, to the obscure *fill or kill*, an order to buy or sell that is canceled if the broker can't execute it immediately. No matter what, you'll want to make sure the instructions you give your broker are direct, clear, and to the point. For those of you find speaking with a broker a daunting prospect, here's a rundown of the more common orders and how to execute them:

MARKET ORDER. A market order is an order that instructs your broker to trade your stock immediately at the best possible price.

Let's try this sentence, shall we?

"Hello. My name is Pepe and my account number is five-five-two-one-two-three. Buy me one hundred shares of GM at the market."

Nice going. You just placed an order.

Moving on.

LIMIT ORDER. This is a type of order for when you want to trade stock at a specific price. You may want to place an order to buy General Motors at 65. Obviously, you'd rather pay less. Limit orders guarantee you the price you quote, or better. You might pay 64 1/2, but won't pay more than your limit.

Okay. Try it:

"Yo. This is Pepe with account number five-five-two-one-two-three. I want to place a day order to buy one hundred shares of General Motors with a limit price of sixty-two."

Every order you give, regardless of the type, needs to be designated as either "day" (an order that is good only for that particular day) or a GTC (good till canceled) order. Day orders expire at the end of the trading day. A GTC order is held by your broker until it is executed, or until you cancel it.

One more: Let's try a hard one.

STOP-LOSS ORDER. A stop-loss order is placed *below* the current market and becomes a market order when the market trades or is offered at or below your price. This order basically serves as a safety net to help you cut losses in the event that things don't go as planned. For example . . . you bought GM at 65 but want to bail should the stock drop lower then 63.

Here's your order:

"Hey again. Pepe here. Five-five-two-one-two-three is my account number, thank-you very much. Listen to me. Sell one hundred shares of GM at sixty-three stop-loss . . . Good until canceled. You got me, maggot?"

I'll go over these terms a bit more in the subsequent chapters, and you'll definitely want to learn them. They give you the flexibility to take advantage of market conditions based on your outlook. And while it might seem a bit new, don't be intimidated . . . You can cancel or change your orders at any time. The broker works for you.

LESS CAN BE MORE

Let's talk trading. The term implies some kind of hyperactive trigger finger, buying and selling on a moment-to-moment basis. I often hear stories about individuals who buy and sell stocks all day long, or "day traders." They carry an array of electronica designed to keep them tuned in to the market—pagers, price-quote machines, real *Mission: Impossi-*

ble type of stuff. These people aren't professionals, or even hobbyists, just morons. Why? Trading in and out of stocks for minuscule profits all day long, even at discount brokerage rates, is one of the quickest ways to get clobbered. As an "off-the-floor" speculator, we're looking to take beefy chunks out of the market, not tiny ticks. You can't risk $1,000 to make $10, no matter what type of analysis you are doing. Besides, most of the time, when it comes to trading, "less is more," that is, it's ultimately more profitable to concentrate on a few good speculative ideas than to be jumping in and out of the market, trying to capture a 1/4 point here and 1/2 point there (1/2 a point refers to 50 cents of a stock price, so on a 100-share trade, 1/2 a point is only $50.00).

A representative example of speculating going sour was provided by **John Wombacher**, a 42-year-old bed and breakfast operator who was interviewed in 1998 by *Smart Money* magazine. In 1997 he made over 150 trades, spending an average of six hours a day surfing investment sites on-line. In 12 months he lost over $70,000 trading stock.

The secret of John's "success" is obviously his highly technical trading method: "I don't do a lot of research. I really play on my gut instincts."

Especially with stocks, don't plan on buying before *Regis* and selling after *Rosie*. You'll simply end up "churning" your account, eating up capital by paying the commissions and the **spread** (the difference between the bid and ask prices of a particular security), over and over. That type of super-quick trading, often called "scalping" is just too tough with stocks, especially those that don't have a lot of volatility, or movement throughout the trading day. If that sort of speed appeals to you, I'd recommend building up a bigger speculative capital and trading options or futures instead, where the "game" moves faster and the stakes are bigger.

> In the same 12-month period the S&P 500 was up more than 33 percent. If **Wombacher** had put his $70,000 into a passively managed index fund, he would have made more than $23,000.

> Floor traders pay pennies in commission and do not have to pay the **"spread,"** which is one of the reasons they generally have an edge over the speculating public.

MORE INDISPENSABLE ADVICE

In addition to separating your speculation "fund" from your investment money, here are some more points you should ponder.

ALWAYS HAVE A PLAN. You can't just buy something and hope things will turn out. That's gambling. Know why you're getting into a particular trade and know what will have to change for you to get out. For example, if you decide to buy a stock because new management is taking over, you've got to think really long and hard about whether you want to hold on once if management leaves.

KEEP YOUR LOSERS SHORT AND LET YOUR WINNERS RUN. Every trade isn't a winner, and sometimes as speculators we're just plain wrong. That's okay. By cutting your losses and letting your winners run, you'll make more much more money on the winning trades than you'll lose on the losing trades. That's a major hurdle for many people to overcome when they first start out speculating.

SPECULATING IS A MENTAL GAME. It's about having the confidence to put your money where your mouth is and take a risk. According to Kathleen Gurny, chief executive of Financial Psychology Corp., "Fear and loss are much greater motivators than gains or profits. . . . If you fail to deal with losses in the past, you will not be able to take on future risks." That's why your spec money must be considered risk capital in your mind. To quote Gekko, "You win a few, you lose a few, but you keep on fighting." As cruel as it sounds, crybabies are not allowed.

DON'T BE IN A RUSH TO MINT YOUR FIRST MILLION. Understand that the "trading" part of speculation doesn't take that long. Call your broker or get on the Net . . . you can "trade" in seconds. But CP says that's gambling.

I can give you 3,104 (the number of stocks listed on the New York Stock Exchange) reasons to trade. Throw in the 700 or so companies listed on the American Stock Exchange, the thousands traded on the NASDAQ markets, not to mention options on stocks and futures, and we're talking well into the tens of thousands of tradable securities. Some will go up . . . some will go down. We're not just going to take a flier and hope for the best. Most of the speculator's time is spent understanding *why not to buy*, trying to understand the various factors that would make the price of a particular instrument rise or fall. That sort of insight comes only with the proper due diligence.

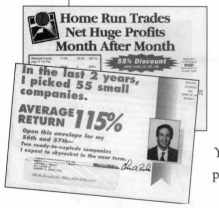

I'm not going to dignify most of this tripe with too much of a response, only to say that if someone had a foolproof, or even somewhat foolproof, way of consistently taking out money out of the markets, why in God's name would they be looking to share their secrets?

WHAT'S TO COME

In Chapters 10 and 11, we'll start with stocks. Picking 'em, playing 'em, and understanding the basic mechanics of speculating in equities. Unlike options or commodities (futures), stocks are unusual in that they have a naturally trending upward bias—over time stocks generally move up (that's why we're investing in them, right?). Consequently, most of your stock plays will probably be from the "long" side, meaning that you'll be buying low and selling high—buying first and selling later, or "going long." But money can actually be made in both directions. You can, strangely enough, sell stock you don't even own by "going *short*." In this strategy, if you think the price of a security will go down, you sell stocks or bonds you don't own (you borrow them from a broker) at one price, hoping to "cover" or buy them back later at a lower price. The difference between the two prices is your profit. We'll talk a bit about shorting, but you generally need a whole hell of a lot of **margin** capital to "get shorty."

Shorting securities requires opening a **margin** account with your broker, an account you are able to use to borrow money to trade stocks in a more speculative manner.

In Chapter 10 you'll learn how finally to live out your deepest and darkest Wall Street fantasies through derivatives like options and futures. These products are the most risky, most volatile . . . and, I hate to say it, the most fun. Options and futures were specifically designed for trading, which is why I think they are among the best choices for people serious about speculation. With the higher profit potential comes, of course, significantly higher risk. We'll explore buying **calls** and **puts.**

Call: The right to buy a stock at a specific price on a certain date.

Put: The right to sell a stock at a specific price on a certain date.

Don't worry about the terms just yet—options trading is like riding your bike. Once you learn it, you never forget it. I'm a big fan of trading options—they allow you to get a lot of leverage on the upside while having a limited loss on the downside.

We'll also dabble in the futures markets, where fortunes are made and lost in a matter of moments. Futures, also called commodities, are way, way, way up there in the nosebleed section of the risk/reward pyramid, mainly because futures are the only type of product we're going to discuss where you can lose *more* than your original investment. For this reason, they should only be traded by the most capitalized and least faint of heart.

10 STOCK SPECULATION

In high school and most of college, my stock speculation was like porno: a dirty little secret nobody knew about. I'd tuck *Investor's Business Daily* behind *Raygun* and hope that friends wouldn't notice when I excused myself from the afternoon kegger to call my broker.

Now the secret is out and everybody wants in. Market mania is everywhere, and for good reason. Speculating in stocks is an intoxicating pastime that, *if you're good*, can make you some serious money as well. This chapter is going to outline some of the more salient points about getting started speculatin' in stocks. Much of the information comes from my own experiences, successes, and (very often) screw-ups. The learning curve can be expensive, so check out my mistakes and make sure you don't commit the same financial faux pas.

DISCLAIMER

Before we begin, please, please, *please* promise me that you've already tucked away some emergency cash and begun to invest regularly in bond and stock mutual funds, and not just a couple of coins. Again: The money you use to *play*, or speculate in stocks, should not constitute more than 10 percent of your entire portfolio. In the Studio 54 of stock picking, only a sound investment program gets you past the red velvet rope. *Seriously!* No mutual fund, no stock-pickin' fun. That's all there is to it.

The disclaimer now done . . . *let's get it on!*

SPECULATIONS
Individual Stocks
Options
Futures

STOCK MUTUAL FUNDS
Actively Managed Funds
Passively Managed Funds

BONDS OR "FIXED INCOME"
Bond Mutual Funds

CASH OR CASH EQUIVALENTS
Savings Accounts, Checking Accounts, Money Market Accounts
Certificates of Deposit

PRICE AND PROFIT

So much to learn! I'm about to talk about dividends, capital gains, stock tables, ticker symbols, and a host of other terms that are probably as familiar to you as a good **Carrot Top** film.

But don't let the vocabulary distract you from the actually quite simple goal of the stock speculator: buy stock at low price and sell it for a higher one. After all the vocab, all the charts, graphs and BS, a price can only do three things in our game: *It can go up. It can go down. Or it can stay right where it is.* Those are the moves the market will make. A speculator, we've got three moves as well: *Deciding what to buy. Deciding when to get in. And deciding when to get out.* While it seems simple, I think you'll find speculating in stocks to be tremendously challenging and a ton of fun.

Recap: So here's what we know: A stock is a piece of a company. It represents ownership. As a stockholder, you own a tiny piece of a much larger entity. Sure, it's minuscule, but make no mistake: the million-dollar CEO and well-heeled board of directors all work for you.

As you remember from Chapter 7, there are two major ways to make money buying individual stocks: dividend income and capital gains.

Not all stocks pay dividends, but most that do pay them quarterly. The **dividend** is expressed on a per-share basis; the dividend, when divided by the price of the stock, gives you the dividend's yield. For example, if AT&T pays a dividend of $1.32/share, it represents a 2.3 percent yield when the stock is at 57 1/4, or $57.25. If the stock's price drops, the yield goes up. That's because $1.32 is a bigger percentage return of, say, 50 (2.6 percent) than of 57 1/4. You also probably remember that dividend income makes up a large part of your investment return.

Your speculative return, however, will come largely from price appreciation, or "capital gains." Two percent a year in dividend is great for our funds, but boring for our speculating. When it comes to speculating, dividends just take too damn long.

Price appreciation is simple. You buy at one price, sell at another, and make or lose the difference. If you buy one share of AT&T at 50 and sell it at 60 you've made ten bucks in capital gains. *BFD.*

But a *sawbuck* (slang for $10) won't get you to Scarsdale, and that's exactly the reason why it's hard to make money speculating when you've only got a small stash to start. You've got to be able to accumulate enough shares to make the upside worth it.

Think about it. You've got $100 to speculate with. If AT&T is at $50/share, you can afford to buy two shares. It's going to cost you at least $10 a "**round turn**," or $5 a trade, to buy and sell your shares.

So AT&T's stock price needs to climb to 55, or make a 10 percent move, for you just *to break even on the* **commission**.

Factor in the capital gains taxes and our "telephonic" winner has actually lost us money. So when speculating in stocks, especially with a smaller bank account, it's often best to concentrate on low-priced stocks, the type of stocks where you can accumulate enough shares to actually make the trade worth your while.

Here's the same example, this time using a $5 stock instead

of a $50 dollar stock. In 1998, TCBY (the yogurt company) was trading at about $5/share, so with $100 we are able to buy 20 shares. If TCBY moves up to, say, $7 a share, we've covered our commissions and are up $30. If we had bought a "round lot," or 100 shares, for $500, as I'd almost always recommend, we'd be up $200.

Let's talk about the concept of a stock's "price" for a moment. Stocks trade in points, or dollars, so a price of 50 means $50/share. As speculators, we want to buy low and sell high, so how do we know when, to quote Bob Barker, "the price is right?" Is AT&T "more expensive" than TCBY simply because the price of its stock is $45 higher? *No.*

Remember that stocks represent ownership in a company. The company issues shares through an initial public offering (IPO), at which time they are sold to the public at a specific price. The investment bank handling the IPO tries to determine how much the company is worth (say $100 million) so they know how much to initially sell the companies share to the public for. But they don't just sell a few shares of stock, they sell millions. So a "high" stock price has nothing to do with dilated pupils, but plenty to do with the **float**, or the total number of shares that are available for trading. The reason they issue so many shares is so we can afford to buy them. Think about it: If a company is worth $100 million dollars and there was only a float of 100 shares, each share would be worth a mighty million bucks. The shares would be so expensive, hardly anybody could afford them. Also, if there were such a few number of shares out there, they'd be highly illiquid—it would be that much harder to enter and exit the market.

Float: The number of shares available for trading by the public.

To avoid this, the company issues a large number of shares. General Electric, for example, has 3,276,837,000 shares outstanding. As of this writing, each is worth 90. Multiplying the total number of shares "outstanding" with the current price per share will tell you how much the company is worth in total. (about $294 billion) So the concept of high and low is always relative to how much the company is worth, and how many shares are outstanding.

Just cause a stock is trading at or near its 52-week low doesn't mean it's time to buy. All too often, cheap stock just keep getting cheaper.

As of late 1998, Disney was trading at about $30/share. Barnes and Noble is also trading at around $30/share. Obviously, Disney is a much bigger company, but they've got more shares outstanding (2,048,690,000 vs. 68,585,000), which explains why their stock price is just about the same as Barnes and Noble's. In short, a "high" stock price doesn't necessarily mean the stock is expensive, and a "low" stock price doesn't necessarily mean it's cheap. *So how do we tell?*

Two easy ways to tell how high a stock price is involve looking where it's been in the past, maybe through the use of a chart. A company that once traded for $50/share and how trades for 10 is obviously a lot cheaper than it used to be. Another good indicator is the stock's "52-week high/low."

This pair of numbers, listed every day in the paper next to the stock price, will tell you the highest and lowest price a particular stock has traded at within the last 52 weeks.

When a company's stock price gets very expensive, usually in the $100–$150/share range, it will sometimes issue a **stock split**.

This piece of financial hocus-pocus is wildly misunderstood, so allow me to set the record straight. In a stock split, the company is looking to decrease the price of its shares so that they will more affordable for investors to buy. So they "split the stock," meaning that they decide to double the number of shares outstanding, while halving the price of the stock itself. So if you owned 100 shares of a stock that was worth $50/share (100 $50 = $5,000) after a stock split, you'd own 200 shares, each now worth $25. It's not like you're getting something for nothing—your stake is still $5,000—but you now own 200, or twice as many shares.

The stock is now $25 a share instead of $50, making shares more affordable for other investors to buy. While they are usually interpreted as a "bullish," a stock split don't necessarily mean the stock will continue to rise. If a stock you own *does* split, you don't need to do anything—the change will appear automatically on your brokerage statement.

On the Net, stock prices are everywhere, although they can still be found, Luddite style, in the pages of most local newspapers. Prices are categorized by exchange, so you need to know whether a stock trades on the New York Stock Exchange, the American Stock Exchange, or the **NASDAQ**.

Your broker will know which exchange a particular stock trades on, although it's pretty safe to say that most of the larger, more established companies—the "blue chips" especially—trade at the New York Stock Exchange. The NASDAQ is home to lots of smaller companies, as well as many technology oriented compa-

Stock split: A division of the total number of shares a company has issued. Stock splits do not change the value of investors' holdings; instead, investors simply have a greater quantity of lower-priced shares. In a 2:1 split, you'd own twice as many shares as before. With a 3:1 split, you'd own three times as many.

The **NASDAQ** actually consists of two markets, the NASDAQ National Market System and the Small Cap Market. Since so many stocks trade on the NASDAQ, most local papers print only the most actively traded issues. The complete listings can, however, be found every day in the *Wall Street Journal*.

nies. The American Stock exchange is loaded with both small companies and a few familiar names, most notably Viacom, or the company behind MTV.

Stocks trade under ticker symbols, a one-to-five-letter symbol that is unique to each stock, for example, General Motors—GM, Donna Karen—DK, Dell—DELL. Stocks are listed alphabetically in the paper, so you'll be able to look up a company's ticker by only knowing it's name.

INTRODUCTION TO HIEROGLYPHICS: STOCK TABLES

Let's talk about stock tables—you know, those three or four pages that usually get thrown out with the ads for commemorative plate sets from the Smithsonian Mint. *Yes, Grandpa . . .* the small numbers *are* hard to see. But don't freak: The listings are standard and simple to understand.

One of the most important pieces of information in the stock tables is the P/E, or price/earnings ratio. Here's the deal with the P/E ratio. Companies that actually earn money (not all do) express their earnings on a per-share basis, hence "EPS," or earnings per share. Who puts the P in P/E? The P stands for price, and the E stands for earnings, so the P/E ratio is simply the current market price of the stock divided by its earnings per share, or EPS.

The P/E tells you how much "times earnings" investors are paying for a single share, and allows you to get a general sense of the stock's "expansiveness." Historically, the overall stock market has had a P/E ratio of about 15, meaning that most of the time, stocks are valued at about 15 times their current earnings per share. A stock with a "high" P/E ratio, either relative to the overall market or to its own historical P/E, doesn't necessarily mean the stock will decline; it just indicates that investors are optimistic about the company's future prospects, and bullish enough to pay a rich price for each share. Often, really hot companies will trade with high P/E ratios. For example, in late 1998, many Internet-related companies traded at a P/E of over 500 or more, while the rest of the market traded at a more modest 25. Investors are betting that the company is growing so fast that the stock will continue to climb even from current lofty levels. Stocks with high P/E ratios are often called "growth" stocks, because the expectation is that they will continue

1 **The 52-week high/low shows the highest and lowest prices the stock has traded at within the previous 52 weeks**

2 **The name of the company**

3 **The ticker symbol, or "ticker"**

4 **The dividend per share**

5 **The dividend's yield**

6 **The P/E ratio: Price/earnings ratio.**

7 **Vol: The volume, or number of shares the stock traded on the previous day, expressed in hundreds.**

8 **Hi/Low: The highest and lowest price the stock traded at during the previous day.**

9 **Close: The closing, or last price the stock traded at.**

10 **Change: The change in the stock's price from the previous session, expressed as a + or -.**

1		2	3	4	5	6	7	8		9	10
52 Weeks Hi	**Lo**	**Stock**	**Sym**	**Div**	**Yld %**	**PE**	**Vol 100s**	**Hi**	**Lo**	**Close**	**Net Chg**
13 3/16	6 3/16	MrgStnMktFd	MSF		...	...	152	9 7/16	9 5/16	9 3/8	– 1/16
13 7/8	5 15/16	MrgStMktDet	MSD	.96a	12.8	...	2117	7 13/16	7 5/16	7 1/2	– 5/16
26 5/8	25 3/16	MrgStn 9.00	un	2.25	8.7	...	40	25 13/16	25 11/16	25 3/4	+ 1/16
26 3/16	25 1/8	MrgStn 8.40	un	2.10	8.2	...	20	25 5/8	25 9/16	25 9/16	– 1/16
26 1/16	25	MrgStn 8.20	un	2.05	8.0	...	33	25 5/8	25 1/2	25 1/2	...
14 3/16	7 1/4	MrgStnOpp	MGB	1.20e	13.2	...	132	9 1/4	9 1/8	9 1/8	...
16 3/8	12 3/16	MrgStnHiYld	MSY	1.38a	8.8	...	124	15 11/16	15 1/2	15 11/16	+ 1/8
9 13/16	5 5/8	MrgStnIndia	IIF		...	...	1213	9	8 13/16	8 7/8	– 3/16
25 3/16	6 7/8	MrgStnRus	RNE	.67e	6.4	...	95	10 5/8	10 5/16	10 7/16	– 5/16
22 7/8	16	MorrisnHlth	MHI	.16	.8	18	49	19 1/4	19 1/16	19 1/16	– 1/16
15 1/4	8 1/8	MorsnKnud	MK		...	13	1376	9 5/16	9 1/16	9 1/4	...
7 3/4	**2 5/8**	**MorsnKnud wt**			**...**	**...**	**17**	**3 7/8**	**3 5/8**	**3 5/8**	**– 3/8**
36 11/16	21 1/8	MortonInt	MII	.52	1.4	24	9483	36 5/8	36 5/16	36 5/16	– 3/16
25 1/8	12 5/8	♣ MortnRestr	MRG		...	dd	1143	16 11/16	16 1/2	16 1/2	– 3/16
16	**1**	**Mossimo**	**MGX**		**...**	**dd**	**2006**	**11 1/2**	**9 3/4**	**10 13/16**	**+ 1 1/16**
32 5/16	**16 9/16**	**MotvePwrInd**	**MPO**		**...**	**12**	**569**	**24 3/8**	**22 5/8**	**22 3/4**	**– 1 3/8**
24 7/8	23 13/16	MtrolaCap pfA	MOTA	.27p	...	...	661	25 3/16	24 1/16	24 3/16	– 1/16
74 7/8	38 3/8	♣ Motorola	MOT	.48	.7	dd	30919	72	70 3/16	71 5/8	+ 1 5/8
40	14 7/8	MuellerInd	MLI		...	11	571	21 7/8	21 1/8	21 5/8	+ 1/2
14 15/16	13 5/16	Muniassets	MUA	.83e	6.1	...	225	13 7/8	13 9/16	13 5/8	– 3/16
14 1/2	12 13/16	MuniAdvntg	MAF	.80	5.9	...	90	13 5/8	13 9/16	13 5/8	...
10 7/16	9 1/4	♣ MuniHiIncо	MHF	.58	6.1	...	206	9 11/16	9 9/16	9 9/16	– 3/16

to grow earnings, market share, and profits . . . all which will lead to an even higher stock price. (Remember "growth stocks" from a few chapters back?)

A low P/E means the opposite, that a stock is trading cheaply compared with its current earnings. Stocks that trade with low P/E ratios are companies that are past their prime growth cycle or have otherwise fallen out of favor with Wall Street. Low-P/E stocks are often called "value" stocks, because often stock bargain hunters check out low-P/E stocks to find some undervalued assets in the market. The "value" mutual funds mentioned in Chapter 7 gravitate toward these types of stocks.

Keep in mind that this notion of value is relative to the overall market. If the overall market (as measured by one of the major indexes like the S&P 500) is trading with a P/E of 15, then a stock with a P/E of 25 is trading at a "premium" and is perceived as expensive. These facts 'n' figures, all of which speculators should be familiar with, can be found in any of the major business newspapers. My personal favorite is **Barron's**, whose "market laboratory" has more market minutiae than you'll ever need . . . or probably be able to stomach.

Barron's Web site can be found at www.barrons.com. Their telephone number is 800-568-7625.

PUTTING THEORY INTO PRACTICE

I like to focus my own stock speculating on securities of which I can buy at least a "round lot," or 100 shares. Brokers used to charge extra for trading "odd lots," or denominations of stock less than 100, but that's hardly ever the case anymore. Again, while you don't have to buy round lots, you'll want to make sure you can accumulate enough shares to make the speculative upside worth the damaging downside.

Here's another example of why it's so important to be able to accumulate enough shares to make a speculation worthwhile. Let's say Mr. Drummond has $1,000 with which he wants to speculate in the market. Now, we all know Mr. Drummond has a lot more than just one measly grand, but he's decided to take it slowly and begin with a small account. Unfortunately, with $1,000, he's only got a few choices. Let's say Mr. Drummond is bullish on Microsoft, which at this writing is trading at about $100/share. With his $1,000, Mr. Drummond can only buy about 10 shares. Even a healthy 10 percent move up in the price of Microsoft (to $110/share) wouldn't make him that much money. He'd make $100. A hundred bucks is barely enough to send all three kids to the movies, let alone replace the sweater Arnold ruined while trying cigarettes for the first time. Moreover, his entire $1,000 is invested in a single company: While he's waiting for Bill Gates to get things in gear, his entire speculative portfolio is tied up in just one stock.

Okay, so what about **Chase Manhattan** Corp., a large banking company that trades at $50 a share. With $1,000, Mr. D can buy 20 shares, making a $10 surge in the stock worth $1,200 toward Sam's trip to Universal Studios. The percentage move in the stock is bigger in this case, but the share move in the stock ($10) is the same. When you're speculating with a small account, you're going to have to veer toward the lower-priced stocks, simply because they allow you to accumulate more shares with your money, and it's the movement in the share price that we're most interested in.

Let's say Mr. D kicked it even smaller, to a stock like, say, **Musicland**. In 1998, the music retailer was trading at $5 a share. Now the grand gets you 200 shares, and it only takes a $1 move

Chase Manhattan Corp. is a large bank holding company that provides banking and financial services to both individuals and institutions across the globe; 1997 revenues totaled over $16 billion.

Musicland is a music and multimedia retailer that operates stores under the names Sam Goody, Musicland, Suncoast, Media Play, and On Cue.

upward in the price of the stock to make that same amount of money that the $10 move of Chase stock would have made. This is because the smaller a stock's price, the bigger the percentage when the prices rises.

Moreover, with a $5 stock, Mr. D could have done a little speculative diversification, meaning that he could have put perhaps only $500 into Musicland, and kept the other $500 on the sidelines, or even better, put it in a different stock.

This method of speculating in **low-priced** stocks is a bit more tricky, because you've got to find companies with both good prospects and low-priced shares. Many of these are found on the NASDAQ, although lots of lower-priced stocks trade on the NYSE as well.

For a more detailed description of how to find these **low-priced** gems, CP recommends *Winning Big with Bargain Stocks,* by Bill Matthews (Dearborn).

PRICES AND COSTS

Prices, prices, prices. Everything has a price. Besides our time here on earth, there's almost nothing that can't be bought and shipped to your door overnight. Ahhh, the beauty of capitalism! Everything is nice—as long as you pay the price.

So "what's the price" is a laudably loaded question, primarily because stocks actually have—are you ready for this?—*three* prices. Anyone who has ever been to a flea market or garage sale will know exactly what I mean.

So we've got this thing—it could be a stock, a pair of shoes, a spatula—whatever. How much it is worth is a function of what someone's willing to pay. That's what I mean when I say stocks have three prices. There's the "bid," the "last," and the "ask." Let's look at the bid, the last, and the ask for XYZ, our Every-stock.

XYZ Stock
50 bid 50¼ last 50½ ask

The bid represents the highest price that someone is currently willing to pay for stock XYZ. If you wanted to sell stock XYZ, you'd have to sell it at 50.

The last is the last price at which the stock traded. Notice that it is slightly above the current bid of 50.

The ask is the lowest price that someone is willing to sell the stock for. So if you wanted to buy XYZ, you'd have to pay the ask price.

The difference between the bid and the ask is called the *spread*. In the example above, the spread is half a point, or 50 cents. *Who gives a shit? You should.* The spread represents one of the major costs of investing, and one of the reasons why speculating in individual stocks is so gosh-darn difficult. Here's why:

Say you bought XYZ. You'd pay 50 1/2 (the ask) for 100 shares, shelling out a beefy $5,050, plus whatever commissions you'd pay a broker (let's say $10 a trade). Your cost for the stock is now $5,060, the price of the stock plus the commission.

Seconds later . . . you want out. A speculative Sybil, you've now decided it's time to dump XYZ. The stock hasn't budged, so how much could you lose? Plenty. You sell your hundred shares at the highest bid, which is still 50, and receive $5,000 back. You'd pay another 10 bucks in commissions, meaning that you'd only get back $4,990.

Your cost: $5,060

Your return: $4,990.

You lost 70 bucks and the stock didn't even move. Ouch!

The spread and the brokerage commissions are part of the cost of speculating. Every time we want to make a move in the market, like buying or selling a stock, we pay these transaction costs. They automatically put you behind the speculative eight ball— so as speculators we've got to make a concerted effort to keep our transaction costs, our expenses, and general "overhead" as low as possible.

DON'T GET GOUGED BY GADGETRY. If the wireless quote machine or Dick Tracy quote watch is costing you $100/a month, you've got to be pulling in over $1,200 in speculative profits every year just to cover its overhead. Real-time tick-by-tick quotes, even at $30 bucks a month, are a luxury that you probably don't need.

USE A DISCOUNT BROKER. There are two major types of stockbrokers, full-service and discount. With full-service brokerages, especially any of the big "wire houses" that operate chains nationally, your account will be assigned to a particular individual, your broker, with whom you'll work directly to pick and choose good stock ideas. The broker will provide research on request, suggest stocks to buy, and give you all the requisite hand-holding you'd ever need. Strangely, full-service brokers like to be called anything but brokers. They're more likely to call themselves something decidedly less-

Wall-Street(y) like financial planners or asset managers. In fairness, the term "broker" is partly passé, because most full-service brokers now handle much more than just stock executions. Insurance, **estate planning**, and **annuities** are among the plethora of products they'll be more than happy to sell you. And *everybody* is a vice president. *Everybody*.

Full-service brokers are ideal for investing, but suck for speculating. Here's why: Full-service brokers make their money in one or both of two ways: They most *certainly will charge* you a commission each time you buy or sell any security—and commissions through a full-service broker are among the highest in the industry. For example, buying 100 shares of Ford though Merrill Lynch, the country's largest full-service brokerage house, could set you back almost $90—much more than the measly $8 it would cost to trade through an on-line discount broker. The other way they make money is through "fee-based" percentage, where they might take up to 1 percent of your account each year.

While you're certainly getting *more* service than from a discount broker, I often wonder how much a full-service broker can really offer a young investor, let alone a speculator. If you decide to *invest* with a full-service broker, most likely they'll put you into a mutual fund anyway (the same one you could have bought directly), although of course you'll pay the broker a commission and/or percentage for his (*ahem*) expertise. *C'mon guys* . . . wasn't *that* the whole idea of mutual funds to begin with? Full-service brokers are best suited for high–net-worth individuals who require individual stock picking or a ton of hand-holding.

Trying to speculate through a full-service broker is even more frustrating because the commissions will kill you. Unless you're trading $10,000 blocks of stock, I'd stick to a discount broker to handle the actual executions of your speculative trades.

Discount brokers are like the prostitutes of the business. *They'll do whatever you tell them to quickly, cheaply, and without consideration.* Call your discount broker and they'll gladly make any number of trades for you for as little as five bucks a pop—just don't ask for advice, guidance, hand-holding, or much of anything. While many discount brokerages offer stuff like stock charts, company research, and earnings estimates, they won't make any recommendations—*period*. They are simply order takers who are willing to execute trades for your account.

No service equals big savings. Competition between discount brokerages have reduced commissions to a pittance at best. Simply put, commissions have plummeted: Most **discount brokers** will allow you to trade for well under 15 bucks a trade.

It's a low fee but not negligible. When you're actively trading, even discount commissions add up.

The best strategy is, of course, is to trade with a reason and only when necessary.

While I was attending Northwestern University, my tuition came to almost 20K/year. Education or extortion? *You be the judge.* But among the niceties of student life was the ultimate in the Internet: An **Ethernet** hookup directly into each student's dorm room.

For someone like me, who *loves to speculate*, it was the equivalent of installing a one-armed bandit. Twenty-four hours a day, my computer tracked every tick of my tiny portfolio. I traded between classes. I traded between chapters of *The Republic*. At night, I monitored overseas markets and traded the S&P 500 futures. I traded. And traded. And charted, and researched, and obsessed, *and loved every minute of it*—that is, until my penchant for pulling the proverbial trigger began costing me money. Commissions were killing me, as were the various quote feeds I eagerly signed up for. I loved the instantaneous feel of trading. Push a button, you buy. Push another, you sell. It's the monetary version of Super Mario Brothers. But I lost sight of the dollars it was costing me and ended losing a big chunk of my portfolio—not to stupid trades, simply to too *many* trades.

Discount brokers, on a $1,000 speculation account, trade one stock per week (buy and sell) and at the end of the year, you will have spent almost $500 on commissions alone, assuming a very low commission rate of $5 a trade. Trading that frequently, you will have to almost double your account, or make a 50 percent return, just to make back the commissions.

Ethernet is a extremely fast method for computers and data systems to connect and communicate with each other via shared cabling.

CONSIDER THE SOURCE OF INFORMATION

Some other realities of using the Net for speculation include the always obvious . . . don't believe everything you read. Just because "techstocksguy392" on AOL hates LSI Logic doesn't mean you need to bail. Consider the *source* of every piece of information you get.

Who's it coming from? Do they have a vested interest in a particular stock or company?

Start trading and you'll get on everyone's mailing list. One of the types of junk mail you'll undoubtedly encounter at some point are "research reports" about some stock. Often couched in a magazine-style or heavy-duty Wall Street tone, these are actually just PR jobs for stocks. Stock promotion is a burgeoning and perfectly legal business—company XYZ will hire a consultant to help prop up a stock price; they do it by trying to get the word out about just how good a company XYZ really is. So understand what the reason might be for a company or individual to recommend a particular stock. While they undoubtedly already have a position on (jargon for owning the stock—if they hadn't bought the stock then I'd really avoid it!) the best research is the research you do yourself.

Again, I also believe that "real-time quotes" are not the necessity everybody seems to believe they are. In fact, if you place the correct types of orders with your broker, you won't even need a quote machine at all. I'll get into the specifics a few pages down the line, but know that with proper order placement, you can "preset" the risk and reward of almost any speculation. For example, let's say you buy a stock at $20, knowing that if it moves to $40, you'll sell it for a profit. At the same time, looking to limit your potential loss, you think that if the stock slid to $15, you'd bail. You could sit and watch the ticker all day (which can actually get boring after a while), or simply give your broker these orders well in advance. By putting in these parameters, you excuse yourself from the often mundane task of constantly monitoring the markets. You also keep your twitchy trigger finger at bay. When your price targets (either the upside or downside one) are hit, your broker will sell the stock for you. That's what he or she is paid to do. You pay a commission so you don't have to watch the markets . . . the broker will do that for you.

Two Schools of Analysis

Gee, Jonathan . . . I opened my account, but what should I buy?

One of the "goals" of speculating that I've talked about is becoming more educated about the markets. Knowing *what* to buy means knowing *why* to buy, and I'm sorry, but "I heard it on CNBC" just doesn't cut it. If you want to put your hard-earned money in Bill Griffith's hands, you might as well send him a check. As speculators, we're going to count on our own ability to research and understand, eventually making an informed decision about the stocks we want to play. Anything less, anytime we merely "take a chance," we're just gambling. When you speculate you've got a chance of making money. When you gamble, it's just a matter of time before you go broke.

So we'll go into picking stocks knowing that it's our own research, understanding, and due diligence that will ultimately make us successful speculators. There are two approaches speculators use when they're deciding where to put their money: **Fundamental analysis**, the study of a company's earnings, cash flow, and overall health; and **Technical analysis**, which is where we use charts and graphs of past stock prices to try and determine future stock prices. Speculators tend to gravitate toward one of these two camps, although I find that using and understanding a bit of both techniques is usually a better strategy than the "all or none."

FUNDAMENTAL ANALYSIS. The idea behind fundamental analysis is that by analyzing a company's books—its financial condition from head to toe—we can understand how much it is really worth. Then, after culling through the mass of statistics, ratios, facts, and figures, we decide if the company is headed toward greater profitability or a financial belly flop. The idea is that companies that are the most profitable and show the greatest rise in income, cash flow, and earnings per share will rise in price. So fundamental analysis is plain old number crunching, the kind of shtick that makes accountants squeal.

It's hard to give the government credit for much of anything, but you gotta hand it to the **SEC** (or Securities and Exchange Commission) for leveling the playing field for us individual investors. In the Securities Act of 1939, basically the SEC mandated that all of a company's pertinent financial information must be publicly released on a regular basis. This means plenty of information, and plenty of paperwork, including "10Qs" (quarterly reports) "10Ks" (annual reports), and a host of other disclosures that indicate how well or poorly a particular company is doing. As speculators, we sift through the information and decide whether or not to buy the stock.

A good place to start is a company's annual report, the yearly report to shareholders that outlines how the business performed during the prior year. In the annual report, you'll find page after page and picture after picture of happy smiling employees and

Fundamental analysis: Analysis of factors such as a company's earnings growth and balance sheets in order to predict its future stock prices.

Technical analysis: An approach to forecasting stock movements based on charts of price movements and trading volumes.

The SEC: The Securities and Exchange Commission, a federal agency created in 1934 to enforce trade regulation, protect investors, and promote full disclosure about investments. You can visit its excellent Web site at www.sec.com.

Page from an annual report.

Cash flow is the total amount of cash a corporation has available to pay dividends and invest in its operations.

Dilution occurs when a company issues additional shares of stock, thereby "diluting" its earnings per share.

responsible-looking management. PR? You betcha. But read it anyway and understand just what the company does, how it makes money, and its strategic plans for the future. Remember, we're looking to be as knowledgeable as possible about the companies in which we speculate.

Next skip right on to the report's financial section, noticeably devoid of pretty pictures and heavy on the numbers. The balance sheet is as good a place to start as any: It shows a company's assets and liabilities, or what a company "has" and what it "owes" Next, take a look at the income statement—this is the main measure of profitability over a period of time. The income statement includes gross revenues, or how much total money the company takes in, the cost of goods sold, depreciation, administrative expenses, interest, taxes, and the like. You'll be able to tell whether these amounts are increasing or decreasing because companies usually put in a the last few years' numbers as well.

A firm's **cash flow** measures how much of the good old greenback actually flows into and out of the particular company. It's the blood that keeps companies happy, healthy, and profitable. When a company runs too low on cash, it might have to borrow money or even issue more stock to meet its financial obligations. Issuing more stock would be considered a **dilution**, because it would dilute the value of the shares you already own—ouch!

The most important number for the fundamental analyst, the "magic number," so-to-speak, is the stock's EPS, or earnings per share. EPS is the number we get when we divide a company's net earnings by it's number of shares outstanding, or shares issued by the company. The best part? We don't even have to do the division. It's listed in the annual report, as well as in the other major financial statements, which can all be found on the Web at www.edgar.com.

The EPS is so important because there is a direct and proven link between a company's earnings and it's stock price. Earnings go up—so does the stock. So we're looking for companies that are *growing* their **earnings** per share, because of an improvement in either sales or profits or because of overall financial health. Something else that can cause the **EPS** to rise is when a company buys back it's own stock, using it's own cash on hand to make "open market" purchases of its outstanding shares. This effectively reduces the number of shares outstanding, and increases the earnings per share of the remaining stock. It's a bit of financial hocus-pocus, and analysts and speculators alike should look for genuine financial improvement, not just a reduction in the number of outstanding shares, before they buy.

On Wall Street, when a company "misses its numbers," or fails to meet the EPS expectations analysts had, *someone's gonna get a beating . . .* and you can bet it will be the stock. Many investors consider a decrease in a company's EPS to be the first sign of financial trouble, and quickly bail out of the stock.

Although EPS is only one of several tools of fundamental analysis, it is regarded as the most important and should be thoroughly checked out when evaluating a stock.

Many of the other important facts and figures regarding a company's financial health can be found through any one of the major information providers on the Web, most notably *Value Line* (www.valueline.com) and *Morningstar* (yes, they do stocks too—www.morningstar.net). Slightly less current versions will surely be housed at your local library.

Ratios to remember: We've talked about the P/E ratio a bit before, and you are definitely going to want to keep an eye on the P/E of the companies in which you invest, because it plays a big part in fundamental analysis. It's useful to compare a company's current P/E to (1) its historical P/E (found in annual reports and research on the Web), (2) to other P/Es of similar companies, and (3) to the overall market's P/E. America Online provides a very useful tool for comparison.

Here's an example of how P/E would be used in fundamental analysis: If a company has always traded between 15× and 20× (× = "times") earnings, and is all of a sudden trading for 30× earnings, you'll want to explore why. Has the business fundamentally changed? Or have the earnings dropped, making the stock more expensive, and poten-

With **earnings**, it's the *expectations* that are most significant, so put your ear out on the street and get an idea of what's being talked up as a possibility for the **EPS**. Despite their free-wheeling propensity for propaganda, the better Net chat rooms are not a bad place to start. A stock price may rise even when a company is losing money, especially if the EPS loss wasn't as great as had been anticipated. The best place to go for information on earnings is Zacks Investment Research, which is found at www.zacks.com. I also like www.ragingbull.com, known for its astute discussion of the more popular Internet stocks.

tially likely to take a fall? Another idea: If all the restaurant stocks are trading at 10× earnings, and your favorite is trading at 6×, its multiple is said to be at a "discount" to that of its peer group. What's causing it to trade so low? Or is it an opportunity to scoop up a bargain before everyone else jumps in?

Another favorite ratio in fundamental analysis is the *debt to capital ratio*, which measures how much of a company's total capitalization is made up of long-term debt. Now, after reading Chapter 2, we all *know* that long-term debt is the devil. It's as dangerous to a company as it is to an individual. To get the debt to equity ratio you divide a company's total dollar amount of outstanding bonds, or debts, by its total market capitalization, or worth. The number, a percentage like .10 (10 percent) or .30 (30 percent), gives you an idea of just how leveraged a particular company is. The higher the debt-to-capital ratio, the more money the company will need to spend to service its outstanding debts. Again, you can use America Online or www.moneynet.com to compare a company's debt ratio to that of other companies within the sector, as well as the overall market.

Ooooh do I love book value, another helpful tool the fundamental analyst uses to determine whether a company's stock is worth his speculative stash. The book value is the total value a shareholder would receive if the entire company's assets—all the machinery, computers, inventory, buildings, file cabinets, potted plants etc.— were liquidated. Sold off. So imagine if a company had a massive garage sale and sold everything it had. After paying off the debt, that remaining money would be the book value. Think of it as representing a company's tangible assets; I say "tangible," because stuff like copyrights, patents, and intellectual property isn't included. The book value is expressed as an actual number, and is often divided into a stock's current price to get the "market-to-book" ratio. A market to book ratio of 1.0 means that a company is trading at its exact book value, whereas a market-to-book of 1.5 means that it's trading for 150 percent of its tangible book value. Oftentimes, fundamental investors will search out companies trading for "less than book," meaning that they'll be buying the company's shares for less than the tangible value of the company's assets if they were sold.

These are just a few tasty hors d'oeuvres of fundamental analysis. You'll undoubtedly want to learn more about evaluating the worth of the companies in which you decide to speculate, and I encourage you to call the shareholder services departments of any company to ask questions about any of these particular issues.

Each publicly traded company has an individual or department set up to answer questions from the investing public. Call the company's main office and ask for "shareholder services."

In your research, you'll encounter the ever-present analysts' reports and research papers written by investment experts at the various brokerage houses on Wall Street. These reports usually contain some nuggets of truth, but they're a shaky way to constantly pick stocks. Brokerage house "upgrades and downgrades" are immediately factored into the market as soon as they are announced; by the time we read them they are the investment equivalent of the Bible. So as soon as a brokerage firm announces an upgrade, it's not unusual to see a stock jump immediately—and I mean seconds later—up two to three points. Not enough time for us to get in on the action. Furthermore, as

Basic Technical Analysis

I've said before, many of these "research reports" are veiled attempts to boost the stock of a company in which the brokerage house holds a stake.

TECHNICAL ANALYSIS. Technical analysis is sometimes compared to fortune telling and is often berated by naysayers who believe you should only stick to the fundamentals. *They miss the point completely.* Technical analysis, or the study of past stock prices to predict futures ones, can be a very useful tool, especially for the shorter-term speculator.

Here's the basic premise: All of the information needed to predict the market is already in the market itself. This is because the market is a function of supply and demand that these recognizable patterns are easily traceable on charts and graphs. Investors tend to act on emotion, and technical analysis allows us to pull a Dr. Joyce Brothers and understand how the prior movement of a stock will affect individuals' future decisions to buy or sell.

Technical analysts look for what's known as "support" and "resistance," meaning that they're looking for a pattern of support for a stock at a particular price. In the preceding example, "support" for the stock would be found at around 97. The concept is that as long as the support line isn't penetrated, the stock will continue to trade higher. When support (or the opposite, resistance) is broken, then it's a signal the market is ready to move to new lows (support) or new highs (resistance).

Support and resistance lines make room for tech analysts to develop a entire verbiage of terms, including the "head and shoulders," the "saucer," and the "rising bottom." Sounds crazy, but this stuff works.

One excellent source of material on **Dow Theory** is located in *Cashing in on the Dow,* by Michael Sheimo (Amacom).

One of the most well-known concepts in technical analysis is called **Dow Theory**. Developed by Charles Dow, the same dude who came up with the Dow Jones Industrial Average back in 1896, Dow Theory divides market movements into three categories: the primary movement, or long-term direction of the market; the secondary movement, or series of brief reversals from the general trend; and daily movements, which are the daily emotional noise that makes up most small market movements.

One element of technical analysis you should know about involves tracking insider trading. An insider is someone in a company's upper management, like the president, a vice-president or members of the board. These individuals know the real deal about a company's prospects. But because they know this "inside information," they are not permitted to trade the company's stock without disclosing their trades. Thus, tracking insider trading can give an indication of whether the smart money is jumping on . . . or bailing out.

Sometimes insider trading is routine. Some VP's kid needs braces? CFO wants to pay off his mortgage? They cash in their stock. But what we're looking for is a *pattern* of buying or selling and an above-average dollar amount for the transactions taking place.

CP'S RECOMMENDED RESOURCES AND BOOKS ON TECHNICAL ANALYSIS

Technical Analysis of Stocks and Commodities (magazine, 800-832-4642 to subscribe)

The Technical Analysis Course, by Thomas Meyers (Probus)

The New Science of Technical Analysis, by Tom DeMark (Wiley)

GETTING THE MOST FROM YOUR BROKER

What are the three things a stock can do? Stocks can go up. Stocks can go down. And stocks can stay the same. And what are the three things a speculator does? Decide what to buy. When to get in. And when to get out.

So you've set aside your speculation money, done your search, and you're ready to buy a stock. *Not so fast.* What's the plan? What are you going to do if it goes up, down, or stays the same? When will you get in? When will you get out? In short, you need some strategy.

Before you buy a particular stock, you should already know what you want to do in all these cases. You should already have these "what if?" scenarios knocked out in your noggin. I hear the stories on CP all the time. "I bought it at twenty and now it's at fifteen. What do I do???" Kinda like asking how to work the parachute after you've jumped out of the plane. You want to set some price targets and loss limits for your stock speculations, either price or dollar amounts where you know you'll get out. This "forced" discipline is easily accomplished when you give orders to your broker that reflect the risks and reward parameters you are prepared to undertake. Don't be a speculator who buys a bit at $20, a bit more at $15 and is *still* holding on when the stock is wallowing at $8. Not only are you not having fun . . . but your capital is tied up in what is obviously a loser of a trade. Orders help give us the discipline to get out when we know we should (stop, stop-loss, orders), or get out while the getting is good (limit orders).

Market order: An order to buy or sell immediately at the best available price.

Limit order: An order to buy or sell at a specified price or better.

Stop order (also called a stop-loss order): An order to buy or sell shares if a stock trades at a specific price. This order is designed to limit your loss to a predetermined amount.

Order Up

The orders you'll use most when trading stocks include **market orders**, **limit orders**, and **stop-loss orders**. A market order is immediate. It means you want to trade at the best price available as soon as possible. If you give your broker a market order to buy stock, he will buy it "at the market," or at the lowest current ask price available. Consequently, a market order to sell stock will be executed at the highest current bid price. Market orders make me a bit nervous, simply because you're not sure where your order gets *filled, or executed,* until it's already done. This is especially troublesome when you're trading smaller or more illiquid stocks that have bigger spreads and less volume— you'll want to avoid market orders when trading stocks like these, opting instead for the always useful *limit order*. A limit order allows you to specify a specific price at which you'd like your order to be executed.

An example: We have good old fictitious stock XYZ again. It's 50 bid (the highest offer to buy) and 50 1/4 ask (the lowest offering to sell) and *you want to buy*. You tell your broker to buy however many shares of XYZ at a limit price—meaning that you'll pay only up to a certain amount for the stock. If you're limit-order if for 100 shares at 50 1/4 a share, you might pay 50, you might even pay 49, but you won't pay more than 50 1/4.

I mentioned using market orders for trades you want done immediately, but limit orders can be used as well. Here's how: You want to buy—the stock is 50 bid, 50 1/4 ask. Give your broker a limit order to buy at 50 1/4 and you'll most likely get your price.

Another way to use limit orders is by setting them at a level away from the current market price. Let's say the stock is trading around $50/share. You can give you broker a limit order to buy below the market, say at $49 or even $48/share. If the stock trades down there, you'll get filled. If not, you just won't end up owning the stock. Don't mess around with orders. Specify a price, put in an order, and wait to get it filled.

You will also use limit orders to sell stock that you already own. Let's say you own a stock XYZ that you bought at $50 share. If it ever got to $60, you think you'd sell. Give your broker a limit order to sell your stock at $60, indicate it's good until canceled, and forget about it. If (or when) the stock ever gets to that price, your broker will sell your stock. You are saved from having to watch the markets every moment.

You'll want to use a stop-loss order, which is appropriately named because we use it to stop the losses on a particular investment. This is an order that instructs your broker to sell your shares if the stock trades below a price that you set. It's designed to limit your loss to a predetermined amount. Here's an example:

Let's say you bought a stock at $50/share, and although you're confident about its prospects, you're also realistic enough to know that anything could happen. Immediately after buying the stock, you give your broker a stop-loss order to sell the stock at $40 a share, good until canceled. So if the stock ever traded at or below $40 a share, the broker would sell your stock (at a loss) and you'd be out of the market. While it never feels good to take a loss, limiting the downside is imperative if you are to preserve your speculative capital. And think about it: If the stock has declined that much, then something in your analysis is wrong. Take your loss and reevaluate the stock. You can always get back in, probably at a lower price.

While it's a good idea to put in a stop-loss order as soon as you buy, don't put the stop-loss order too close to the current price. Stocks normally fluctuate by a few points or more, so pick, say, a 10 or 20 percent decline as your benchmark of when to bail. Also, remember that stop-loss orders should be designateded "GTC," or good until canceled, meaning that your broker will keep your order until either he has executed it or you have canceled it.

Think about it: You buy a stock at 10. You set 8, or (−20 percent) as your maximum risk, so as soon as you buy the stock you place a sell stop-loss order to sell your stock at 8, GTC. At the same time, you place a price target on the upside, say 60 percent, giving your broker a standing order to dump the stock if it should venture up to 16.

There. You're done. You've taken an aggressive speculative position in the market. You are long stock at 10, you've limited your risk with a protective sell stop-loss order, and you've set a price target on the upside at well. Now go play ultimate Frisbee or something, because staring at the ticker isn't going to make any difference.

Of course, you can always change your orders. In fact, one popular speculative technique is to move your stop-loss higher as the stock climbs higher. Okay, you buy a stock at 10, placing with your broker a stop-loss order to sell out at 8 should the stock trade that low. The stock rallies up to 15. You're a genius, or just really lucky. At this point, who cares?— because you're up money and *this party is just getting started.* But before you savor that sweetness of a winning speculation . . . move your stop, your stop order, that is. Remember when you initially set a −20 percent stop-loss from your long position at 10? Now that the stock has rallied up to 15, you might seriously consider moving your stop up to say, 12, to again reflect a −20 percent stop-loss from the current market price. That way you are protecting your gains (locked at 20 percent, or 13). Making money in the markets is tough. When you've got a decent profit, don't blow it. Use money management techniques like stop-loss orders to limit your losses and, in this case, protect your gains.

THE HORROR OF HOW BAD IT CAN BE

The horrible tales of speculations gone awry could fill an encyclopedia, so I'll save you the gruesome details and distill some common themes. Remember, the story below illustrates the *wrong* way to speculate.

In keeping with the horror-story motif, let's use Corey Feldman as one fictitious example of potential gone bad. So Corey Feldman, still receiving residual checks from *Licensed to Drive*, decides to clean up his life and start speculating. He plans on using his speculation winnings to invest in a mutual fund, and opens up an account with an on-line broker into which he deposits a few thousand dollars. *Okay, slow down there, cowboy.* Like so many of his movies, he's already off to a shitty start. Corey should *not* be speculating until he's got an investment program already in place—which he does not.

On with our torrid tale: So using his high-level brain capacity, the Corster picks a stock he heard mentioned on CNBC and instructs his broker to immediately buy as much as possible at "the market." Obviously, this guy hasn't yet kicked his drug habit. He's picking a stock without doing any research (which is basically gambling) and has given his broker an order to buy as much as possible, putting his entire speculative account into one highly concentrated position. Moreover, he used a "market order" with his broker without even asking the spread (or the bid and ask prices), meaning that his trade will undoubtedly be executed at the worst possible price.

Q rating: An advertising research rating that gauges how easily a celebrity is recognized and how much liked by the public.

Also, he failed to give his broker the corresponding stop-loss and limit-sell orders, so his risk and reward are totally undefined. Corey goes back to the crack pipe, and a few days later he notices his stock has dropped as badly as his **Q rating**.

He's lost over 20 percent and decides to "wait it out." Bad move! *Focus, Corey, focus!* When you are speculating, you don't want to have to *wait* for a stock to come back. We're playing stocks, not throwing boomerangs. First, it might never come back. Second, all the time you are waiting for it to "come back," you are essentially out of the game. Corey's speculative money is completely tied up at this point. Six months later, he's still waiting for it to come back, although at this point he's probably got a better chance of getting a guest booking on *Keenan*.

Ultimately, the worst thing is that Corey wasn't speculating at all. He was gambling. His gambling became a speculation, then his speculation became an investment.

Gambling → Speculation → Investment

How'd that happen?

Don't let this happen to you. Short of renting *Stop or My Mom Will Shoot*, waiting for the market to "come back" is a really foolish way to spend your speculative time. If you were wrong on a stock, you were wrong. No big deal. Don't let a small loss turn into a huge one. Set protective sell stops and limit orders and have a ball.

DON'T MESS WITH MARGIN

There are two types of accounts you can set up with your broker. One is called a **cash account**, which simply means that every stock you buy will be paid for with the cash out of your account. Simple and safe: When you pay for stocks in cash, the most money you can lose is your initial investment. The other way—and the *wrong way*—to speculate in stocks is with a **margin account**, an account that lets you speculate with money you have borrowed from your broker.

I've been mauled by margin. During one particularly nightmarish afternoon at college, I was beeped during biology. It was my broker. My stock pick, Sunglasses Hut, had fallen sharply, and since I had bought the stock on margin (dumb idea), the broker was giving me a **margin call**, a request that I deposit more money in my account to cover the escalated losses from my bad call on da hut. I had borrowed money from my broker, 50 percent of the purchase price, to buy the stock. The stock had fallen so low, the broker was demanding more money to cover the loss, or else . . .

Cash account: A brokerage account used to buy and sell securities in cash.

Margin account: Brokerage account that allows the customer to speculate on stock and other securities with money borrowed from the broker. Your broker lends you a portion of the money you use to speculate.

Margin call: If your purchase goes down in value—below the amount you have in your margin account—you'll get a margin call, in which your broker will demand additional cash or securities to cover your losses.

Puke out: To close out at a big loss, effectively puking your entire position from your portfolio, as a result of having a leveraged (made with borrowed money) position move against you.

Not having the cash in a . . . let's just say, *liquid* form at the time, I was forced to **puke out** my position at a major loss, only to watch it immediately reverse. Simply put, I got walloped. To add insult to injury, remember that with margin, you're borrowing the money you use to buy the stock at a rate anywhere from 7 percent on up. So I not only took the loss on the stock but also had to pay interest on the damage. Take a tip from Nancy Reagan and "Just say no" to margin accounts. Margin is a dangerous way to play and I'd advise you to learn from my mistake. Don't mess with margin.

DON'T SHORT STOCK

Another dance with the devil is "shorting" stock, a speculative technique that involves selling something you don't even own. Here's how it works: Instead of buying low and selling high, shorting involves selling high and buying low. Your broker borrows shares from someone else, and you sell them on the open market, hoping to be able to buy them back at a lower price and later date. The borrowing process isn't something you need to worry about. Your broker would handle it without much difficulty. But there are a couple of major dangers in shorting stock: First, a stock can only fall to zero, but there's no limit to how high it can go. When you short stock, you are obligating yourself to buy it back. You want to buy it back lower . . . you're expecting it to fall . . . but what if it doesn't? It could go to Pluto. And you have to "cover" your short, or buy back the stock. If you're wrong, you'll have to buy the stock back at a much higher price than you sold it at. Technically, your losses are unlimited. Second, shorting stock tends to be quite difficult because the odds are stacked against you: Stocks have a historical tendency to rise over time; stock prices are more often than not going to be higher, not lower. Between 1790 and 1997, stock prices have gone up 73 percent of the time. Only 27 percent percent of the time have they declined, so by shorting a stock you are definitely going against the odds, setting yourself up for a speculative splinter . . . big time. So don't short stocks. Play the long side or don't play.

HOW TO LOSE MONEY IN STOCKS

Let's talk about some of the specific risks involved in picking stocks.

The first risk is the risk of being undercapitalized—not having enough cash to spend. Simply put: Do you have enough? If you decide to speculate and just don't have enough money or time, you are subjecting yourself to an inordinate amount of risk, inasmuch as you really can't afford to lose. The expectation that we can't (or won't) lose money just ain't realistic. Speculating in stocks is risky for anyone, let alone those of us without the **Ron Perelman** style of pennies. So know what you're getting into.

Economists like to differentiate between **stock-specific risk**, the risk that the price of your specific stock will fall, and **market risk**, the risk that the entire market will fall. For our purposes, it just gets back to the old diversity diatribe. Don't bet the farm, even your little speculative one, on one horse—I mean, stock.

There are a few other types of risks worth noting. One is **political risk**, which is the risk that some series of political events could upset the stock markets. This is present in places like Libya (with Muammar) and America (with Monica). As the saying goes, the "markets hate uncertainty." There's also **inflation risk**, the risk that the speculations we choose won't outpace inflation. This risk, although real, is more applicable to our stable investments, not our spec buys.

The Wealth of Nations: by Adam Smith. The book noted the economic concept of free enterprise.

The kicker: You're not going to find this in **Wealth of Nations**, but the biggest risk we face in speculating in stocks is ourselves.

Ronald Perelman, one of the Forbes 400, is worth an estimated $4 billion.

Stock-specific risk: The risk that the price of your particular stock will fall.

Market risk: The risk that the entire stock market will fall.

Political risk: The risk that political events could upset the markets.

Inflation risk: The risk that our speculations won't grow as fast enough to keep up with inflation.

DON'T TOUCH

We touch too much! Not ourselves, mind you, but our portfolios. According to a University of California study by the doctoral student Terrance Odean, investors using discount brokerages stocks tended to sell stocks that went up and buy stocks that went down.

Run-up: A stock's upward movement.

Called the "bandwagon" effect, this term describes our tendency to buy stocks that have had a recent **run-up**. Most people hear about a stock because it's been going up—but at that point, the "smart money" has already made its money. We, the public, tend to jump on the bandwagon . . . but alas . . . too late.

Odean's study presented a telling analysis of these mind traps, based on the psychological effects we feel as "winners and losers." The researchers assign a "+1" to represent the feeling of buying a stock and having it go up and a "−1" to represent the feeling of buying a stock that moves downward. Subjects had a "+2" feeling when they bought a stock that initially went down but then recovered and a "−2" feeling when a stock initially rallied but then fell.

Conclusions: We tend to sell our winners when it's too early and hold our losers until it's too late. Why? We'd rather sell small winners because we'd hate to lose any of what we've already made on paper. Kind of "take the money and run" type of vibe.

Consequently, we tend to hold on to losing trades because we adopt a bit of a "how much further can it go" attitude. The psychological impact of a stock's reversal feels much better to us than losing a few more dollars. Ironically, after a stock reverses, most of us tend to sell out as soon as we break even—cashing out with minimal damage as the stock continues to rally even higher. This is speculating like a sheep. ***Don't be a sheep. Sheep get slaughtered***.

If you think speculating in stocks sounds fun, exciting, and educational (which it is), in the next chapter we'll unpack the plastic explosives: derivatives. Yowza, yowza, yowza!

More than anything, the most important rule of thumb to remember about speculating can best be gleaned from the old McDonald's ad campaign for their BLT, which stated that you must keep the "hot side hot" and the "cool

INDIVIDUAL STOCK DATA BANK

Where: Stocks are traded on stock exchanges and traded through licensed professionals called brokers.

Investment return: While stocks are regarded the higher-returning asset class over time, the performance of individual stocks will vary widely.

Safety of principal: Varies. It is not uncommon for a more speculative or "penny" stock to fall all the way to zero.

Purpose: Unless you have enough assets to build a diversified stock portfolio, buying individual stocks is a speculative endeavor more likely to deliver excitement and education than consistent returns.

Tip: Concentrating on lower-priced stocks, the ones that allow you to amass a greater quantity of shares, is one effective way of speculating without a lot of money.

side cool." For our purposes, this means you've got to remember to keep your speculative and investment money well separated, and not be tempted to dip into your investment cash in case you need an additional speculative "fix." Your spec money should not be more than 10 percent of your overall portfolio, and once it's gone . . . it stays gone.

So preserve your capital. Don't just take a flier to get some action . . . Relish the opportunity to do the research and preparation necessary to make money without doing any actual labor for a change. Set realistic stops to protect your downside, trade with patience and care, and read everything you can about the companies that interest you.

11 | *KNOW YOUR OPTIONS*

DERIVED, NOT CONTRIVED:
A QUICK INTRODUCTION TO DERIVATIVES

At the supercharged and uppermost tip of the investment pyramid we find options and futures, both commonly called derivatives.

If you thought stocks were cool, just wait, because these suckers are pure speculative speed, solidifying their rep as the riskiest and most dangerous financial "products" of them all. For one thing, unlike stocks, bonds, or mutual funds, where in the worst-case scenario you could only lose your initial stash, when you speculate with certain derivatives you can actually lose *more* than you originally put down. So while speculation of any sort should only be attempted by those with risk capital, futures and options also necessitate a strong stomach and an extralarge bottle of Maalox.

In this chapter I'm going to discuss one major type of derivative: **stock options**. The next chapter is wholly devoted to **futures**, another, potentially even more dangerous kind of derivative. Before I go into depth about options, however, I'll go over some of the basics of derivatives in general. While options and futures are decidedly different members of the speculative species, they are both found at the uppermost tip of the investment pyramid, meaning that they both offer the highest combination of risk . . . and reward.

Ever dance with the devil in the pale moonlight? For those of us who speculate on derivatives, part of their allure is that hardly anyone

A **stock option** gives the holder the right, but not the obligation, to buy or sell 100 shares of stock at a predetermined price on or before a date in the future.

A **futures contract** is an obligation—a legally binding agreement—to buy or sell a particular commodity at a specific future date.

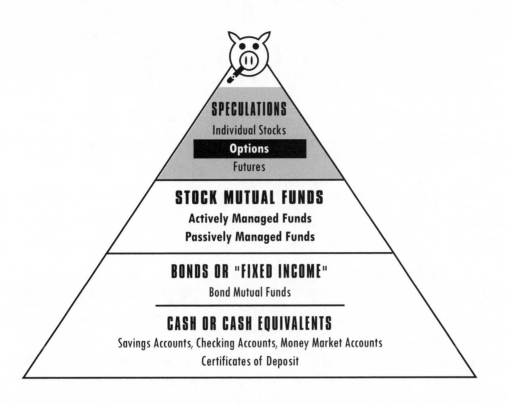

SPECULATIONS
Individual Stocks
Options
Futures

STOCK MUTUAL FUNDS
Actively Managed Funds
Passively Managed Funds

BONDS OR "FIXED INCOME"
Bond Mutual Funds

CASH OR CASH EQUIVALENTS
Savings Accounts, Checking Accounts, Money Market Accounts
Certificates of Deposit

understands them. From **calls** to **corn**, most speculators avoid dipping into derivatives simply because they don't know how they work. *Smart move.* Speculating can be dangerous to your financial health, but speculating with derivatives can be downright deadly.

So why try? For one, derivatives are **leveraged**, meaning that they allow you to control large amounts of a stock or **commodity** with very little money down. It's like getting to drive the Ferrari for the cost of a Fiero. Second, the profit potential of trading derivatives dwarfs that of the stock market. When trading options and futures, the money can be huge. Made 20 percent on your stock pick? *Whoopee, junior . . . go back to the sandbox.* If you had bought a call on the same stock, you'd probably be looking at 200 percent instead of 20 percent.

Here's a reality check: It is estimated that over 80 percent of traders lose money speculating in options and futures. Unlike stocks, which have a historical tendency to rise over time, derivatives are **wasting assets**, which have a definite life span. These are

A **call option** represents the right but not the obligation to buy a specific stock at a specific price on or before the expiration day.

One Chicago Board of Trade **corn futures contract** obligates the holder to buy or sell five thousand bushels of corn on a specific date.

To leverage: The use of borrowed money to control assets much greater in value than that of the actual cash you've put down.

A commodity is a basic and relatively homogeneous product that can be bought or sold. Commodities are usually agricultural or mineral, but the term can also be applied to foreign currencies and financial instruments and indexes.

Wasting assets: Assets that have a finite life span, such as natural resources deposits, business equipment, and derivatives.

---

products designed for trading. So whereas investing takes time, speculating (especially with derivatives) takes timing. Even for the professionals, it's a mighty difficult task.

As with any sort of speculative endeavor, it's important to delve into derivatives with some realistic expectations of what's going to happen. Since no one can promise payouts, let's be honest about why we're speculating in the first place. The money might come. But excitement and education are almost guaranteed.

After trading futures for a few years, my threshold for excitement has skyrocketed into the stratosphere. It would take a Led Zeppelin reunion, a bikini-clad Alyssa Milano, and several cases of Jägermeister to get my blood pumping harder than it does most days on the floor. It's this excitement and action that draws most of us to derivatives in the first place, so consider the rush one of the value-added benefits of the game. When the adrenaline rush comes, as it inevitably will, *enjoy it!* Speculating should be fun—and if you're not digging it, *simply stop*.

Trading derivatives also demands learning an entire new lexicon of terms, concepts, and applications. Some involve the stock market, although many derivatives deal with the various other financial markets, from soybeans to Swiss francs. I find this to be one of the coolest parts of the whole deal. You'll become more in tune with the economy, you'll read more business publications, and what was once arcane terminology will soon become second-nature slang. Even if you find that speculating doesn't suit your style, having a better idea of the relationship between interest rates, commodities markets, the stock market, and the overall economy will simply make you a more well-rounded person. Others may have learned it from a book, but you'll have learned it from *life*. As most of us would agree, the latter is ultimately a more meaningful method.

Just as with speculating on individual stocks, you're not going to want to do the derivative thing until you've got *a chunky investment program already in place*. And to make sure you've got enough chips in your pocket before you slide up to the table, Take note that many of the same money management rules for individual stocks apply here: *Don't speculate with more than 10 percent of your overall portfolio.* I see you salivating at the prospect of playing in the big leagues, but if you are undercapitalized, you'll just have to wait it out in the minors for a few more months.

DERIVATIVES: THE WHAT, THE WHY, THE WHO

THE WHAT. A derivative is a financial instrument, the value of which is determined (or derived) from the value of some other underlying asset or security. The derivative itself is worthless; it merely reflects a change in the value (or perceived value) of an underlying asset.

THE WHY. Besides fulfilling our wildest Wall Street fantasies, derivatives actually are used by businesses and institutions worldwide for a variety of important reasons.

I've already described how supervolatile, highly leveraged, and essentially danger-ous these risky rockets of speculation are, so why do you suppose they are used by thou-sands of investors worldwide?

To reduce risk. As loony as it may sound, the economic purpose of the derivatives market is to reduce the risk inherent in various areas of the business world. That's why derivatives professionals are often called "risk managers." Large corporations, **pension funds**, and even governments use derivatives regularly to hedge against different types of risk, most notably price fluctuation. By using derivatives to hedge risk, companies can lock in a price for almost anything.

Pension fund: Money set aside by an employer to provide retirement income to its employees. Pension funds are some of the largest investors in the stock market.

THE WHO. Who are these risk managers? Let's say you are a big-time mutual fund manager who, after researching a particularly volatile technology stock, decides to include it in your fund. The stock, however, has a history of erratic price swings, and you're worried it'll dive as soon as you buy it and crimp your fund's otherwise stellar per-formance. You could buy the stock, paying cash for a few thousand shares while rabidly rubbing your rabbit's foot . . . or you could buy call options, which would give you the right to buy the stock at a certain price before a certain date. Your options purchase would cost less than buying the actual stock, and your risk would be limited to the price you paid for the option. In short, you would be able to participate in any upward movement of the stock, but limit the risk of its tanking your portfolio.

Here's another options example: A pension fund manager has 20,000 shares of IBM stock. She's reluctant to sell the stock and pay capital gains tax, but at the same time she's worried that IBM might drop rapidly in price, pulling down the value of her fund and jeopardizing thousands of people's pensions. So instead of selling her IBM, she buys put options on IBM. A put option represents the right to sell a particular stock at a particular price for a limited amount of time. So by buying put options, she has effectively reduced the risk to her fund if IBM drops in value over the short term.

In the next chapter, I'll show you how entities from farmers to fast-food joints use futures contracts to hedge themselves against risk.

SO WHERE IS ALL THIS RISK GOING? If people and corporations are able to reduce risk by selling and buying these futures, just whom are they buying them from and selling them to?

You and me. The speculators. As speculators, we take on the risk the hedger wants to get rid of. Speculative trading provides an active and liquid market so that hedgers have someone to trade with when they look to limit their risk. If nobody were willing to "take a chance" as speculators do, the markets would simply be unable to function. Remember: A trade of any sort has two parts. If someone buys, someone else must sell.

Speculators are the liquidity that an active marketplace needs to survive. When a pension fund manager is looking to hedge his exposure to interest rates, I might very well be the one taking the other side of his trades. Whether he manages your pension fund— *or the fund of someone you love*—it's the willingness of us speculators to take a chance that ultimately makes this world a safer place for all.

Or at least that's what I tell my mother.

EVERYTHING YOU NEED TO KNOW ABOUT STOCK OPTIONS

The Price of Admission

So are you ready? According to the clergy, most parents, and almost every high school health educator, it's better when you wait. While I don't necessarily agree when it comes to sex, I'm an enthusiastic supporter when it comes to speculation. I know you're probably anxious to get in on the action, but simply put, it's just not a whole hell of a lot of fun to speculate when you've only got a tiny bit of cash to play with. Nobody has the magic touch; everybody experiences losses at some point, and if you've only got $500 in the first place, one or two trades could easily wipe you out for good. Then you're done. Through. Kaput. Gee, that was fun.

That's why I think you'll definitely have more fun and probably more success if you instead choose to wait until you've got *at least* $1,000 to play with before you begin playing options, and quadruple that for futures. I know, I know . . . it's a hell of a lot of money, but there's just no getting around the fact that this is a big-money game. To play, you simply need to have that kind of dough, especially since discount options commissions haven't yet caught up with the rock-bottom rates of stocks. If you don't have it now, start saving and don't stop. Reread Chapter 3, become a bit more frugal, and you'll get your grand in no time.

With $1,000, you can easily buy options on more than one stock, allowing you to diversify your speculative risk from being too **stock-specific**. You'll also be able to cut your losses without cutting off your legs, meaning that with $1,000, you'll have some wiggle room in which you can take smaller losses and still have enough capital to get back in the game. Think about it: If you lose $100 of $1,000, you've still got plenty to play with. Lose $100 of $500, however, and it's do or die at best. That's why waiting until you're a bit better capitalized is a smart and solid idea.

> As you recall from Chapter 10, **stock-specific** risk refers to the risk inherent in owning stock in just one company, as opposed to smaller risk of owning stock in several companies.

The Basics

In simplest terms, an option is the right to make (or not make) a particular choice. In the case of stock options, that choice is to buy or sell 100 shares of a particular stock.

An **option** gives the holder the right, but not the obligation, to buy or sell 100 shares of stock at a predetermined price on or before a predetermined future date.

The **underlying asset** is the actual stock on which the option trades.

Buying an **option** gives you the right, but not the obligation, to buy or sell 100 shares of stock at a predetermined price on or before a future date. Got it?

Because options are derivatives, their value is derived from the price of another asset, called the **underlying asset**. Underlying assets can be stocks (like IBM) or even entire stock indexes, like the S&P 500. For our purposes, let's stick with stocks. For stock options on IBM, for example, the underlying asset is IBM stock. So changes in the value of IBM's stock price will directly affect the value of the options on IBM.

Why would we would want to incorporate options into our speculative strategies? If you think IBM is headed upward, why buy IBM options instead of the stock itself? In a word, *leverage*. Options allow us to control large amounts of stock for much less *dinero* than it would cost to buy the actual shares. Here's how that works:

Say **Urkel** expects the price of IBM to rise over the next few months. He has been doing research, looking at charts, and he is confident that now's the time to buy, or **go long** IBM. Here's the problem: IBM is trading at over $164/share, meaning that a round lot of 100 shares of IBM would cost him $16,400 ($164 × 100 shares = $16,400). With the **residuals** from *Family Matters* waning and a marginal movie career ahead of him at best, Urkel just doesn't have that kind of money to shell out. So instead of buying the actual stock, he decides to buy a **call option** on the IBM, which will allow

Going long refers to buying a security at one price in anticipation of selling it at a higher price later.

Residual: The extra pay an actor receives each time a broadcast in which he or she appears is broadcast.

A **call option** gives the buyer the right but not the obligation to buy 100 shares of stock at a predetermined price on or before a future date.

Exercise: To buy or sell the actual stock (underlying) of an option.

him the right (but not the obligation) to buy the stock at a specific price at or before the future date. The single "call" that Urkel buys costs him 2 1/2 points, or $250, much less than it would cost to actually buy 100 shares of the stock, although he still "controls" as much of IBM as if he actually *had* bought the stock.

But he won't. Most buyers of call options (Urkel included), have no intention of actually buying the stock. They are just expecting the price of the underlying asset (IBM, in this case) to move up, making the options more valuable and allowing them to sell their options to someone else at a profit. They make money on the difference between what they paid for the option in the first place and what they sell it for later. What would make his option go up in value is if the underlying asset went up in value, in this case, IBM.

Options give you the right to buy or sell stock. Most of us won't choose to **exercise,** or actually demand that your right to buy or sell be fulfilled. If IBM is trading at 85 and you have bought an call with an 80 strike price, you could conceivably exercise your right and buy IBM at $80/share, even thought it is trading on the open market for $5 higher. As I said before, most options players prefer not to exercise the right, merely to sell back the option and make a profit on the difference between where they bought and sold.

WHAT'S YOUR TYPE? There are two types of stock options: A **"call"** option represents the right to buy, and a **"put"** represents the right to sell. Buying an IBM call, therefore, would give you the right to buy 100 shares of IBM at a certain price on or before a future date. Buying a put would allow you to sell 100 shares of IBM at a predetermined price on or before that same date. Either way, you can own the option without owning the stock. Many people find it helpful to associate "call" with "calling the stock in," as in getting it, and "put" or the right to sell, with "putting it on someone else," or getting rid of it.

Call = Right to Buy

Put = Right to Sell

If you thought a stock was going to move higher, you'd buy a call, or the right to buy. Conversely, if you thought the stock was going down in price, you'd buy a put. Besides **shorting** stock, buying puts is one of the few ways to profit from a stock's decline. When you buy a put on a stock, the further it falls, the more money you make. Puts, which give you the right to sell at a certain price, become more valuable as stock prices decline. Calls, on the other hand, become more valuable as stock prices rise.

Shorting stock: Selling borrowed stock at one price in anticipation of buying it back at a lower price, effectively profiting from a stock's decline.

But you've got to choose the right stock. If you thought IBM was moving higher, buying a Microsoft call wouldn't do you much good.

Every option has four major variables we need to be aware of. The type, either put or call. The underlying asset, the particular stock we want to buy an option on. The expiration date, meaning when the option will expire and become worthless. The strike price, the specific price at which we have the right to buy or sell.

Strike prices are usually offered in increments of five, each strike price representing an entirely different option. One underlying asset might have several hundred different options available to trade, each at a slightly different strike price. For example, there are several different strike prices available from IBM, from strike prices nowhere near the current market price of the stock (called "out of the money") to strike prices much closer to the current market price (called near or even "at the money"). The owner of an IBM 80 call would have the right to buy 100 shares of IBM at a price of $80 a share anytime before the option expires.

Options are wasting assets; like coupons and frequent-flier miles, they expire. They die. They cease to exist. They just become worthless. So the **expiration** is a predetermined date when the option becomes worthless. For most equity options, it has been standardized as the third Friday of the expiration month. An IBM October 80 call would give the owner the right to buy 100 shares of IBM at a price of $80/share anytime before the third Friday in October. After that final Friday, the option can no longer be traded.

Expiration: The last date you can exercise your options. You can buy options that expire as far as two years in the future.

Here's an example of how strike prices and expiration dates work. Let's say you buy an at-the-money call (more about this later), meaning that the strike price of the option you buy is the same as the current market price. With IBM stock trading at $80/share, you buy an IBM October 80 call, paying a premium (or price) of $4 1/2 ($450) for the right to buy 100 shares of IBM anytime before the third Friday in October. If IBM moves up, your call will become more valuable, allowing you to sell it at a profit. But if IBM falls, or stays right where it is, the option expires worthless in October. You lose the entire $450, the entire premium you paid for the option in the first place. Of course, you could have salvaged some of your cash before expiration, selling your option for less than what you paid as soon as it became apparent that IBM wasn't going to make it above 84 1/2 (the strike price, 80, plus the 4 1/2 you paid for the options) before the option expires. In this example, because you paid 4 1/2 ($450) for the option in the first place, IBM would need to move to about 84 1/2 for your option to be worth more than you paid—and for you to make money.

Let's try another example, this time with puts. With IBM trading at $80/share, your (*ahem*) exhaustive research indicates the stock is due to drop. Expecting the price of IBM's stock to go down, you buy an October 80 IBM put. It gives you the right to sell 100 shares of IBM stock at a price of $80/share anytime before the third Friday in October.

For this right, you pay a premium of 5 ($500). At expiration, the stock will have to be below 75 (your strike price, which is 80, minus the cost of the put, which is 5) for you to make any money. Of course, you could always sell your options before expiration if market conditions warrant a change in your game plan.

The put is the best example of how options can act as a hedge, or protection, against adverse movements in stock prices. If you wanted to protect a stock portfolio from decline, you could easily buy put options on the various stocks that make up the portfolio. You'd shell out some money for the puts, but your stocks would be hedged against loss. If the stocks dropped in value, your value of your puts would rise. Of course, if the market didn't drop when you anticipated, the puts would expire worthless and you'd be out the premium paid, but your portfolio would have been protected during the entire period.

Put options are often described as insurance, because they can quickly and easily be used to protect against falling stock prices without actually having to sell the stock. You pay for the protection, not unlike the way a homeowner buys insurance to protect herself in case a fire breaks out. The premiums we pay on fire insurance aren't a waste just because the house never burns down.

I don't advocate worrying about or constantly trying to hedge *your* investment portfolio—over time you'll pay too much out in premium, and since the long-term trend of the market is up, you'll waste a lot of money attempting to time the market's decline. But in terms of speculating on an individual stock . . . put options are perfect for making money on the downside.

HOW MUCH TO PLAY?

Options aren't free. You pay a price—it's called the premium. The premium is the cost of the right to buy or sell, the option itself. So if you buy an IBM 80 call for 4 1/2 ($450) you

> When you **buy options**, you're tak-
> ing a risk, but the risk is limited. The
> most you can lose is the premium
> you've paid. Traders who "short"
> options, that is, selling options they
> haven't previously bought, are
> exposing themselves to potentially
> unlimited risk. Because shorting
> options is a *highly* risky affair, and
> because it's so damned detailed,
> I'm not going to cover it here.

are essentially buying the right to buy IBM for $80/share before the option expires. Our risk is minimized. *Options buyers can only lose the premium they pay to buy the option in the first place.* This is one of the advantages of buying options: at all times, your risk is known and limited. the most you can lose **buying options** is the price, or the premium, you pay for the option in the first place.

What determines the price? The price (premium) on an option is determined mainly by three factors: the current market price of the underlying stock, the time remaining before expiration, and the underlying stock's volatility. I'll outline below.

The *most* influential of these factors is the current market price of the underlying stock. Think about it: When IBM stock is trading at $85/share on the New York Stock Exchange, how much is the right to buy IBM at 80 worth at that very moment? At the *least*, it's worth $5/share (or $500/option contract), because as the holder of the option you could conceivably exercise that option and buy 100 shares of IBM at 80, immediately selling them on the open market at $85 for a $5 profit ($500) on 100 shares.

In this example, the IBM 80 call is said to be $5 "in the money," meaning that as long as the market price of the underlying stock is higher than the strike price of the call, the call is intrinsically worth the difference between your option's strike price and the current market price of the stock. And if IBM were to rise to 90, the right to buy IBM at 80 would be "intrinsically" worth at least $10 ($1,000). Why? Because with the stock at 90, you could conceivably exercise your right to buy it at 80 (with the call) and immediately sell it at 90.

When IBM is at 85, your 80 call would be worth at least $5. But what if IBM was lower, say, 75 . . . how much would your option be worth then, smart guy? Call options that have strike prices *above* the current market price of the stock are said to be "out of the money," meaning that they have no intrinsic value whatsoever. After all, how much is the right to buy IBM at $80/share worth when you could buy it on the open market for 75?

Actually, it *is* worth something, because of time. Time represents another main factor in determining an option's price. Take our above example. The right to buy IBM at 80 when it's trading on the open market at 75 isn't necessarily worth $5, but it's worth something. That "something" is the time value—or the chance that the stock will move "into the money" before the option expires. In the above example, that would happen if IBM moved from $75/share to any price above $80/share. It would have moved from being "out of the money" to being "in the money."

Time value is another factor that determines an option's price. Time value reflects the length of the option and the corresponding possibility that the price of the underlying stock will move in your favor before the option expires. The longer the option "contract," the greater the possibility that a stock will at some point move in the direction you'd like it to; for that reason, contracts that expire further in the future usually cost more.

The more time before an option expires the more the time value costs. An option that expires in six months has a greater *time value* than one that expires in six weeks, simply because there's more of a chance the stock will have enough time to rise above the strike price.

Some specifics on our scenario: It's September and IBM is trading at $75/share. The October 80 call, even though it's "out of the money," might still be trading at $2 ($200) because there's still a very significant chance IBM will move above $80/share, or "into the money" before the option expires in October. The January 80 call would be worth even more than the October 80 call, perhaps $5 ($500), because the extra three months represents even *more* time in which IBM could conceivably move above the strike price, which in this case is 80 bucks a share.

As time marches on, time value starts to decline. Options lose their time value as expiration approaches, and when the third Friday of the expiration month finally comes, *time's up.* If your option isn't in the money by expiration it's worthless, and you've lost the entire premium you've paid. Just know that the more time before an option expires, the more time value the option will have—time value that will slowly erode as the expiration date approaches.

The third major factor influencing an option's price (premium) is the volatility of the underlying asset. If a stock has historically experienced large price movements or **volatility**, there's a greater chance the stock could move into the money before expiration. This is why volatile stocks will usually have more expensive options premiums.

The insurance analogy works again here: Which would cost more, fire insurance that expired in a week or in a year? Obviously, fire insurance that expired in a year would cost more because there'd be a greater chance of your house burning down in 52 weeks rather than just one.

One way of measuring a stock's **volatility** is it's beta rating, which is a measure of a stock's price sensitivity relative to the overall market. Stocks with a beta higher than 1.00 are said to have above-market volatility, while stocks with a beta less than 1.00 have a lower-than-average volatility.

Take IBM vs. Yahoo!. Because Yahoo! has historically been a more volatile stock than old Big Blue, one could expect that Yahoo!'s options would be comparatively more expensive than IBM's.

MAKING THE TRADE

So you've decided to try your hand at options. You've been following IBM since the Carter administration, and feel confident the stock is ready to rally within the next few months. The stock is at $80/share, and since you don't have enough cash to buy many shares, you decide instead to purchase call options which will rise in value when (or if) IBM (the underlying asset) rises. But which IBM option to choose? After checking out the Chicago Board Options Exchange's Web site, you see there are literally hundreds of different combinations listed for IBM calls. There are strike prices raging from 65 (which would give you the right to buy IBM at 65 before expiration) all the way up to 120 (which would give you the right to buy IBM at 120). Furthermore, the expiration dates on each of those range from a few months out to a few years. How do you chose?

First let's talk about choosing the expiration date. This is where the timing comes in. It's not enough to know *if* IBM is going to make a move, you've got to know *when*. If you buy a call that expires in January, it's not going to do you much good if IBM doesn't rise until February. In fact, it would be worthless. At the same time, buying options that expire too far in the future will cost you way too much in a time premium that will inevitably be lost once expiration does roll around. For example, with IBM trading at 80, a one-month "at the money call" (a call that expires in one month with a strike price of 80) might set you back 3 points (or $300). The six-month call might cost 7 points (or $700), reflecting five months more of price fluctuation and uncertainty. While you might feel safer knowing that there's more time before you option expires, buying options too far into the future is a bad move. More often than not, you're paying for time premium that will slowly erode as expiration nears closer, dragging the value of your option down with it.

I like to buy options that expire anywhere from two to four months in the future. That way, if the stock isn't performing as planned, I can usually sell the option back in the last few weeks before expiration, recouping some of the premium and moving on to the next trade.

When deciding on which strike price to choose, CP recommends one particular strategy: *Don't buy options that are too far* **"in the money."** For example, when IBM is trading at 80, the 65 strike call will intrinsically be worth at least 15 (stock price - strike price = intrinsic value, or $1,500). It sounds tempting, because if IBM ticks up to 81, your 65 call will immediately be worth at least 16, giving you a $100 profit ($1,100 shares). But you'd be paying out way too much in premium for so little control—you'd be controlling only 100 shares but would still be paying well over $1,500. A better choice would be an at-the-money call with a strike price of 80. The premium will be much less, allowing you to make a more leveraged bet and buy more contracts. Think about it: If the 80 strike (**at-the-money**) call is trading at 5 per option ($500), you'll be able to buy three contracts with $1,500. You'll control three times as many shares as you would buying the 65 call. If the stock moved to 81, your three calls would immediately (intrinsically) be worth 6, giving you a profit of $300 over the $1,500 you originally bet.

AN OPTION IS:

At the money: when the stocks price is the same as the strike price.

In the money: when the stocks price is higher then the call's strike price.

Out of the money: opposite of "in the money"—when a stock's price is lower then a call's strike price, or higher than a put's strike price.

Even *more* leveraged would be the 95 call, which would give you the right to buy 100 shares of IBM at $95/share any time before expiration. With IBM stock tracking at 80, the 95 call might only cost you 3/4, or $75/contract. With the same $1,500, you can now buy 20 contracts at 3/4 ($75 × 20 = 1,500) giving you the right to control two thousand shares of IBM. Of course, there's a much less chance that the 95 call will move "into the money," meaning that there's a fairly slim chance IBM would rise 15 points before the option expired. But if IBM moved closer into the money, say to 85, it's quite likely your 95 call would move up in price to 1 point (or $100) from the 3/4 point (or $75) you originally paid. Now your 20 options are worth $2,000 (20 contracts × $1 [$100] contract), and you've made $500.

Even more amazing is the percentage return. Your $1,500 options speculation is now worth $2,000, which represents a 33 percent return. *Ya gotta love the leverage!*

CP recommends sticking to call and put options that are slightly **out of the money**. This means calls that are *above* the current stock price and puts that are *below* the current stock price. That way, the value of your positions will increase much more when (or if) the stock actually does move in your favor.

Currently, options are traded on thousands of different stocks, and the majority of options trading occurs at the Chicago Board Options Exchange, located in my own

A **bid** is the highest price someone is willing to pay for a particular security.

The **ask** is the lowest price at which someone is willing to sell.

The **last** refers to the price at which the last transaction took place.

home town. They trade in basically the same fashion as stocks: there's a **bid price**, **ask price**, and **last price**. *When you want to buy, you pay the ask. When you want to sell, you sell at the bid.*

Be sure to check with your broker as to the bid and ask price before you trade. Some options, especially the less actively traded, or less liquid, ones have wider spreads between the bid and ask price. If a spread is over 1/2 a point, *don't even bother trading the options.* Wide spreads indicate there's not a lot of interest in trading that particular option, which makes it harder to trade in and out at a fair price. For example, the at-the-money IBM call might be quoted at 5 1/2 bid, 5 5/8 ask, a spread of a point or more ($12.50). Far out of the money options, calls or puts, might have a spread of 1 or more.

Just like with stocks, we're always going to *buy first, sell later.* While it is possible to "short" options, doing so exposes you to unlimited risk and requires way too much margin capital for most of us to handle. I'm talking, like, Oprah-type money. We will concentrate our options trading to going long, meaning buying calls or puts at one price and expecting to sell at a higher price later on.

The most active options are listed daily in the **Wall Street Journal** and even a few of the larger regional newspapers. To find out if options are traded on a particular stock, or to check on the price of a specific option, you can always call your broker. CP recom-

---

OPTIONS DATA BANK

Where: Options are traded on several exchanges located throughout the United States and can be bought or sold through a stockbroker.

Investment return: High. Options afford the speculator lots of leverage. When you're right, you're *right.*

Safety of principal: Very low, although controlled. When you buy options, the most you can lose is the premium you paid.

Purpose: Options are perfect for speculating on the short-term price movement on individual stocks. Because options are wasting assets with a limited life span, speculating on them is generally more exciting than speculating on individual stocks.

Tip: Concentrate on the most liquid and actively traded option to avoid paying the spread.

Financial professionals the world over consider the *Wall Street Journal* the bible of the business world. Published by Dow Jones and Co., with editions every weekday, the paper covers all aspects of business, with special emphasis on markets, trading, and the securities business. The paper comes in three sections. Section A includes the front page and contains the day's top news with a general business focus. Section B, also called "Marketplace," is more focused on marketing, advertising, and general business trends. Section C, "Money and Investing," contains the listings of almost every market imaginable, from stocks to futures and everything in between. Section C also contains the "Heard on the Street" column, which usually includes a tasty tidbit that might actually have an impact on that day's trading. In *Wall Street*, the character Gordon Gekko instructs Bud Fox to call the *Wall Street Chronicle* at an inside extension and tell the editor that "Blue horseshoe loves Anacott Steel." While never explicitly stated, this is assumed to be Gordon tipping off the fictitious paper's "Heard on the Street" column.

mends an easier route, namely, the Chicago Board Option Exchange's Web site at www.cboe.com, where all listings and prices are always available.

Unlike mutual funds, which are long-term investments, options are the securitized equivalent of a heroin hit: powerful, potent, and short-lived. I've given you a broad outline, but before getting started, you'll want to check out a few of the excellent, no-bullshit primers on options trading that are readily available at most bookstores. The best quickie is *Getting Started in Options*, by Micheal C. Thomsett (John Wiley), although George Angell's excellent *Sure Thing Options Trading* (Penguin) provides even more specific strategies. The very sophisticated (and patient) will enjoy Larry McMillan's voluminous *Options as a Strategic Investment* (New York Institute), considered by many to be the Talmud of options trading. Everyone who intends to trade needs (and is required by the SEC) to read "Characteristics of Risks of Standardized Options," available by calling 800-OPTIONS (800-678-4667) or by checking out the Chicago Board Options Exchange's Web site at www.cboe.com.

12 | *FUTURES*

A religious reading from the Book of the Capitalist Pig: *And on the sixth day . . . God created commodities.*

First things first, and I'm going to say this right at the outset: *Be careful!* Commodities, also called futures, occupy the highest point on the Pig Pyramid, meaning that they are, *sans doute*, the riskiest of the lot. With this level of risk, comes, however, a correspondingly delectable level of return. Trust me: If trading stocks gets you off, try futures. You won't leave the house.

What did the market do today? Every newscast in America includes an obligatory mention of the Dow's performance. As more people invest in mutual funds, it increasingly seems as if everybody is talking about the market, which is something I love to hear. I could talk about it all day.

Almost always, when people are talking about "the market" they are talking about the stock market. Kind of ironic that the "market" has come to mean the stock market, since the U.S. stock market is dwarfed in size by both the bond and foreign exchange markets. It's not too often you'll hear anyone griping about how weak the grains have been lately, or how the Canadian dollar has been performing relative to the U.S. dollar. These are both examples of futures, or commodities, markets.

That's why I love commodities. There's definitely a cool elitism in following and trading markets only a few people are tuned into. Also, the U.S. stock market just doesn't always move enough to generate good trading opportunities: The Dow could be in the dumps, or just plain quiet for months at a time. Not so for the futures markets. In the world of commodities, *there's always something moving.*

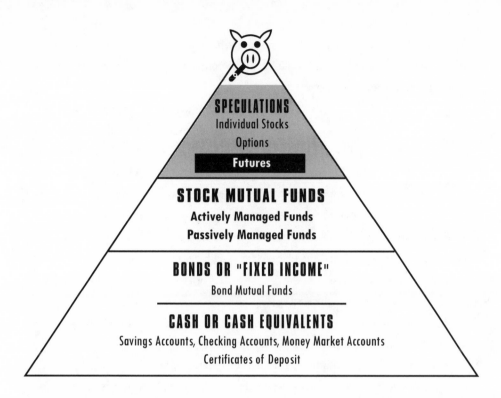

SPECULATIONS
Individual Stocks
Options
Futures

STOCK MUTUAL FUNDS
Actively Managed Funds
Passively Managed Funds

BONDS OR "FIXED INCOME"
Bond Mutual Funds

CASH OR CASH EQUIVALENTS
Savings Accounts, Checking Accounts, Money Market Accounts
Certificates of Deposit

THE "WHY" OF IT

Just as I did with options, I'm going to spend a few lines discussing how professionals use futures markets—in a sense, why we have them in the first place.

Even though you've never grown anything of note (well, not legally, anyway), pretend for a moment that you are a farmer. If it takes a few *Little House on the Prairie* reruns to get into character, so be it. You're a farmer growing soybeans. After a year of tilling the field (or whatever it is farmers do), you've got 10,000 bushels of soybeans ready to sell, same as every year. What's different, however, is the price. Soybeans are a commodity, and the price can and does fluctuate. So the amount of money you will get when you go to sell your soybeans is highly dependent on a number of factors, but it all comes down to supply and demand. Bumper crop (oversupply) or disastrous drought (undersupply)? Tofu's hot (high demand), or has everyone ditched soy sauce for salsa (low demand)? Supply, demand, and even the weather play a part in determining how much people will pay for soybeans. If you thought stock prices were hard to predict, these factors are even more difficult.

So you've got soybeans but have no idea what you'll be able to sell them for once you've gotten 'em out of the ground. When this is your source of income for the year, you can imagine how frightening that might be.

This is one of the reasons we have futures markets. As a farmer, you can lock in a price for your crop by selling futures contracts to speculators like me, even when your crop has yet even to be harvested. That's what a **futures contract** is: *a contract to buy or sell something at a specific future date.* So if you, the farmer, sell November soybean futures at $6/bushel, you are guaranteed to be able to sell your crops at that price once November rolls around. Even if market conditions by that time have caused the price to fall, you'll get your guaranteed price; it's the speculator who takes the loss. On the other hand, if prices rise, you'll still only get your $6—and the speculator gets the rest.

But you've controlled your risk. You're exchanging the risk of uncertainty as to how much you'll get for your crops for the certainty of knowing how much you'll be able to sell them for, in this case . . . $6 a bushel. In this example, the farmer is the *hedger*; selling futures allows him/her to protect against the uncertainty of the future price of soybeans.

Another one: In the above example, the hedger needs to limit the risk that prices might fall—but sometimes hedgers need to limit the risk that prices might rise. Futures can be used for that as well. Let's say you're a financial officer at McDonald's. You know you're going to need a few thousand pounds of bacon for those beefy BLTs six months out. How much will that cost the company? Right now, pork bellies are trading at 46 cents per pound. As the financial officer in charge of procuring the pork at the lowest price, you could wait and see how much bellies cost, taking the risk that the price might rise. Or, you could lock in a price by buying futures on pork bellies now. This would reduce the risk that the price would be higher later, and allow McDonald's more effectively to balance their books.

THE "WHAT" OF IT

As you can tell, futures are a lot different from stocks. Sure, both futures and stocks trade on exchanges, and both can potentially be bought and sold at a profit or loss, but the fundamental difference is this: When you buy stock, you become a part owner of a company. You pay cash to receive shares of stock. As a stock owner, you cannot lose more than your original investment. You can sell your stock at any time.

A futures contract, on the other hand, is an agreement to buy or sell at a particular time. When you enter into a futures contract, what you're contracting for is not a stake in a business or (as with stocks), or a *right* to buy or sell later (as with options). When you buy or sell futures, you are contracting yourself—entering into a legally binding obligation—to buy or sell a particular commodity at a predetermined price and on a predetermined date, no questions asked, *period*. That's right, an obligation. With futures, you *must* make delivery (sell) or take delivery (buy) the commodity in question when the contract expires. A deal is a deal.

When I buy November soybean futures, I am entering into a legally binding contract to buy 1,000 bushels of soybeans at a specific price once November rolls around. Of course, I have no intention of actually receiving **delivery** of the beans. As a speculator, I am merely hoping to profit on the price fluctuation inherent in any active marketplace. So I'll be selling back the contracts I bought before the contract expires. This is called **offsetting**.

Almost all futures contracts are offset before they expire, meaning that speculators will sell back the contracts they've bought (or buy back the contracts they've sold) before the delivery date. They'd like to do so at a profit, but, in order to keep from having to take or make delivery of the actual goods, they may very well have to sell or buy futures at a loss. This process of offsetting is also called "flattening" your position. If, for example, you buy 10 corn futures contracts, you will have to sell 10 futures contracts before the delivery month rolls around—even if you have to sell them at a price much lower than what you bought them for—or risk having a cargo load of carbohydrates dropped on your davenport.

Of course, in the best-case scenario, the price of corn futures rises before the delivery date, and you can sell your contracts at a profit. So just remember to offset. It's not too tough.

The need to offset is one of the major differences between futures and all of the other financial instruments on the Pig Pyra-

In the instances when **deliveries** are made (fewer than 2 percent of all futures contracts are fulfilled by delivery), the products are actually sent to specific warehouses located around the country so as best to accommodate the professional farmers who use the underlying commodities.

If you take delivery, then you have to figure out what to do with all that corn, sugar, or, heaven forbid, that herd of cows. You also have to pay the full price stipulated in your contract.

Offsetting: Selling back a futures contract you have bought or buying back a contract you have sold short. The purpose of offsetting is to "flatten" your position in a particular market, so that you are neither long or short in a particular commodity.

Shorting: Selling a futures contract first, hoping to buy it back later at a lower price. In the futures market, it's just as easy to go short (bet on a price decline) as it is to go long (anticipate a rise in prices).

Most of the large multinational corporations use currency futures to hedge their exposure to fluctuations in foreign exchange rates. For example, a U.S. carmaker selling automobiles in Japan would be paid in yen. The company might sell yen futures to effectively lock in an exchange rate, lessening its risk and helping to maintain a steady balance sheet.

mid. If you bought stock and then the price went down, you could wait forever until the price went back up so that you could sell at a profit. But when you buy a futures contract on, say, soybeans, you've entered into a contract to buy soybeans, you can't just wait around for the price of soybeans to go up. You've got to flatten out your position before the contract comes due or else be prepared to take delivery on a few thousands bushels of beans. And this rule doesn't apply just to the agricultural commodities, either: If you sell **short** gold at $300 an ounce, you must buy that contract back before expiration or start smelting your mom's wedding ring.

Another major difference between futures and everything else is that you don't have to actually finance the various commodities you are buying and selling. In the commodities game, you don't pay for the contract—you merely put down a "margin," a small portion of the contract's overall value, to finance your position. This is serious leverage. For example, the margin on the bond contracts I trade, about $1,200, allows me "control" a contract worth $50,000. Without a doubt, futures give you the biggest bang for your buck.

I hate to admit it, but ultimately, the best metaphor to describe trading commodities is that of a good old-fashioned bet. This is fortune-telling here, folks: From **pesos** to **potatoes**, the futures markets allow you to express an opinion about the relative value of almost anything. Is the price going up or down? If you believe prices will rise in the future, you'll want to buy. If you believe prices are going to fall, you'll want to sell short. It's that simple. When we take a position in the market by buying or selling a particular commodity, we are expressing an opinion about where we think

Peso futures trade at the Chicago Mercantile Exchange. **Potato** futures trade at the New York Board of Trade.

prices are headed. If we're right—we make money. If we're wrong—we lose money. But it's our market opinion that's either correct or incorrect. The market is just a market. It's never "wrong."

THE "WHO" OF IT

So you're thinking about trading. Who will you be trading with? Part of the elegance of the futures markets is their anonymity in the sense that you could conceivably be trading with anyone. A farmer. A portfolio manager. An automobile manufacturer, a floor trader, or "**scalper**."

It could be anyone. Contracts trade at a centralized exchange, and your order gets executed just the same as anyone else's. It's quite democratic: may the best price win.

Frankly, it doesn't really matter with *whom* you're trading. Remember the time Tommy Jamison said he'd agree to be Cindy Brady's secret admirer only if Bobby gave him his Kennedy half-dollar? How did Bobby know Tommy would actually deliver his side of the deal after he got the half-dollar? He didn't. That kind of uncertainty can't happen in the futures markets, which are regulated to insure there is no "counterparty" risk. The counterparty is the person who is on the other side of the trade: the buyer if you're the seller, the seller if you're the buyer. No counterparty risk means that you never have to worry whether the person you trade with will be able to cover her losses. The futures exchanges have a variety of safeguards in place to make sure no one weasels out of a losing trade (more about some of these later). If you lose, you have to cover your losses. If you win, you'll get the money that's coming to you. No weasels, welchers, or whiners allowed.

Just as with the stock exchanges, buyers and sellers meet at a centralized location: a futures market. Orders are sent to a "pit" of traders and delivered "open outcry." Each order to buy or sell is announced to the entire pit of traders, who verbally (and physically) compete for the best trades. Think of it as a mosh pit of finance. What emerges as a result of all the screaming and shouting that takes place there is simply a price. The price of corn, wheat, T-bonds, or any of the other futures available for trading doesn't just "exist"—it is created by the current status of supply and demand of the particu-

Every day over 4,000 people work in the Chicago Board of Trade. The product of their exhaustive labors? The price of many of our nation's most ubiquitous commodities, the most important being money. Futures on the United States Treasury Bond, which reflect current interest rates or the "price" of money, are the exchange's most popular and actively traded contract.

lar commodity. If there are more sellers than buyers, the price goes down. If more people want to buy than sell, the price goes up. The floor traders don't control prices, nor do they set them. Prices are set by supply and demand—what people are willing to pay.

This process of arriving at a price is actually one of the economic benefits of futures markets: They tell us how much things are worth to society at a given moment. This process is called **price discovery**.

Think about it. A compact disc might be priced at $15 bucks at one store and $13 at another. That's because there's no centralized exchange for CDs. With commodities, on the other hand, because they are all traded in a centralized location, we get an immediate and accurate indicator of their current worth. Want to know the price of gold? You don't have to call all over town: Gold is traded at the New York Mercantile Exchange. Just look in the paper and you'll see—the price is listed every day.

KEEPING THE MARKETS IN LINE

Keep in mind as well that we're trading contracts on commodities, not the actual commodities themselves. The latter would involve actually buying the commodity with cash. Futures prices are kept tightly aligned because of opportunistic professional traders called arbitrageurs, who exploit small and fleeting differences in price to make a profit. For example, a stock index arbitrageur might seek to profit between momentary differences cash S&P 500 (the actual value of the stocks listed in the S&P 500 index) and the S&P 500 futures price (the futures contract based on the 500 stocks). If the futures price rises significantly above the cash value—or the actual value of the stocks being traded on the stock exchanges—the savvy arbitrageur might sell futures and buy a representative basket of stocks in the S&P 500, making a nice, riskless profit. On the other hand, if the futures value fell to far below the price of the cash market, the arbs would buy the futures and sell the stocks, thereby pushing the price of futures back up and bring the **basis**, or the relationship between the prices, back into line. While arbitraging is better left to the professionals, the important thing to know about them is that their trading effectively brings price relationships back into their theoretical alignment.

So for our purposes, the futures markets are simply a highly leveraged way to speculate on the price movements of almost any financial or agricultural commodity. Speculators' trading helps to bring liquidity to the marketplace, allowing hedgers to use the markets as a means of reducing risk, while permitting us to potentially profit on price movement. Liquidity is the active and often speculative trading that allows the markets to function efficiently.

MARCHING TO A DIFFERENT DRUM

Part of the allure of commodity markets is that they are overwhelmingly uncorrelated with the equity markets. This means that they move in different directions—when stocks sink, commodities might do very well, or vice versa. One commodity, gold, tends to rise in price whenever inflationary fears enter into the marketplace—yet fear of inflation is bad for stock prices. The less-than-perfect correlation is also one reason that many large-asset fund managers are increasingly using the commodities markets as a means to further diversify a portfolio of stocks and bonds.

At one point in 1998, the billionaire investor Warren Buffett had invested in over 20 percent of the world's available silver supply.

Maybe for the $1 billion pension fund manager, commodities can diversify a portfolio. Of course, those of us with slightly smaller portfolios can't serve up the old "diversification" BS when we're still long soybean futures even after the position has moved a few hundred dollars against us, and we didn't have enough discipline to get out of the trade, and now we've got *bubkus* left in our spec account! So again: Don't think of your spec money as part of your overall investment portfolio. Keep them separate and unequal: Most of it in the stock market. A bit on the side to play with.

GETTING SOME ACTION

HOW DO I PAY FOR THE ACTION? As I mentioned earlier, the sweetest thing about futures is that you don't have to pay cash for the various commodities on which you want to speculate. To buy (or sell) a contract based on the future price of wheat, for example, you'd only have to put up a small portion of the contract's overall value, called margin. Think of it as a bit of collateral in case you lose money on the trade. When you trade stocks, margin refers to borrowed money, say, from your broker. In the futures game margin is a good-faith deposit each investor must deposit with his or her broker before trading. Each futures contract has its own margin requirements and is usually a small percentage (less than 10 percent) of the contract's overall value. This means you are getting to control a hell of a lot of wheat for a small slice of bread.

Despite the small percentage of the contract that a margin represents, futures cost more than options to get into, mainly because futures expose us to the risk of unlimited loss. Unlike equities, bonds, funds or even buying options, when you play futures, you could conceivably lose more money than your account even holds. *Awww yeah!* Because of this obviously higher level of risk, most futures brokers won't let you even *open* an account for less than $3,000, making the futures game significantly more expensive to crack into.

BROKER BASICS

Above I mentioned that I was able to buy futures on a $50,000 bond by only putting up a mere 1,000 bucks. So why, you might ask, do futures brokerages require $3,000–5,000 to open an account? *Because shit happens!* When you trade futures—unlike with any other type of product we've talked about—you can lose more than you originally paid up. The **futures broker** is ultimately responsible for keeping your account in order, and so he or she wants to be sure you'll have enough money in your account to cover any losses that might occur when a speculative position falls apart. The higher minimums protect the broker in case your well-laid plans go awry. So most retail futures brokers, brokers catering to the individual "off-the-floor" trader, actually require *more* than the exchange-mandated minimums.

THE MAGIC OF MARGIN. Margin is different for different commodities, depending on the size of the contract and the relative volatility of the commodity. For example, the initial margin for one soybean futures contract (traded at the Mid-America Commodities Exchange, a subsidiary of the Chicago Board of Trade) is $216, while the initial margin for one Australian dollar contract (traded at the Chicago Mercantile Exchange) is $1,620. Set by the various exchanges, margin requirements can be changed

Whereas stocks, mutual funds, and stock options are federally regulated by the SEC (the Securities Exchange Commission) futures fall under the jurisdiction of the CFTC, the Commodity Futures Trading Commission. This means that in order to trade futures, you must use a separate **futures broker** (also called a commodities broker), not a stock broker as you'd use for stocks, bonds, or stock options.

Minimum margin: In the world of futures contracts, the term "margin" means, basically, a down payment toward the overall value of the contract. In the world of stocks, "margin" means money borrowed toward the purchase of stocks.

Futures speculators who want to buy or sell futures are not required to fully finance their purchase, only to deposit a small percentage of the overall value of the particular contract they are interested in trading. This dollar amount, called the minimum margin, represents a good- faith deposit on the part of the speculator that he or she will be able to cover any losses that might occur if the trade becomes an unprofitable one.

at any time to reflect changes in the market. Many times, when contracts become more volatile, the various exchanges will raise the margin requirements, effectively making sure that everyone who is in the market can truly afford the added risk that more volatility brings. Your futures broker will keep you informed of any changes in margin requirements.

The **initial margin** is the money you have to deposit with your broker to put on a position. Traders refer to buying or selling contracts as "**putting on**" or "**taking off**" a position in the market.

At the end of each trading day, the positions in your account are "marked to market," meaning that if you've bought a contract that has risen in value, your "winnings" for that day are immediately deposited into your account. Of course, if a position has moved against you and you're down money, it will immediately be taken out of your account at the end of the day.

Futures trading is what they call a "zero-sum" game, meaning that every time someone wins, someone else loses. As William Gallacher notes in his excellent trading primer *Winner Take All*

Initial margin is a kind of security deposit that your broker will require you to put down as an assurance that you can cover the total cost of a contract if necessary. If your position moves heavily against you, your broker will require you to put up even more cash.

Put on a position in the market: Futures trader lingo for buying a contract.

Take off a position in the market: Futures trader lingo for selling a contract.

(Irwin Professional Publishers), "Traders can only redistribute their own funds among themselves—there is no infusion of money from any other source." When you win . . . someone else loses (and vice versa). Strangely poetic, huh?

So let's say you put up a few hundred dollars in margin money and get into the soybean market. Over the next few days, the trade begins to "move against" you, depleting your account of the original margin money. As speculators, we must maintain a certain amount of our margin money in our accounts as long as we have positions on in the market. This "maintenance margin" is a further safeguard to protect the integrity of the entire system. The maintenance margin works like this: You buy or sell a contract and deposit an initial maintenance margin. Then you must maintain a certain level of cash to cover any losses, which will be taken out of your account. Let's say the initial margin requirement for T-Bonds (traded at the Mid-America Commodities Exchange) is $1,200/contract. You'll be required to deposit that amount *before* you can make the trade. The maintenance margin is $900/contract, meaning that you must maintain at least $900 in cash in your account if the position moves against you, and you start to lose money. If you go long on a T-Bond and lose $400, you'll get a call from your broker asking for an additional $100 to be deposited in your account, bringing it back up to the $900 maintenance level, as long as you want to keep your position in the market. This is what's known as a *margin call*.

You'll usually need to send or wire the money right away, and if you can't meet the maintenance margin, your broker will quickly close out your position. And probably your account. Why is he such a bastard? Ultimately, it's the broker's responsibility to cover any of your trading losses. He's just trying to cover his own ass.

The best way to avoid a margin call is to keep your losses small before they turn into big ones, and to trade with enough money so that you are never just "skimping" by when it comes to margins. For trading one contract like a T-Bond with a $1,200 margin, I would keep at least $3,000 in my account.

FINDING A FUTURES BROKER WHO WON'T BREAK YOU. As I mentioned earlier, you'll need a separate futures broker to trade commodities. Just like stockbrokers, futures brokers come in a variety of shapes and sizes. Discount futures brokers are similar to discount stockbrokers: They'll take your orders and execute your trades, and that's all. They also offer the cheapest commissions; a "round-trip" futures commission through a discount broker might cost anywhere between 10 and 25 bucks.

The discount futures brokerage Lind Waldock is the nation's largest, and I've had good experiences with them. Others include Saul Stone Futures and Ira Epstein and Company. They offer very reasonable rates and access to every futures market in the world. Other brokers are listed in the business section of the newspaper or can be found on the Net. You'll definitely want to check out a broker's record with the National Futures Association (NFA) and Commodity Futures Trading Commission (CTFC) to make sure there's no litigation or criminal action pending against the broker you're looking to open an account with. Their respective Web sites can be found at www.nfa.futures.org and www.ctfc.gov. A full-service futures broker will offer specific trading ideas, keep a careful eye on your positions, and even provide research materials upon request. You pay for this stuff: Full-service commissions usually start at about $50 per round trip.

MAKING THE TRADE

When you give your broker an order, it is written down, time-stamped, and immediately routed to the appropriate futures exchange and pit by a runner. It is then given to a broker, who executes your order through "open outcry" in the pit. You receive a telephone call moments later with the details of the trade execution. Seem archaic? Perhaps. In recent years, more and more futures trading is being done electronically. While this is not as colorful and cool as "open outcry," most industry insiders expect that because of the cost savings, it's just a matter of time before trading cards are replaced with computers. A romantic at heart, I'll be sad to see the old system go. One good example of an electronic system is the Chicago Mercantile Exchange's e-mini, a smaller version of the much larger-margin S&P 500 futures contract. Both contracts follow the movements of the stocks listed in the S&P 500 index. The e-mini is traded exclusively via an electronic system, allowing you to see real-time bids, offers, and trades on your own computer screen. More information on the e-mini is at www.cme.com, the Chicago Mercantile Exchange's Web site.

Here's an example of how you'd speculate with futures: From his secret hideaway on Fantasy Island, Mr. Rourke has decided to start speculating in commodities. Because of the comparatively low margin requirements, he checks out the contracts traded on the **Mid-America Commodities Exchange** and finds they perfectly fit

Mid-America Commodities Exchange: A subsidiary of the Chicago Board of Trade that offers smaller-sized contracts. Their Web site: www.midam.com.

the $4,000 speculative portfolio he has opened with a discount futures brokerage. After following the markets for several weeks and even doing some paper trading, he decides to try his hand at trading soybeans, an agricultural product that (according to the charts he got off the Internet) he thinks is destined to fall in price. Because he is betting on a price decline, he will be going short, or selling first at one price, hoping to buy back later at a lower price and profit from the difference.

According to material provided by his broker, the Mid-Am corn contract is sized at 1,000 bushels and quoted in cents per bushel. The minimum price fluctuation of the contract is 1/8 cent, which represents $1.25. This is known as the tick size.

Let's say the initial margin requirement for Mid-Am soybeans is $216 for one contract. With $4,000 in his account, **Mr. Rourke** has more than enough to put on a short position. He gives his broker a market order to sell one soybean contract at the best available price currently trading on the floor of the exchange. The order is filled at a price of $5.45 1/2 cents.

Immediately, Mr. Rourke calls back his broker and gives him two additional orders. One is a stop-loss order, in which Mr. Rourke instructs his broker to buy back the contract he sold if the price goes above $5.65 1/2 cents. Because he is short beans, he wants the price to go down. The stop-loss order at $5.65 1/2 cents protects him in case beans go up instead of down. With a stop-loss order in, the most Mr. Rourke can lose on this trade is about $200.

In addition to the stop-loss, Mr. Rourke puts in a limit order to buy one **soybean** contract at $5.05 1/2 cents, meaning that if the price of the contract drops to that level, the broker will cover Mr. Rourke's short position by buying back the contract he originally sold. If things work out as planned and soybeans drop to that level, Mr. Rourke will make $400 (sold at 5.45 1/2 cents, covered at $5.05 1/2 cents). The orders are designed as "one cancels the other," meaning that if one order is executed, the other will be immediately canceled.

Each 1/8 cent is worth $1.25, which means each dollar movement in the price of **soybeans** is worth $10. A 20-cent loss (sold at $5.45½ cents, bought back at $5.65½ cents) would therefore equal $100, less commissions.

PROTECTION. I can't overemphasize the importance of putting in these additional orders. First, they allow you to protect yourself against loss: If beans rally, Mr. Rourke would be "stopped out" around 5.65 ½. I say "around" because the actual price the trade gets filled at might be slightly different, depending on market conditions. It loses him some money but protects him against the possibility of further loss. If soybeans should rise to $6.00 or even higher, the stop loss would allow Mr. Rourke to cover before things get too far out of hand.

You see, theoretically, the loss in futures markets is unlimited. Soybeans could go to $7, $8, $10. The higher the price went, the more money Mr. Rourke would lose on his short position. So stop and limit orders are mechanisms of forced discipline that allow us to immediately set the risk parameters for any one trade. In Mr. Rourke's example, he is risking $200 to make $400. Not too shabby a deal.

Furthermore, placing these orders with your broker spares you from having to watch the market every second. The broker will keep your order in his **deck**, and if either one is executed, you'll immediately get a phone call and a subsequent written confirmation.

Deck: The physical stack of GTC (Good Til Cancelled) orders a broker is waiting to execute.

SETTING STOPS. For the love of God: *Don't speculate without stop-loss orders.* The markets are hard to predict, and a reasonable stop-loss order will protect you if (when) things don't go as planned. I use the word "reasonable," because you don't want to set your stop-loss order *too* close to the current market price. Set it far enough away from the current price so that your stop won't be "hit," or executed, in the normal price fluctuations of a particular market.

I like to keep it strictly dollars and cents. Before putting on a trade (even on the floor) I've already noted in my mind where I'll get out, on both the losing and winning sides. This keeps trading more disciplined, efficient, and fun.

I have found, in my own trading, that derivatives, both options and futures, are actually much more fun than stocks. For one thing, they move faster and the payouts (and losses) are larger. And by keeping my eyes glued to other markets besides the stock market (like agriculture, for example), I'm never tempted to dabble in my mutual funds, which are long-term holdings not to be messed with.

Not to sound alarmist, but when dealing with derivatives, remember that any sort of gain comes with an equally substantial amount of risk. Being ready to accept the gains—*and losses*—while still enjoying the trade is ultimately the only reason to speculate in the first place. It should be fun. Before opening an account or trading anything, you'll definitely want to follow the markets and maybe even do some paper trading to see if you like it.

Although these last few chapters by no means fully explain the nuances of speculating with derivatives, I hope you have a better general idea of what they are and how they work. In the not-too-distant future, we'll be able to speculate 24 hours a day on almost anything. Think of these past two chapters as merely a crash course for the future.

CONCLUSION

I am not a tough guy. I am not Jack Kerouac. I don't own a baseball mitt. I don't drink aged whiskey neat. I don't fix my own car. I don't have a "six-pack." I can't go all night. My dress suits are not actually suits but hand-me-down combinations of almost identically colored jackets and slacks.

But you know what? I don't give a shit. And with money in the bank, neither will you. What is so deliciously undeniable about money, is that when you have some of it, you call the shots. You are in charge. Let the proverbial beach bully kick as much sand as he pleases—when you've got money in the bank you can simply buy the beach and kick his sorry ass off.

I can't see the future. One thing I am certain of, however, is the life-affirming power of resources. When you have resources you can take risks. You can explore. You have choices. You have freedom. Without resources you are a "have-not." You are simply at the mercy of the "haves." Unfair? Perhaps. Surprising? Not a bit. That's capitalism. That's America. And it's how the game is played.

What do you value? What has worth? Two questions that could elicit 2 million responses. Without much coaxing, most people are more than willing to share their feelings regarding the relative merit of just about anything, from stocks to Stravinsky. Opinions are never in short supply, while money often tends to be.

When you spend money on a particular item—on a particular experience, good or service—you are effectively making a value judgment. You are exchanging a resource (money) for an item, product or service that, at the very least, you value as highly as the cash. You are casting an opinion about relative and comparative worth. Ask yourself if the products and services you buy are really worth the effort, the time, and the resources it takes to obtain them. Most often, they are not.

What I hope you now realize is that the "secret" of amassing wealth starts not with a stock or even with savings, but with deciding what, out of everything this world has to offer, you actually hold to have meaning, importance, value, and worth. When it comes to the material world, nothing is "born" with a price tag on it. This is the beauty of a market economy: Goods and services are worth exactly what the market is willing to pay.

So be smart. Start asking questions about what it is you value. What is "worth it" for your hard-earned resources. The individual choices are yours to make, the point is simply to make then in the most informed and responsible manner.

Investing is the other half. Once you've gotten into the habit of saving and spending with sense . . . start investing. Slowly but surely wins the race here. Take prudent risks and keep a long-term focus. Do the numbers: In a matter of years, the big bucks can really start to compound. Now that you've made your way through this text, I hope you will include savings and investing among your arsenal of intellectual weaponry.

One of the most powerful arguments for why you should care about money is that spending is the most powerful form of expression we have. When we appreciate or believe in a particular cause or product, we support it: with our time, with our money, with our resources. Everybody complains about trashy television, cigarette companies, and drugs. If nobody supported these "vices" with their resources, they would simply cease to exist. The power of money is even more powerful than freedom of speech. Talk is talk. Money gets things done. And having money gives you the freedom to express your opinion any which way you choose: to directly support whomever and whatever you choose.

While this stuff ain't rocket science, getting your finances in order does demand consistency. Financial independence isn't going to happen all at once. You are simply not going to hop from Baltic Avenue to Park Place after one quick skimming of any book, let alone this one. But by starting to develop the Capitalist Pig mentality of being critically aware of your spending, diligent in your savings, and aggressive in your investing, you've begun to play the game. And you'll collect much more than $200 every time you go around the board.

And once you get your finances in order . . . once you have some money . . . to paraphrase Dr. Seuss, *Oh the places you'll go!* The limits of your life seem to fade away and you begin to remember the childlike fascination of the impossible becoming possible. With money anything is possible.

You can buy the tangibles, of course . . . but beyond the items you could put on your Discover Card, money affords you choice, expression, independence, and freedom. Who knew the Constitution and the cash machine were so closely related?

I encourage you to continue reading about money, how to invest it, save it, store it, and, ultimately, use it to its fullest potential. Get started sooner than later. You've seen how compounding works—how small changes to our daily routine can add up to make substantial differences later on. Start slowly. Start small. But start.

And finally . . . dream. With money in the bank, you'll finally have the means to one day make your dreams a reality. So make some plans. Think about everything you love to do, every mountain you've wished to climb, every boundary you thought could never be crossed. Think about everyone who told you that you "couldn't" or "shouldn't." Write their names down. You'll want to inform them when you accomplish the "impossible."

> *"I who can have, through the power of money, everything for which the human heart longs, do I not possess all human abilities?"*
>
> —Karl Marx

INDEX

IBM, 58, 68, 216–22
Image marketing, 29–32
Impulse buying, 35–36. *See also* Risk
Income statement, 197
Indexes:
  of bonds, 113–14
  of stocks, 64, 113, 128–30
Index funds. *See* Passively managed mutual
  funds
Inflation, xix, 53
  cash investments and, 79
  interest rates and, 78–79
  risk and, 74, 75
Inflation risk, 56, 89, 208
Initial margin, futures contracts and,
  233–34
Initial public offering (I.P.O.), 123, 185
Insana, Ron, 138
Insider information, 45
Insider trading, tracking, 201–2
Intel, 127
Interest, 68
Interest rate, 68
  banks and, 81
  on bond mutual funds, 117, 118
  on bonds, 68, 71, 93, 94, 96, 97, 102–4
  on cash investments, 78–79, 80, 84, 85
  on certificates of deposit, 88, 89–91
  on credit card debt, 15–16, 17, 97, 102
  on government bonds, 98, 99
  on money market accounts, 85, 86, 87
  on savings accounts, 84, 85. *See also* Com-
    pound interest
Interest-rate risk, 89, 98, 118
Internet, information from:
  on bank accounts, 85, 90
  on company's financial health, 198, 199
  Ethernet and, 194
  on mutual funds, 109
  on public debt, 98
  on speculating, 174, 177
  on stock speculating, 194
  on stock tables, 189
In the money, stock options and, 220, 221, 223
Investing, xviii, 44–72, 239
  asset allocation and, 69, 72–73
  broker recommendations on, 66–67
  compound interest and, 43, 50–53, 59–62, 70
  definition, 48–50
  diversification and, 67–69, 70
  full-service brokers for, 193

goals and, 53–55, 64, 65, 69, 70
gurus and, 65–66
investment pyramid and, 70–72, 73
knowing reasons for, 62–63, 65–66
money and, 3
pacing oneself with, 72–75
portfolio, 67–69
reckless, 74–75
return on, 26–29
risk and, 55–57, 59–61
risk tolerance and, 63–65
speculating *vs.*, 57–58, 70–71, 170, 172
 spending as, 28–40
stock market crashes and, 80
time and, 50–53, 70
trading *vs.*, 137–38. *See also* Bonds; Cash;
  Stocks
Investment risk, 74
Issuing debt, 121. *See also* Bonds
Izod, 32

Jefferson, Thomas, 10
Jetsons, The, 39
Job, money from:
  investing and, 53
  savings and, 40–41
Junk bond funds, 116
Junk bonds, 97

Kandel, Myron, 74
Kaufman Fund, 120, 121
Kerouac, Jack, 35
Keynes, John Maynard, 92
Kill, 177
Kravis, Henry, xi

Laddering maturities, on certificates of deposit,
  89
Large-cap stocks, 60, 69, 80, 124–25,
  164
Last price:
  stock options and, 224
  stock speculating and, 191
Lehman Brothers Aggregate Bond Index,
  113–14
Leveraged buyout (LBO), xi
Liabilities, 14
  living beneath your means and, 40, 41
Lifestyle marketing, 29–32
Limit down, 168
Limited liability, of stockholder, 126